Husband, Lover, Spy

Husband, Lover, Spy

A True Story

Janice Pennington

with

Carlos de Abreu

Custos Morum Publishers
Los Angeles

Grateful acknowledgment is made to all sources that provided information and/or materials that enabled the authors to complete this book.

It was the policy of Custos Morum Publishers to change some of the names in this book in recognition of the importance of preserving and protecting people's identities and privacy.

Library of Congress Catalog Card Number: 93-72895

Pennington, Janice
Husband, lover, spy: a true story
by Janice Pennington with Carlos de Abreu

ISBN 1-884025-03-X

Printed in the United States of America

First Edition

Contents

In the name of Truth

Some names have been changed in recognition of the importance of preserving and protecting people's identities and privacy.

1.

The Dreamer

Los Angeles
1975

T he plot was twisted, complicated and elusive, unlike those in the Nancy Drew mysteries of my childhood. I couldn't just set the book down on the nightstand and be done with it when I didn't like the way things were unfolding. This story was real. This was my life. My husband, Fritz Stammberger, mysteriously disappeared on September 27, 1975, in the restricted area around Tirich Mir Mountain, along the Afghanistan, Pakistan, and Russian borders.

I straightened the sheets on the bed and threw on the comforter. Through the window I watched the sparrows land in the yard and hop around. They left feathered tracks in the wet dirt. Footprints. Indentations scratched into the earth remained until another bird wandered by.

I loved my home: a gingerbread house north of the Santa Monica Mountains, a rustic haven in Los Angeles. The lush growth reminded me of my childhood in Washington surrounded by Douglas firs. Those times were simple, peaceful.

Because I was raised that way, I wasn't prepared for the chaos that followed. I was brought up during the Fifties, a carefree time which promised a happy future. It was the era of bubble gum, net petticoats starched in sugarwater, Buster Brown shoes, Davy Crockett, and Hollywood musicals—feel-good movies with happy endings. My heroes and role models were the movie stars: Elizabeth Taylor, Jane Powell, June Allyson, Elvis Presley, Roy Rogers, and the Lone Ranger.

When I married Fritz, I believed that I married my prince. He was all my childhood heroes rolled into one, everything I dreamed of in a man: handsome, interesting, strong but gentle, and a risk taker.

The movies, magazines, and books I read told me about men like Fritz, larger than life, the epitome of the dashing adventurer.

During the Fifties, there were only two options for women. You were either a nice girl or a bad one. If you were nice, you went to church on Sunday, then Bible school. You did what you were told. You didn't question authority. We were led to believe that the world and our lives would be perfect.

The struggle with being imperfect was something I knew. During my childhood in Seattle, my home was perfect, at least on the outside. Like a scene from *Ozzie and Harriet*, meals were always on the table promptly, and the family ate together every night. There was order. Chores. Homework. Playtime. Weekends with cousins, aunts, and uncles. On the outside it looked good, and it was. But living in the midst of all this perfection made me feel that perhaps I was not perfect enough. Deep inside I didn't feel I belonged there. I was scared that they would see my flaws.

I can't say exactly where my fears came from, but I think my childhood visits to my grandmother's house had something to do with it. I was shy, and my cousins were all performers who took piano and voice lessons. I would sit on the couch and listen to them play and sing. Their voices were beautiful, clear and high. I wanted them to keep singing, because when they finished, my grandmother and my aunts would call on me. "Come on, Janice, why don't you get up too. Show us something." I had nothing to show. I couldn't sing or play the piano. I only playacted when I was off by myself in the woods or in the privacy of my room. After my cousins finished, I tried to shrink back into the couch. I wanted to evaporate, to be invisible. But I had to stand up. Eventually, someone would comment about how I looked. "She's put on a little weight . . . ," they would tell my mother, as if I couldn't hear. I cringed, feeling self-conscious.

I remember one day in particular when I sat near the piano with my cousins, under the huge portrait of my great-grandmother Mamie. She was an adventurous woman who had gone to teach in Alaska at the turn of the century. My grandmother sat nearby in her high-backed velvet chair. She told my aunt how beautiful and talented my cousins were. My cousins started teasing me, calling me pudgy. From that moment on I decided not to eat another bite until I was thin. I hardly ate anything for weeks, until the weight was gone. Still, the shyness stayed. Old habits, old fears, stayed with me.

I was so shy that in school I ate my brown-bag lunch in the girls' restroom rather than with the other students in the cafeteria. I was afraid of attention, because for me it led to rejection. I was sure that if they had the chance to look at me closely, they, like my family, would see my imperfections, and then they wouldn't like me. When there was a school dance and I knew one of the boys was going to invite me, I avoided him. I didn't want to be asked. I didn't feel confident.

I dreamed about getting married and envisioned someone just like Fritz. In spite of my shyness, I knew what I wanted. I didn't think about the boys at school, the ones who wanted to ask me to the dance. I dreamed about someone with experience, like my heroes in the movies. I wanted someone exciting who would show me the world. I wanted to be more than a housewife. I wanted independence, glamour, excitement, and romance.

Every week I spent my allowance on the Saturday matinee at the Lake City Theater in Seattle. If we did our chores well, my mother would give each of us twenty-five cents. I always saved up for the serials—features that arrived in installments. When I got in trouble, I wouldn't get my allowance, and missed a week at the movies. That was the worst. After seeing the heroine in peril and the swashbuckling hero coming to her rescue, it was torture to miss the finale, the love scene.

At night, I lay in bed and thought about their lives, and about mine. In order to get rewards at home I had to play by the rules, do what I was told without questioning authority. Sometimes I did things I didn't really want to do just to keep the peace. I went to bed at the same time each night. I did my chores. I forced myself to concentrate in school when I really wanted to daydream. I knew it was just a matter of time until I could leave. I had a mature mind trapped in the body of a young girl. I felt ready to leave, ready to meet the man of my dreams. I wanted a life like Liz Taylor's. She was so beautiful, always on the arm of a dark, handsome man, traveling in Europe, attending elegant parties. I knew I had to wait to meet the man of my dreams, the one who would rescue me from my routine existence.

It was 1956 when I first saw Elvis; he was on the *The Ed Sullivan Show*. He was the man I dreamed of, larger than life. I listened to him on the radio and collected all of his forty-fives, playing them endlessly, singing along, again and again. I pored through the latest movie magazines, scanning the pages for the familiar, darkly handsome face, hoping to spy a photo I had not seen before. Elvis in a shocking pink shirt and black pants cradling a mike and crooning over it. Elvis standing, legs astride. Elvis in a leather jacket, leaning on a long pink Cadillac.

From the age of fourteen, I saw my life as I had never seen it before. The things I counted on, the fixtures of daily life, looked different. Bedtime, school, regular meals, the whole routine seemed like a trap, keeping me from what I wanted. By following the pattern, I risked never doing the things I wanted, having the things I wanted, or going to the places I wanted. I was not the only one. My whole generation was growing up in a world that was trying to be perfect. We were starting to rebel. The atom bomb was a decade old. World War II was long over. Rock and roll was in the air. James Dean was the symbol of a new era. Teenagers started to question authority—their parents, their teachers, their government.

I knew that my life had to change.

I stepped outside and laid a crust of bread for the birds on the porch rail. The sparrow tracks had disappeared in the earth beneath the fig tree, vanishing like footprints in snow, covered over by the wind.

Until Fritz disappeared on Tirich Mir, I thought that when I found the man I loved nothing would ever separate us. In the movies, if the leading lady remained faithful, the hero returned, no matter what. That was the Hollywood ending. Love always triumphed; it was just a matter of time. I thought that if I had enough faith, and enough courage to wait, Fritz would come back to me. He had promised: "Time will play into our hands . . ."

2.

Love at First Sight

Aspen
July 1973

We just finished taping the last show of the season on *The Price Is Right*. I had been working for two years as a hostess on the national game show, emceed by Bob Barker. Now I looked forward to my summer vacation in Aspen, Colorado, with my mother.

I still remember the day we met. It was July 1973. As I walked out of the Jerome Hotel, my eyes met his. He was a big man. His shirt—blue flannel, printed with cartoonish red and yellow Volkswagens—strained over his shoulders and arms. The sleeves rode higher up on his arms than they should have. In a shirt and jeans, with his brown hair disheveled and a sculpted profile, he looked like a great Indian chieftain. Yet, when he took my hand there was no condescension; his handshake was firm. His hands were powerful, with thick wrists, but he had a calm, gentle way of crossing them. Those hands could do anything, I thought. He seemed unpretentious, a man who knew himself and was comfortable with who he was. He appeared to have an inner strength, a certainty of self. I watched him as we spoke, trying to understand my attraction. He asked me to dinner and I accepted.

That night, when we passed into the hazel glow of the candlelit restaurant, the first date tension dissipated as though a stifling cloud had been removed. Simply being in his presence warmed me. He had an attentive, quiet air about him. As we spoke, I looked into his eyes, which opened like a passage into a different place, a place disconnected from this world, a place I knew.

"So, what have you done with your life?" he asked a little too seriously. I was tempted to laugh, but I didn't, sensing that laughter might offend him.

"Well," I replied, "I've traveled a lot. I like to explore the world, find adventures. I lived in New York for a while. Now I'm in Los Angeles." Trying to redirect the conversation, I asked, "How about yourself?"

Fritz reflected for a second, then said, "Well, I too left the place I grew up—Europe, Germany—although I go back there once in a while. But my life . . . that subject is not so good before dinner, yes?" He said it more as a statement than a question, then changed the subject. "Ah, we haven't even ordered yet. What would you like? The paella is nice."

"Why don't you order for me? You know what's good here," I said.

After dinner, Fritz's reticence eased; he began to open up, to share things with me. His voice altered as he told stories of his past, his childhood, the war.

"You must understand, my upbringing was not a traditional one. My parents tried to give me the best they could in the middle of the war, World War II that is. Life was very different then. People say the world is crazy. They do not know. Nothing I have seen so far can compare to the world I grew up in. There the only order was inside a person.

"When I was five, my father was captured and put in an Allied POW camp. I didn't see him until I was nine. Many members of my family— including my mother—died when our house was bombed.

"It happened one day when I was late getting home after school. When the air raid sirens began to howl, I ran. A few hundred yards from the house I saw the American bombers. Big steel monsters in the sky. I remember looking up to see them. Strange, I felt more curious than afraid.

"When I was just crossing the railway lines, I heard the whistling sound. I looked up again, and I'm certain I saw it, the silver capsule. Then, an enormous explosion. When I looked at our house, through the dust and smoke, the whole front of the building had disappeared and there was a big pit in the ground. The walls lay in shambles. A kitchen sink dangled from the second story. I ran toward the rubble and scrambled about, burning my shins on the metal fragments still smoldering

14

from the explosion. With my hands, I tore through the shattered planks and broken plaster. I hardly felt the splinters and glass. I kept digging until I saw a body. I remember backing away, then starting to run again. I didn't know where I was going. I was only trying to get away, to go as far as I could.

"By the time I stopped, exhausted, I didn't know where I was or where to go. I sat down on the street. It was dark. A family friend recognized me and took me to my grandmother's house. My brother was there already. Nearly everyone else was dead."

I could hardly answer. My greatest childhood adventures involved camping out in the backyard and listening to horror stories on the radio. To lighten the mood I asked him about his mountain climbing. I'd heard that he had adventured around the globe. He told me of the early days, how he began. By the age of seventeen, he had climbed every famous mountain in Europe. At twenty-two, he had conquered, on his own, nine peaks in North Africa, the Middle East, and the Indo-European subcontinent. Solo climbing was what he enjoyed the most. Nobody to hold him back.

Fritz explained how he was able to evade government restrictions, crossing borders without visas in Turkey, Vietnam, and Tibet. All in the name of adventure. To top off his story, he proudly told me how he became famous in the mountaineering community. He was able to rely on his lung capacity, not using oxygen tanks while climbing altitudes higher than twenty thousand feet—the death zone.

We were a balance of opposites. I couldn't wait until the next time we'd be together.

The next morning I awoke in my hotel room with a feeling of euphoria. Fritz had invited me to the ballet that night. As the hour approached, I felt a calm excitement. I wanted our time together to be special, magical. After a long, calming shower, I went to the bathroom and carefully made up my face, choosing blue shades of sky and water, and rusty hues of earth, joining the elements with me. These colors were also in my dress, made of soft brown suede with jagged edges at the hem. I looked for a pair of shoes to finish the outfit.

Leather heels seemed too heavy. I put on black flats, but they weren't right either. Fritz was supposed to be there in ten minutes. My frustration mounted. I would have to change.

My mother tried to help. "Maybe I have a pair you can wear," she offered. At a loss, I waited as she headed toward her room. I felt myself withdrawing, becoming the quiet, sullen child that I sometimes had been. Here I was thirty-one years old and still everything felt beyond my control.

"I can't do this anymore. I'm going to have to find something else to wear," I called after her, riffling through the closet.

There was a knock. My mother had left the door slightly ajar.

"Come in," I said. The door nudged open and there was Fritz. "I am sorry to come early. . . . It is okay, yes?" he questioned. I tried to compose my face as I said hello. He took in my expression. "What happened?" he asked as he sat beside me, looking into the open closet. I told him the problem, joking and laughing at myself as I explained.

He said seriously, "Oh, then go barefoot."

At first, I was not sure that I heard him correctly. Wear a dress without shoes?

"It's lovely. I wouldn't want you to wear anything else." He took my hand. Barefoot to the ballet, I mused to myself as we left. It was very romantic. When we reached the parking lot, he swung me up in his arms and carried me over the rough asphalt to his car.

That was how it began. The moment we met, I knew that I loved him. I did not know why. It made no sense. When he turned toward me and touched my mouth with his warm hands, parting my lips, his touch felt familiar. That delicate gesture, that tender touch with those big hands. Days later at the airport, I was hardly able to say good-bye. I broke down and cried. My tears moved him. Even though we were living in separate cities, we began to see each other, flying back and forth, dating. We began a dance on air, and the dance was not over yet.

3.

Missing

The snow thundered down on the men trapped inside their sleeping bags. Chunks of ice and rock mingled with the powder as the avalanche rumbled through the valley, echoing off the mountain walls, the Himalayas. The three men yelled, and wailed, intoning a death knell. Then, as suddenly as it had begun, the noise died out, until it was replaced with an ominous silence. Their breath rasped in and out as they greedily took in oxygen. A small pocket of air had been trapped under the snow. It would keep them alive for maybe an hour. Long enough to suffer. Long enough to think about the end that awaited.

Fritz's climb the previous August had ended under that avalanche. In spite of the odds, he managed to dig his way out, saving himself, and then his companions. Back at home he told me how he clawed through the weight of the snow, not knowing if he would survive. It made him rethink his whole life, he said.

He was gone again. And although he had been two weeks late from climbs before . . . this time was different.

I thought about our life together. Moments from his courtship, our wedding, the honeymoon surfaced like a rapid montage. We'd been seeing each other for three months when he proposed: "Will you share your life with me?" We spent our honeymoon in Europe, living on coffee, croissants, and each other. A series of pictures whirled by in a sweep of pastels and picturesque scenes like Monet paintings. The days and nights we spent in Aspen.

I desperately tried to recreate his image. I remembered how he looked in the first light of dawn, his hazel eyes, aquiline nose, full lips. I captured each feature for a moment, then it faded: the way one arm would be raised above his head, its well-defined muscles leading to his broad shoulders, his chest, his taut belly. His sensuality was powerful. Pictures of our intimacy flooded through me. I could almost feel the warmth of his mouth as he bathed me with his kisses, the smell of his hair and his body, the feel of his skin.

I touched my body as if he were touching me—gently, tenderly, passionately. Making love to Fritz was like stepping out into space, floating free in a world of our own making. We knew we had found something rare and special; we had found the other half of ourselves. The illusion faded. Tears streamed down my face and neck. No matter how I fought to bring him back, I couldn't. I was alone in our bed.

My whole family was with me. I heard my mother moving around. She was straightening up, fixing the place. It was the waiting that was doing me in. I hadn't talked to Harry Conway, Fritz's partner and the head of the search party, since the end of October, two weeks after Fritz was supposed to return from Pakistan. Since then I receded into a cocoon of waiting. I wished that I'd gone myself, not let Harry go for me. I shouldn't have listened to him when he said that I would be in the way, that I would hold them back. I should have gone regardless of what anybody said. I hoped I wouldn't live to regret this.

Through the window I saw Aspen Mountain in the distance. It was filled with holiday skiers. I used to watch Fritz from this window. He would come home from the office in the afternoon, burst through the door and head for his skis, talking to me all the while. After he left, I would wait to start dinner, giving him time to get to the top of the mountain. Then I would walk to the window and look out, just as I was doing at this very moment. I could always spot him in the middle of a throng. His speed and finesse set him apart. He created his own way, leaving a flurry of snow in his wake. I would watch him continue down the mountain and come right up to our door. That was my favorite part of watching him ski, seeing him come home to dinner, to our time together, to me. It was at times like those that I wished I was a skier or that I was more athletic so I could share the things he loved, but I wasn't.

This time as I watched, I saw no familiar figure making its way through the crowd. No one turned off the path and skied down to my doorstep.

"Janice? Phone's for you." My mother's voice filtered in from the other room. "It's Vicky, Harry's girlfriend." There was a pause. "Should I ask her to call back?"

I composed myself. "No, Mom. Thanks. I'll be there in a second." My face was still turned toward the window. It was in these last few weeks that I mastered the art of silent crying.

"Hello," I heard myself mumble into the receiver.

"Janice . . . Harry just called me."

My pulse quickened.

"They found Fritz's knapsack in Parpish."

His knapsack . . . he couldn't be far. This was the closest we'd been to knowing anything in weeks. I listened to Vicky as she unraveled the story.

"Harry was passing through the village, the last village on the mountain, when he ran into these merchants. They said they remembered seeing a man who fit Fritz's description. He'd hiked across the river bridge about one month before. They said he hadn't stopped in the village, and they never saw him come down from the mountain.

"At first Harry took their word and continued on to see if he might find someone with more information. On an outside chance, he went back to the same hut a few days later, and there was Fritz's knapsack in the corner."

Why hadn't the locals told Harry about the knapsack? Were they trying to hide something?

"What was in the knapsack?" I asked. Maybe Fritz had left behind a clue.

"Harry said there wasn't much . . . an electric blanket, a notebook, a map of the area, a few books . . . " She paused.

"Books," I said, a little startled. "What books?"

"One of them was about a climb of Nanga Parbat, a mountain near

19

there. Another was a book called *Dear America*. And there was some book on Lenin. I don't remember the title of the last one. Harry would know."

Why did Fritz leave the books behind? It made no sense. Books are sacred to him; he always carries one with him, especially when climbing. He would never have abandoned his books. He would never have given them up. The one time I had cleaned up his bookshelves, he was furious with me for moving them around, for having even considered throwing out some old paperbacks. His vehemence surprised me. I loaned him *Dear America* just before he left. I knew that book. I hadn't even finished it yet. He would not have left it behind willingly.

"Janice . . . Janice, are you there?"

"Yes . . . Vicky, Fritz wouldn't have left those books . . . that means something, he never would have left them behind."

"Well, Harry's decided to hire a helicopter. It's the one option he hasn't tried yet. If Fritz is on the mountain, that's how they'll find him."

"They have to find him," I said. "They have to."

She didn't say anything for a moment.

"Janice, are you all right? Do you want me to come over?"

"No, no, Vicky. I'll . . . I just need some time to let this all sink in . . . I really appreciate everything you two are doing."

"Yeah, well . . . " her voice trailed off.

"They'll find him. I know they will."

* * *

It had been one week since I last heard from Vicky. There was a faint knock at the bedroom door. "Janice, come out and sit with me for a while. I've made some snacks, and there's an old movie on TV," my mother said.

I got up from the bed and followed her into the next room. She sat down on the couch, and patted a spot next to her. I nestled into the warm brown fabric and rested my feet in the hollow where the cushions gave, sinking under her body. The movie flickered on the screen.

She leaned forward and stood up. "Would you like some tea? I put the kettle on a little while ago."

"Sure, Mom. Thanks," I replied, rubbing my feet in the spot where she had been sitting. It was warm. The pictures on the television danced before my eyes, drawing me into the characters' lives. The movie had started before my mother coaxed me out of my room. I watched a man in a top hat stroll down a cobbled road, passing brownstone after brownstone. He was off to meet someone. I resisted the urge to ask my mother where he was going. As a child, I always assumed that she knew more about the plot than I did. The man in the picture found the address he was looking for. Cane in hand he jaunted up the stairs, then stopped in the entryway to lift up the large brass knocker.

Our doorbell rang. I kept watching the movie. It was probably my sister. I listened to my mother talk quietly with the person at the door. It didn't sound like my sister. They were coming toward me. I quickly combed my hair with my fingers, trying to make myself marginally presentable.

Harry Conway walked into the room. He sat down where my mother had been sitting. His face was puffy, tender. His eyes were bloodshot, red and bleary. He just arrived from Pakistan. I wanted to turn away from him to shut out his words, but they rushed after me.

"I'm so sorry . . . so sorry." His voice lost itself. "We didn't find Fritz. He . . . he's gone."

Gone. I couldn't digest what he was saying. What did he mean, gone? How could he be gone?

I turned away. The blood chilled in my veins.

"Oh, God," I said. "What do I do now?" There were sobs rising in my chest. Why was this happening to me?

In the midst of my turmoil, I heard my three year old niece Jessica, her voice a high-pitched beacon, "Don't worry, Aunt Janny. Fritz is okay."

My heart wrenched at her words. What did she know that I did not? She was so confident. I looked at her.

Hesitantly, Harry continued to tell me what had happened.

"We hired two Jeeps to drive the thirty-five miles to Parpish, inside

Pakistan . . . the road was nearly impassable; it took four hours. Along the way, we stopped to show villagers a picture of Fritz and asked if he had been by. Most of them said that Fritz, or someone who looked like him, had been seen climbing in the area.

"The next day we hiked up steep trails to what had been his base camp. Some woodcutters had seen a man climbing up the same path with a huge pack a few weeks before, but no one had seen him come down.

"When we reached the base camp area, we searched for any sign that Fritz had been there—a piece of clothing or equipment, food, a campfire pit—but we didn't find anything. We went on to the advance base camp area, but again, there was nothing. If Fritz was the man the villagers had seen going up, he had vanished without any trace of making camp or coming back down."

"If he made it to camp, how could there be nothing?" I asked. "He would have at least stopped for the night. There were no signs that he slept there, no markings on the ground?"

Harry hurried on, anxious to make me understand. "Well, we did find some clues. One of the men noticed tracks in the light snow."

"So Fritz had been there." Harry couldn't meet my eyes. He looked away. Something felt wrong.

He continued: "The weather was clear enough to follow them, so we hiked along the slope parallel to the glacier for maybe three hours."

"And?"

"And then the snow became too deep. It was getting dark, so we had to turn back."

"You turned back? How could you turn back?" I began, but stopped. "Did you go back in the morning?"

"We tried, but it was too late. The weather had warmed, the tracks had vanished. We went to Parpish the following day. There we got word from officials who had been questioning villagers on the north side of the mountain that Fritz had not been seen in that area. There was, however, a rumor circulating in the villages that a porter accompanied Fritz on the climb to base camp, but no one knew who the man was."

The more Harry told me, the more unclear the situation became.

"I want you to know the four of us in the search party had a long discussion about his chances, and agreed that if Fritz is still on the mountain, he's probably alive. There are actual cases of people who managed to survive in subzero conditions for up to ninety days. If Fritz was able to build any kind of shelter, he was skillful enough—and strong enough—to survive."

I believed that. I knew Fritz's stamina, his will. I felt that Harry knew more. Perhaps it was just that my mind wanted to know more, wanted an answer. I could not reconcile the facts with my intuition. So much of what I was being told was conditional, uncertain, tentative.

"Vicky said something about a helicopter," I said. "Why did you decide to hire a helicopter?"

"It was our last hope: we couldn't go any farther on foot. It took us another day and a half to make it back to Peshawar. We contacted the local German consul about getting one. He told us we would have to return to Islamabad and go through official embassy channels. It took us another day to get there and begin making the rounds. The consular officer at the American embassy thought it would take ten days or more to scrounge up a helicopter. Bernard Sawatzki, the assistant military attaché at the German embassy, was more helpful. Through his contacts he was able to get in touch with the Pakistani defense minister, who authorized the use of a jet-powered Alouette 3 helicopter. We needed the Alouette to inspect the upper slopes of the mountain. It had never been done, but we thought that this particular copter could land at eighteen thousand feet if it was stripped of all unnecessary weight.

"The next morning we flew from Islamabad over the pass to Chitral, where we dropped off everything to gain maximum altitude. I went alone with the crew, but even so, we only had enough fuel for twenty minutes of flying time over the upper slopes of the South Tirich Mir Glacier, where the ascent route would be visible. The weather, fortunately, was in our favor. It was sunny and clear."

Twenty minutes. All they'd had was twenty minutes to look for my husband.

"The pilots spoke excellent English. They asked me why Fritz would attempt such a dangerous climb alone. Was it possible he was here for another reason? What could I say? I told them that he liked to climb alone so that he wouldn't be slowed down, and that solitude was important to him. It was hard to explain."

I nodded. He used to say that climbing replenished his soul.

Harry was silent for a moment before going on. "I scoured the face of the mountain. I studied the glacier, the steep snow along the upper ice fall, and the ridge linking Tirich Mir to the main summit. But all I saw was snow, rocks, ice blocks, and the black crevasses. No tent, no tracks, no signs of clothing or equipment. There was nothing human there.

"After twenty minutes of circling, the pilots were forced to head back. When they made the final turn down the glacier, I cried. I just can't believe he's gone."

So Fritz was gone. Not dead, but gone. That was what I was left with. Harry fell silent. Looking at his face, I saw his eyes ringed with fatigue, his skin tightly drawn. His body slumped. He had failed. After a while, he rose to leave.

As he started for the door, a thought struck me.

"The knapsack. Fritz's knapsack. Where is it?"

He stopped. An unreadable look flickered across his face.

"I didn't bring it," he said.

"But you said you went back to Parpish."

"We did. And we picked up the knapsack, but we couldn't bring it back. Our luggage was already overweight. There was nothing in it of value, so we left it."

"How much could it weigh? Those few things."

"I'm sorry, Jan. I didn't realize . . . I didn't think it was that important."

I stared at him in disbelief.

"Not important?" I cried. "I wanted everything that was in that pack. Those were his things. I should have them."

"I don't know what to say. I'm sure they're gone now. Disposed of. They meant nothing to anyone there. I am sorry."

What he said sent a chill through me. Fritz's things meant nothing. Nothing. They were gone. I let Harry go. He assured me he would try to get the knapsack back. It was too late. The murmuring voices in the living room receded as I went to my room. The knapsack and the books were gone. Fritz was gone.

My stomach started to churn. I couldn't believe what Harry had told me. Why didn't he bring the books back?

4.

Nellie the Psychic

Aspen
November 1975

The alarm went off beside the bed. Morning. I reached over and slammed my hand down on the switch. Sunlight warmed my face, resuscitating me against my will. I resisted the call and kept my lids shut tight. Scenes of Fritz loomed before my eyes. I remembered how it was when we lived together. Sometimes, he would wake before me, and move around softly. He would go to the kitchen, make tea or coffee. Unfolding the paper, he would sit near the kitchen table and prop up his feet. Then he would tip the wooden chair back. I would hear it creak. He would settle in to read. If I slept late, he would come back in and start preparing for his day, still quiet, careful not to wake me.

I could almost hear him in the shower, as if the water was running, streaming down in rivulets of sound, interrupted occasionally by the obstruction of his body. In my mind's eye, I saw him soaping his chest, his arms, his legs. The suds ran down along the curves and contours defining his muscles, parts, indentations, shapes. The stream thickened where his waist narrowed into slender hips before dividing into his two powerful legs.

I wandered into the living room. A handwoven rug from Afghanistan lay in front of the fireplace. Fritz brought it back from a previous climb. Photographs of the mountains he scaled adorned the walls, and Eastern figures decorated the shelves and mantelpiece. The miniature sculptures were different from one another. I noticed them the first time I came to his condominium. That first night, he took my hand and led me around. He motioned at the figures: "This one is Buddhist, this, Hindu—in Nepal, Buddhists and Hindus live peacefully side by side. The two religions even share the same temples," he told me.

He stood up to light the fire. As he knelt on the hearth, I watched the flames start to blaze fiercely as the wind began to roar and whip outside. I stretched out on the rug as he moved to turn off the lights.

Through the window I saw the onyx sky studded with diamonds. Then he kissed me. My mouth opened instinctively to receive him. For one long slow moment we were joined. I slowly laid my body down beside his.

It was late afternoon when I headed toward town to visit Nellie Hendricks, a respected Aspen psychic. I wanted to see if she could help me in my search for Fritz.

The mountains rose grandly around me, solid wedges covered with patches of snow. Clouds topped the peaks, dotting the otherwise flawless expanse of clearwater blue that was the sky. The main stretch of town, filled with handicraft stores and ski shops, lay ahead. Fritz and I spent so many hours in this town. There were so many places: the cafes where we ate breakfast together, the store where he bought my engagement ring, his print shop. The beauty of Aspen hurt.

Snow crunched beneath my feet as I walked. The long sloped descent reminded me of the road leading away from my grandmother's house in Seattle. She lived at the top of a hill. The curving road ran from the front door to the main thoroughfare. The last time I had looked down that road, my grandmother was dying. No one knew. She had been sick for a year or two, on and off. I had a feeling, and I knew that I had to visit, that there might not be another visit.

There was a snowstorm. It was difficult to get into Seattle. I took the train, not knowing if it would arrive, or when. My aunt and uncle met me at the station. Outside, it was pitch black. They drove me straight to the house, but I asked them to drop me at the bottom of the hill. I wanted to walk up alone. I stayed with my grandmother for three days. She smelled of violets. Certain things had to be done alone. She knew, I knew.

I walked, looking for Willow Road, Nellie Hendricks's address. I checked my watch. Twenty minutes. The place was farther than I thought. I had left the business district behind, and was on a residential street. Victorian homes, delicate and upright, lined the street. They all looked the same; gables with painted trim. Lamplight was already beginning to show through the picture windows. Curtains were drawn closed. I kept walking, passing house after house. Then, at a distance, I caught sight of a residence that stood out. Nellie's house resembled an enchanted fortress with tree trunks, like a line of sentries guarding the path to the door. Leaves cast shadows deeper than the darkness that was falling. A black gate shrouded by thick green growth stood before the entrance. It opened silently. A carved wooden sign hung on the door. I read the name, etched like an incantation on the varnished plaque: Nellie Hendricks, Spiritualist. The hanging chimes tinkled. I lifted the heavy brass knocker, and it fell with a thud, reverberating through the wood. I resisted a momentary impulse to flee; the door opened.

Nellie greeted me. "Hello. Come in, please. Make yourself at home." Her gaze drew me in. There was an intensity about her as if she'd concentrated the energies of the universe into one small place: her being. She glowed. She looked into my eyes and took my hand. "Welcome," she said.

In her home, I noticed only the light. An amber incandescence emanated from the candles set about the room. The light flickered as the flames moved. She led me to a table of uneven shape. It seemed to have been cut directly from a tree trunk. Its irregularities suited it. I sat in the chair she placed before me and stared at the table's surface. Honey, gold, and walnut blended into waves, small curls of change marking the slab of wood. I broke the silence.

"I came here because my husband has disappeared," I offered. There was no response. She brought over a china teapot and one fragile porcelain cup. The painting on the cup did not resemble the usual golds and stark blues that decorate china. Rather, watercolor hues of gray and faint maroon stained the surface in no clear picture. The shades washed into one another in ways that intimated shapes, forms, bodies. I watched her set the pot and cup on a thin square of linen which she had laid down and smoothed out straight in preparation. Two twisted metal candlesticks emerged from a corner curio cabinet and were set on either side of the china. The black wrought-iron contortions contrasted with the delicate white candles.

Nellie sat facing me. She began. One at a time, she lit the tapered candles. Then, with a practiced gesture, she shook some leaves into the cup. From the teapot, she poured a small, steaming waterfall onto the leaves. They swirled in unanticipated motion: a flood of sorts had descended. I looked at her again. She was contemplating me, her eyes enveloping mine.

"Janice, this may be difficult, but you must do what I ask. Focus inward. Remember Fritz. See him as you loved him best. Close your eyes and feel, feel the time shared between you and him. Rejoin him."

I did as she asked. I felt him near me. An energy surrounded me. I could almost feel him in the room. The intensity of his presence entered.

"Now, relax; go within. Ask the spirits questions."

I let my mind go. The questions came. Where was he? Why wasn't he here? What happened to him? Did he want to be where he was? Did he want to return to me? How could I help him? When would we be together again? Was he alive?

The words flowed out of my heart. The silence seemed nonexistent, so many unspoken thoughts filled the air. Finally, the torrent slowed. I opened my eyes. She sat quietly, concentrating. We did not speak. She turned the cup over onto its rim. I waited for her to lift it and reveal the message written in the sodden leaves. Slowly, she unveiled the cryptic pattern and stared down, deciphering the code.

"There's more to this than meets the eye," she said.

I waited for her to speak again.

"He's alive," she said with confidence.

She studied the mound of leaves calmly for another minute. "He's with a tall slender man. . . . There is someone talking to him, a woman with black skin. A woman was involved in his disappearance."

As the phrases emanated from Nellie, she fell into a trance and started reciting revelations. As I listened, my questions mounted. Who was the woman with him? Did she know the man? How were these people connected to Fritz?

Nellie kept talking. I listened.

"He will come back at night. When he returns, he will be in a different business. He's been spared a catastrophe. He will have to make a serious decision about his marriage. He is not feeling well."

He would return. When? I had to know. But she had finished.

She looked up and smiled. "Your Fritz is by nature a very lucky man. He'll be back in the country long before anyone knows."

I thanked Nellie for her help, then called a cab and returned home.

The silver moon glittered like a sliver of ice. The building hulked large and black against the sky. I climbed up the stairs toward the muffled noise inside the condominium. The whole family would be there, wondering where I had been, worried. I turned the key gently in the lock, knowing that the slight motion would engender an onslaught of greeting and concern. I walked in.

I heard my mother and Jessica in an inner room. Mom was probably putting Jessica to bed. I put my purse down. I made tea before joining them. I needed some time to put the pieces of this day together.

5.

The Stranger

Aspen
November 1975

In a few days I was returning to Los Angeles, back to work, back to *The Price Is Right*. My family tried their best to make it easy for me, but to no avail. Since Fritz's disappearance, Aspen was no longer a hospitable place.

I heard a knock at the door. Looking through the peephole, I did not recognize the man outside. He was tall, well-built, athletic. I could make out his long, sandy blond hair and a tan. He looked young.

"Who is it?" I asked.

"My name is Jim MacGeyver."

I cautiously opened the door and looked out.

"Yes?" I said, more as a question than a statement.

"So, that's who you are," he began.

"Excuse me?" I said.

"I just read about Fritz's disappearance in the *Mountain News*. I wanted to offer my condolences. I skied with Fritz once, and I admired him quite a bit."

"What was your name again?" I asked.

"Jim MacGeyver," he repeated, then continued as if I hadn't spoken. "Yeah, the article said that Fritz went climbing and disappeared in Pakistan. I thought I'd stop by and see if there was anything I could do to help. And I have to admit, I was curious to see the woman he married. Any woman Fritz would marry had to be special."

In spite of his explanations, I still wasn't quite sure why he'd come by in person instead of calling. I didn't remember ever seeing him with Fritz.

"Conway's article in the paper," MacGeyver continued, "said that Fritz was climbing around in the Tirich Mir region. I know exactly where that is. I grew up in Pakistan. My parents were missionaries."

I let down my guard and invited him in.

"I don't know how you'd feel about having me search for him," he went on, "but I'm going over there soon, and I think I could help."

I didn't respond.

"Conway probably knows a lot of facts," MacGeyver said, "but take it from me, it's hard to get inside the local culture over there. The whole country's pretty tightly knit. Everything travels by word of mouth. Most of those villagers probably knew the search party was coming before it even got there. Word travels fast. There's sort of a telegraph system, but instead of having transmitting poles they have people scattered about, outposted in the middle of nowhere. A foreigner would never guess. The whole thing is pretty much of a local deal. I doubt that the search party ever tapped into it. The locals have to trust you before they'll tell you anything. I know. I've talked to them for years. Growing up there and all I learned the language and I really got into this human communications system that they had going."

This was not all new to me. I'd already suspected that Conway hadn't found out everything. I wondered what MacGeyver might be able to tell me. He continued.

"Conway probably had that system working against him more than it was working for him. I bet there were a lot of things he didn't know."

This man was offering to look for Fritz. He was volunteering to do exactly the thing I couldn't do for myself, at least not well. "Please," I said. "Anything you can do. The worst part is just not knowing."

He stared at me peculiarly for a moment. "Well, I'll do everything I can to find him," he said, taking his leave.

While we talked, my mother heard our voices and peeked into the room. She returned at the sound of the door closing.

"Who was that?" she asked.

"It was someone who knows Fritz. He offered to help find him. He's going to Pakistan," I told her.

Seattle, Washington.
July 8, 1952.
My tenth birthday.

Los Angeles. 1984. Publicity photo taken to announce my fifteenth consecutive year on national television. Before joining the game show *The Price Is Right* in September 1971, I was a principal for two years on Rowan and Martin's *Laugh-In* and on Hugh Hefner's *Playboy After Dark*.

Aspen, Colorado. July 1973. Fritz and I. After taping the last show of the season on *The Price Is Right,* I went to Aspen to spend my summer vacation. That's when I met Fritz Stammberger.

Beverly Hills, California. May 12, 1974. Fritz and I during our
wedding ceremony at the Beverly Hills Hotel. He was 33 and I was 31.
It was love at first sight when we met in Aspen in July 1973.

Yugoslavia. 1974. Pictures I took of Fritz while we were on our honeymoon.

Munich, Germany. 1974. Fritz and I visiting with his father, Opa, while on our honeymoon in Europe. *Right:* A photo of the two of us in Austria.

1974. Throughout his life, Fritz always fought for what he believed in. By the age of 17, he had climbed every famous mountain in Europe. At 22, he had conquered, on his own, nine peaks in North Africa, the Middle East, and the Indo-European subcontinent. He was able to evade government restrictions and crossed borders without visas in Turkey, Tibet, and Vietnam during the Vietnam War. He was famous in the mountaineering community for climbing solo without the use of oxygen tanks.

Aspen, Colorado. 1970's. Fritz the activist. He chained himself to a tree that the city was going to cut down in order to pave the parking lot. Due to Fritz's action, the tree was saved.

MY DEMAND

EITHER
The trees remain where they are

Or

2000 signatures requesting their removal

The Himalayas. April 25, 1964. Fritz climbing without oxygen tanks on Cho Oyu, the sixth highest mountain in the world (26,750 feet), located in Nepal and Tibet.

Left: Nanga Parbat. Rupal Wall. East Face. The "holy mountain."

1974. Fritz climbing Makalu in the Himalayas. Makalu, the fourth highest mountain in the world (27,824 feet), is in northeast Nepal, southeast of Mount Everest.

1974. Fritz at one of the base camps during his Makalu expedition. This time he was unsuccessful at reaching the summit. Fritz had tried to get Elvis Presley to sponsor the climb. Elvis didn't go for it.

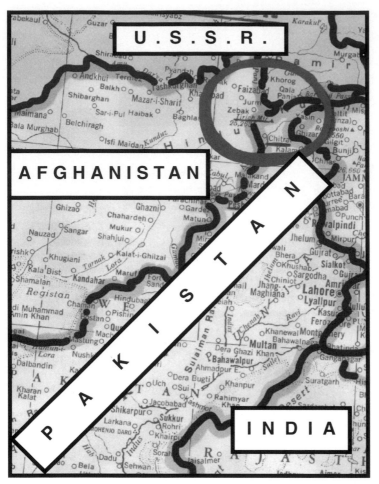

The circled area on the map indicates the region in which Fritz disappeared on September 27, 1975, while he was on a solo climb of Tirich Mir (25,230 feet), the highest peak in the Hindu Kush mountain range. Tirich Mir is in the restricted area along the Pakistan, Afghanistan, and Russian borders.

Makalu, 1974. Fritz checking his knapsack. He was an avid reader. He would never go anywhere, much less on a solo climb, without books. I could not believe that his partner, after his failed search for Fritz, did not bring the knapsack back to the U.S. because it was "too heavy."

Aspen, Colorado. 1975. Fritz Stammberger at age 34. The stainless steel Rolex watch had been a gift from me. I had engraved "To my darling" on the back and signed it "Janice." Later, in one of my searches, it became an important missing piece of evidence.

1975. The envelope from a letter sent by Fritz before his disappearance. Even though he was in the Chitral area in Pakistan, it was postmarked Osaka, Japan. Why?

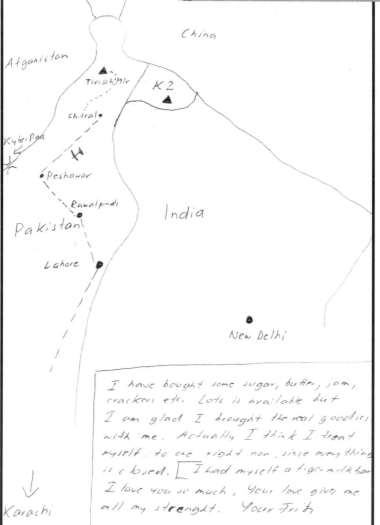

Fritz's handdrawn map showing his airplane going in the opposite direction from Tirich Mir, his destination. Why?

I have bought some sugar, butter, jam, crackers etc. Lots is available but I am glad I brought the real goodies with me. Actually I think I treat myself to one right now, since everything is closed. ⎡ I had myself a tiger milk bar I love you so much. Your love gives me all my strength. Your Fritz

Bumburet, Pakistan.
November 7, 1977.
Ted Noble, the Jamaican citizen whom Jim MacGeyver found in the Kalash Valley while searching for Fritz.

From left to right: Jim MacGeyver, unidentified woman, Ted Noble, and unidentified guide.

تلاش گُمشدہ

فرز سیمبرگر

۲ ستمبر ۱۹۷۵ سے لاپتہ ہے

آخری اطلاع چترال پاکستان سے آئی تھی جہاں سے اس کا پروگرام ترچ میر کے پہاڑوں کی کوہ پیمائی کا تھا۔

اس کا صحیح اتہ پتہ بتانے والے کو مبلغ دس ہزار روپے (۱۰۰۰۰ روپے) کا انعام دیا جائیگا۔

حُلیہ :۔ عمر ۳۰ سال (پیدائش ۲۲ رجون ۱۹۴۰ء بمقام میونخ جرمنی) قد :۔ ۶ فٹ ۲ انچ

Left: Poster, written in Urdu, which was distributed by Intertel throughout the area around Tirich Mir. It offered a financial reward for any information related to Fritz's whereabouts.

Below: Document released by the Justice Department stating that Fritz may have been involved in a covert action for which he might have been imprisoned in Pakistan.

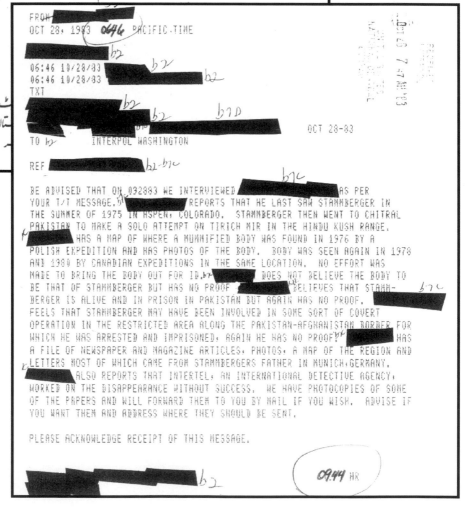

FROM
OCT 28, 1983 0646 PACIFIC TIME

06:46 10/28/83
06:46 10/28/83
TXT

OCT 28-83

TO   INTERPOL WASHINGTON

REF

BE ADVISED THAT ON 092883 WE INTERVIEWED   AS PER
YOUR T/T MESSAGE.   REPORTS THAT HE LAST SAW STAMMBERGER IN
THE SUMMER OF 1975 IN ASPEN, COLORADO. STAMMBERGER THEN WENT TO CHITRAL
PAKISTAN TO MAKE A SOLO ATTEMPT ON TIRICH MIR IN THE HINDU KUSH RANGE.
         HAS A MAP OF WHERE A MUMMIFIED BODY WAS FOUND IN 1976 BY A
POLISH EXPEDITION AND HAS PHOTOS OF THE BODY. BODY WAS SEEN AGAIN IN 1978
AND 1980 BY CANADIAN EXPEDITIONS IN THE SAME LOCATION. NO EFFORT WAS
MADE TO BRING THE BODY OUT FOR ID.   DOES NOT BELIEVE THE BODY TO
BE THAT OF STAMMBERGER BUT HAS NO PROOF.   BELIEVES THAT STAMM-
BERGER IS ALIVE AND IN PRISON IN PAKISTAN BUT AGAIN HAS NO PROOF.
FEELS THAT STAMMBERGER MAY HAVE BEEN INVOLVED IN SOME SORT OF COVERT
OPERATION IN THE RESTRICTED AREA ALONG THE PAKISTAN-AFGHANISTAN BORDER FOR
WHICH HE WAS ARRESTED AND IMPRISONED. AGAIN HE HAS NO PROOF.   HAS
A FILE OF NEWSPAPER AND MAGAZINE ARTICLES, PHOTOS, A MAP OF THE REGION AND
LETTERS MOST OF WHICH CAME FROM STAMMBERGERS FATHER IN MUNICH, GERMANY.
         ALSO REPORTS THAT INTERTEL, AN INTERNATIONAL DETECTIVE AGENCY,
WORKED ON THE DISAPPEARANCE WITHOUT SUCCESS. WE HAVE PHOTOCOPIES OF SOME
OF THE PAPERS AND WILL FORWARD THEM TO YOU BY MAIL IF YOU WISH. ADVISE IF
YOU WANT THEM AND ADDRESS WHERE THEY SHOULD BE SENT.

PLEASE ACKNOWLEDGE RECEIPT OF THIS MESSAGE.

09.44 HR

Portugal. 1973. Carlos, age 20, during his pilot training at Air Force Base No. 1 in Sintra, twenty miles from Lisbon.

On April 25, 1974, after the coup d'état led by the Portuguese armed forces, Carlos went back to Mozambique via South Africa.

One of my favorite photos of Carlos.

Beverly Hills. 1980. Carlos and I when we started dating.

Me in 1976.

Carlos in 1984.

Encino, California. 1984. The Spanish hacienda, built in 1920, once belonged to English actor George Arliss. Carlos and I had bought it to start our life together. What was supposed to have been a sign of change and good luck soon became the opposite.

Left: The living room, showing one of the seven fireplaces.

Right: Carlos in the pool.
Below: The den.

6.

"The Price Is Right"

Los Angeles
December 1975

Q uiet!" came the call on the set. The director raised his hands to
cue the audience, "Five seconds." The chatter died. A thousand
cables and lights hummed in readiness. Then, with one signal,
a rush of applause flooded the studio. Theme music poured from the
speakers as the cameras maneuvered, rolling silently across the floor.
Johnny Olsen's voice rang out, "Come on down!" One by one the lucky
contestants jumped up and ran down the aisle, clapping ecstatically on
their way to the foot of the stage.

I stood behind the doors at the rear of the set trying not to cry, my nails
pressed into my palms. Physical pain kept me in the present. I had to stay
in the present, to be ready. I bit the inside of my lip. It seemed my cue
would never come. Then the doors flew open.

My face smoothed into a smile for ten million people staring at their
TV sets. While I glided about the stage, the unrelenting cameras dollied
closer, pressing in like inquisitive strangers. I forced myself to concentrate, to keep my mind working, to remember the cues. I didn't want to
break. I had to keep smiling, moving, at least until the costume change.
Then I could run backstage for a moment.

Moving to the right, I gestured along the edges of a television set: the
contestants were about to bid.

The lights felt suffocatingly hot. Just in time, I remembered to move
to the other side of the television set. Finally, the shot was over. I ran to
my dressing room.

I had been working for four years as a model on the show and I loved it. Now, for the first time, I felt uncomfortable.

Hours later, it was seven o'clock. Finished for the day. Numbness quickly replaced relief. A dull buzz filled my head as the thoughts I had pushed down stirred, and began to surface. I reached back and groped for the zipper. I pulled it to my waist, unsheathed my arms, and sat down, overcome with a weariness that had become all too familiar. I laid my head on the dressing table, the plastic surface pressed coldly against my cheek.

It was hard to believe what had happened on the set earlier that day. Someone had heard the story of Fritz's disappearance and found it amusing, interesting, a good idea for a game. I watched the screen fill with the words. "Cliff-Hangers." It had to do with climbing. The contestant determined the fate of a mechanical mountain climber. If the player guessed the price of an item correctly, the mountaineer was safe. If he guessed incorrectly, the climber moved up the mountain one step for each dollar away from the correct price. Too many steps, and the mountain climber plunged over the edge, and fell to his death. The contestant lost the prize. The producer had tried to convince me that the game had nothing to do with Fritz, that they hadn't meant to be insensitive, but the game went on. I had to go to my dressing room. I couldn't watch.

I raised my head up and looked around. The dressing room was oddly silent and removed from the normal bustle. The noises that filtered in seemed dimmed, as if they had passed through a huge distance, an endless moat. The only distinct sound was the buzz and crackle of lights. Fluorescent sticks. In their bright bluish glow, the room looked surreal. I rested my head in my hands. No one knew how close to the edge I really was.

Quickly, I finished changing and grabbed my bag. I walked through the silent hallways until I reached the final door and stepped outside. It was darker than usual when I left, and the lot was nearly empty. I glanced about nervously and hurried to the car, fumbling for my keys. I rummaged through my purse, and my wallet, lipstick and compact fell out. I found the key, and shoved the other contents back in the bag.

In the car, the residue of the day's warmth still remained. There was a certain security to being closed in, where I knew where everything was. I turned on the engine. As the car wound through Benedict Canyon, the curves in the road lulled me. I pulled to the side of the road, tears streaming down, blocking my vision. What if Fritz wasn't alive? I lay down on the seat and listened to cars whiz past, my car shuddering in the wake of each wave of sound. I pleaded silently for someone to help. Another wave of traffic passed: motion, silence, motion, silence. The cold of the seat belt buckle digging in my side prodded me back into the insistent present.

I picked myself wearily up off the passenger seat, and took a deep breath. My fingertips wiped away my tears as I started my car and listened to it hum. Pulling away from the curb, I continued home.

7.

Honeymoon

Yugoslavia
1974

I couldn't help but retrace my time spent with Fritz. Yugoslavia was
one of the countries that we visited during our honeymoon. My
basic intuition about authority, oppression, and the lack of basic
human rights was confirmed. It was the first time that I had visited a
communist country. It started when we crossed the border. We were
taken into a barren room with gray cement walls where a grim-faced
man questioned us as to our reasons for entering the country. Simple
curiosity or interest would not suffice. Fritz told him that we had just
been married. We were traveling. He looked up, almost in disapproval.
"Traveling?" his look seemed to say. He made it seem so frivolous.
Wrong almost, as if we were committing a crime. Behind him was a
floor-to-ceiling portrait of Marshal Tito, the only decoration in the
room. He emitted a few terse commands to the man standing next to him.
Authority.

We were led out to our car, only to wait while the guards searched
under every seat. They stuck their hands in each crack, went through the
trunk, checked under the frame. After a half hour they stood back and
allowed us to approach the car. We passed inspection. We drove down
the highway leading away from the border crossing.

After the grilling, we sat silent. The land itself was beautiful. The road
ran alongside the coastline, ocean stretching away beneath us, woods
above us. Off to the side there was a narrow dirt road leading toward an
open field with a thick forest behind it. On impulse, Fritz drove onto the

path. We could lie in the sun for a while, eat the food we'd picked up in Austria. Relax.

We spread the blanket out in the sun and were dozing off when there was a sound of rustling near the woods. I looked up and faced a wall of soldiers. They were dressed in fatigues, belts of ammunition across their chests, knives on their hips, machine guns in their hands. They motioned with their guns for us to get into our car. I tried to show them that we were having a picnic. They did not respond, but kept motioning with their guns. For some reason, Fritz did not seem disturbed by them. He attempted to speak with them in German. They said nothing, but began surrounding us, still motioning, gesturing toward the car. We began to gather our belongings. Fritz took my hand and began walking. They followed close behind. Fritz tried to speak with them again, this time in French. I understood fragments of what he was saying. "We're only on vacation . . . stopped to eat." The soldiers kept walking, inching closer with each step. A claustrophobic tension was building. I wanted to run, leave, move, change the situation, break the vise of their authority. But any rapid action would have set them off. That was why Fritz was moving so methodically. Regularly. One step at a time. Nothing to change the status quo.

We reached the car. Fritz loaded the few things we'd brought. We walked to our doors, opened them, sat down, closed them. He started the engine. The soldiers moved, flanking us. They were moving in front of the car. I tensed. Fritz shifted into first gear and the car began rolling forward. The soldiers hesitated. The car sped up slightly. I heard the engine strain to pull our weight. The men fell back. The wheels dug in; we lurched forward. I looked over my shoulder out the rear window. The soldiers stood motionless, rearranged in rows. That is what authority does to people. It takes away their will to think for themselves, to do anything out of the ordinary. They begin to think that they can't function without someone else telling them what to do.

Yugoslavia was a satellite of the Soviet Union. Even though they were quite independent from their "master," they still had the same guidelines to abide by—communism. The secret services and the military ruled everything. No freedom of any form was allowed. I had left home and school to liberate myself from limiting principles, and as if by accident, here I was in Eastern Europe experiencing it firsthand.

During our trip I questioned myself about Fritz's choice of places for us to spend our honeymoon, but then I pushed it out of my mind. I remembered thinking to myself as we drove along the beautiful coastline of Yugoslavia, "My God, I am married to this man and I don't even know him."

8.

Pieces of the Puzzle

Los Angeles
1976

I f anyone could do it, Fritz could," he said. I hung up the phone. It
had taken hours to get through to Christopher Wren, a *New York
Times* correspondent in Moscow. He knew Fritz. They'd skied
together.

I got up and walked to the window. In Aspen the hours stretched on
without end, but the last few days at work in Los Angeles passed in a
blur. Time was moving in jumps and starts.

Wren told me that Tirich Mir bordered on the U.S.S.R. and is near the
border of Afghanistan. It was conceivable that Fritz had gotten lost in
the area. But Wren said that he didn't think Fritz would have gone that
way, at least not by choice. "The climb down the back of the mountain
into the Soviet Union is treacherous," he stated. But he said that he
thought Fritz could make it, if he had to.

The people I talked to these days—foreign correspondents, senators,
embassy officials—came from Fritz's circle, not mine. During our
honeymoon in Europe, the difference in our social styles became
apparent. Fritz was so comfortable in that milieu, he hardly noticed how
far out of my element I was. Now I was seeking out these people, even
though I wasn't entirely comfortable around them. They had knowledge
that escaped me, an international knowledge.

I put my hand up to the windowpane and felt the chill on the other
side. In Southern California the weather shifts in an almost impercep-
tible way. Slight increases or decreases in rain demarcate seasons. The

occasional drizzle can turn into a downpour. Sometimes, when winter really sets in, the sky remains overcast and gray and the temperature stays below sixty-five for more than a week. That is what southern Californians call a stretch of winter.

I was raised much farther north in a region with four distinct seasons. What people here called winter resembled the beginning of what I knew as fall. When I first moved south, I loved going to the beach and getting a tan in any given month. But the constant warmth became oppressive. The constant life in the blooming trees and green grass suggested that no time was passing or changes occurring, but I knew that was untrue.

I stared out at the gray street shaded by oaks, and watched the wind rustle the leaves. They were red, gold, brown. I ventured into the living room. On the polished mahogany table, pictures were displayed as if on an altar. Ensconced in silver or brass, the faces looked out, eyes crinkled, cheeks plumped in smiles.

I picked up a photograph of Fritz climbing a mountain. It was a favorite of mine. It was taken from above him, caught, suspended inside a crevasse. Above him the sky peered through a hole that resembled a woman's opening. Sunlight shone down between the rocks, then passed through Fritz's legs. It formed a stark contrast to the black rock. The whole shot was rather symbolic. I always envisioned mountains as Fritz's mistresses. And there was the lure: the thrill of hanging in midair, suspended between life and death. No encounter could compare to that: a delicate balance between imminent disaster and salvation at the same moment. He could never experience such a mind-boggling rush of blood with me.

He was not even looking up to see where he was going. Thousands of feet in the air, his head was turned to the side as he grinned madly for all posterity. He risked his life to climb up big heaps of earth. I would never fully understand that. My brain heard all the words about the thrill, the rush, the victory; but my soul, my heart, never understood. He chanced everything for a few moments at the top. Now he was there and I was here. We were both stranded.

I went into the bedroom and pulled open the nightstand drawer. There lay the stack of papers, his letters. I read them often.

I reread the first letter he had written to me.

Aspen, July 28, 1973

Dear Janice,

I loved seeing your tears when you left Thursday afternoon, even if they were painful for you. For only if fractions of what you said during those days was true, there was no reason at all to weep. And I have a good feeling that everything was true. Something truly beautiful could come from our meeting. The fortunate circumstances that surrounded our meeting tempts me to think "Things were meant." Shall I thank "Fate" or you?

I took another from the nightstand:

Punta del Inca - Argentina, March 5, 1974

Dear Janice,

When I hike or climb, every step ends and begins a new thought of you. Already in the first half year we have acquired enough memories for a lifetime. And this is only the beginning. So many sweet nights and lovely mornings to look forward to. I thank God that I met you, yes God, not predestination. I am now certain I will love you forever. If I am lucky you will one day say to me when we are sixty, "I still don't understand you," yet I say to you my soul is more exposed with you than it ever was and it is prone to open even more as time passes, for it is my soul that loves you most and best. When will I hold you again?

Your Fritz

I reached for another letter:

. . . All my hopes concerning you have been fulfilled. If tomorrow we would be bombed out like my grandmother was twice after two world wars, I know now that I could stand in front of the ruins with you, fully convinced that we had lost nothing.

I could not finish it. I put the letters back, but I could not erase the sight of his handwriting. Everywhere I looked I saw the gilt-edged papers filled with his writing, precise and strong, lining the paper. It revealed his character, his style.

I had to make more calls. The phone stared back at me accusingly. The dial looked like a mutated face, a circle of vacant eyes. A modern monster. I began again. The spinning lottery ran from one to zero, a series beginning with little and ending with nothing. Which combination would I choose this time? The U.S. embassy in Pakistan had not told me much; I would call our embassy in Afghanistan. Geographically, it was right next door to where he had last been seen. The dial settled. The line was ringing.

An accented voice answered. "U.S. embassy."

"Hello, this is Janice Pennington. I'm calling from the United States."

"Ms. Pennington . . . How may I help you?"

"I don't quite know where to begin. . . . Last September 27, my husband was climbing in the Tirich Mir region close to the border when he disappeared," I said and explained my story yet again. "I haven't heard anything from him, no phone calls, no letters," I concluded.

"Well, is this unusual?" the voice asked.

"Well, yes. It is," I replied.

"I'll need some information from you," he stated impersonally.

I reeled off Fritz's full name, date of birth, and physical description. After asking me a few more questions, the voice at the other end stopped. There was one question I had to ask.

"Excuse me, but what do you think would have happened if my husband wandered near the border?"

There was a pause.

"Well, Ms. Pennington, I really don't know what to tell you. His situation would depend on who found him."

"What does that mean?"

"Afghanistan's border lies near the region your husband was climbing. Russia and China are also rather close. If he wandered off course, after a couple of days he may have ended up in very dangerous territory. I don't know how much you know about this part of the world, but the region is extremely volatile. If your husband crossed our border, he'd be considered politically dangerous. He could be imprisoned. Where was he when you last heard from him?"

"Chitral."

"Well, Chitral is about forty miles from the Afghanistan-Pakistan border."

"But wouldn't you have heard if Fritz was arrested? Isn't the embassy notified?"

"Not necessarily . . . your husband is not a U.S. citizen. You must understand, Ms. Pennington, this is not the United States. Whoever found your husband would know nothing about him. He would be seen as a hostile foreigner, perhaps even as an enemy or spy. What might happen to him after being discovered is an unanswerable question."

"What about the German embassy?" I asked. "Since Fritz is a German national, might they know something?"

"Yes," he stated drily. "We will contact them. That's standard procedure." His abrupt silence signaled the end of the conversation.

I was not done yet. "Please call me if you find anything."

"We'll do what we can" was the noncommittal reply. A dial tone followed.

I sat for a moment, holding the receiver to my ear, unable to put it down. I learned nothing.

Things the embassy official said stuck in my mind. The facts moved like wooden horses on a carousel: they went up and down, spun around and around, but took me nowhere. The U.S. government did not want to get involved because Fritz was not a U.S. citizen. There were international considerations involving any actions in that region. Local officials would probably consider Fritz dangerous. They might think he was a spy.

I dug out the pack of his letters again. One of them had said something about spies. Here it was: "I just learned that the CIA posed as a mountain climbing expedition and installed nuclear blast monitoring devices directed at China—and got caught. I fear that this affects custom inspection seriously."

CIA agents had masqueraded as mountain climbers. If Fritz was mistaken for a spy, there would be no justice. He wanted so much to do good for the world. During the Vietnam War, he wrote to the North Vietnamese government requesting permission to climb in their country. He wanted to investigate the situation so that he could inform people of what was really going on. One bit stuck in my head. "On the way to the mountains, I met the people of the world," he'd written. "Mountains are no longer the main goal of my travels. They are now rather a means than an end. The end is the people." He was twenty-two when he wrote that.

The government denied Fritz permission to enter Vietnam, but he found another way in. Fritz never allowed paperwork to stop him. He entered Pakistan without a climbing permit this time, intending to procure one once he arrived. Prince Burchanadin, a member of Pakistan's royal family, was a friend. With the prince's help, Fritz expected to avoid administrative difficulties. He kept a copy of the letter he sent the prince.

July 1975

Dear Prince Burchanadin,

Yes, it is time to visit with you again. I have told the entire world your stories, now I need new ones. I hope I will find you as rigorous as always when I come to Chitral at the end of September. However, before I come to Chitral, I would like to hike to the base of Nanga Parbat via the Babusar Pass and Bunar. I know that I need some minor permission. Most likely I will get it here in the States. But if, for some reason, time or otherwise, I cannot get it here, could I ask your good offices to help me get the papers in Rawalpindi? I will come with my wife who is eager to meet you.

Everyone knows you here from pictures and stories I passed on. I look forward to returning to Pakistan, which I find one of the healthiest countries, yes, in the world. The warmth and strength of the people is the subject of a great many conversations. If time permits it, could you answer me? If not, I will see you in Rawalpindi or Chitral. Perhaps you could deposit or leave word in the Intercontinental Hotel in Karachi or Rawalpindi.

Your friend,

Fritz Stammberger

The letter to the prince mentioned a permit for him to hike to the base of Nanga Parbat, with no mention of Tirich Mir. Why? I asked myself. The letter was written when I'd been planning to go with him. Because my work schedule changed at the last minute, I wasn't able to make the trip. I didn't know whether he had planned to visit with the prince before or after climbing Tirich Mir. If the visit preceded the climb, Fritz probably would have acquired the papers he needed. But if he hadn't seen the prince, he might not have obtained a climbing permit.

Tomorrow I had to go back to work. Monday, Tuesday, and Wednesday would vanish before I had a chance to catch my breath, just as this day had vanished. It had passed in a whirl, a panic. Sometimes I felt as if I was in a hall of mirrors trying to find my way out. A hundred doors surrounded me. Ninety-nine were reflections. One was real.

I stood up gingerly and returned to the living room. Sunlight streamed in through the window, which opened on the vacant street. I hadn't spent much time with friends since Fritz had vanished. Talk sounded like a formality, a chore. If I lay still too long, this silence would cover over me as it had covered Fritz. No word had emerged from him, no voice that I could hear. It was almost as if he never existed.

9.

At Home in Los Angeles

Los Angeles
1976

I turned away from the framed picture on the nightstand. Fritz and me hugging in front of the condominium in Aspen. I had no idea how late or how early it was. The sun was streaming in through the bedroom window. I didn't want to get out of bed. The alarm repeated a series of beeps. I fumbled with the snooze button.

The night before, Harry Conway called to let me know that he learned a few more details. He heard that Fritz had never contacted Prince Burchanadin. So, Fritz had never received a climbing permit. The U.S. embassy in Pakistan had been less than enthusiastic about that information. I'd already decided not to rely on them. Feeling weary even though the day had not yet begun, I dragged myself out of bed.

For all I knew Fritz was lying in a cold, dirty prison cell. Injured. Fritz would not surrender quietly. I put some water on to boil and leafed through the photographs left out on the table.

I began to search through our old pictures with the hope that I might recognize someone I had not yet contacted. Fritz's climbing buddies knew the region he was in better than I did, and they might also know of plans he may have had. I kept hoping that one of them would tell me something definite. I passed a picture of Fritz and two others looking grungy and rugged beside a pristine snow-covered peak. I knew one of the men, but did not recognize the other.

I flipped to the next shot. There we stood, poised on a mountain on the edge of Aspen Valley. Below us the valley lay arrayed like a carefully spread picnic blanket. The folds of road were set here and there with wooden chalets and huskier log cabins. Fritz and I had spent so many hours strolling the streets, sitting in the restaurants and cafes, and hunting for odds and ends to fill our home.

I got up and went to turn off the kettle, which was whistling in the background. I watched the steaming water spill into my mug, drowning the teabag.

There was a crisp knock at the kitchen door. Tea in hand, I went to unlatch it.

"Just stopping by to see how your lawn was doing. Wouldn't want it to turn brown in this heat." It was my father. He'd fallen into the habit of stopping by in the mornings. The occasional visit became a daily ritual after Fritz disappeared.

"Thanks, Dad, but you don't have to bother."

"Oh, it's no trouble," he responded. "Now you just go ahead and drink your tea. This is no trouble at all." He always said that people thought there was more to do in life than there really was. Dad liked things simple, basic. Funny how I had always chosen men who were the opposite. Trailblazers. I felt that men like that would be a catalyst for my freedom. With them, there might be an element of danger, but no risk of boredom. My father never understood the men I was with.

Back inside the kitchen, I watched him walk through the yard, put out the trash, putter about the garden. This was the way he knew how to comfort me. With words, he was at a loss, unlike my mother. She and my sister would probably be here soon. They usually came by with my father.

The regularity of his morning visits did not feel like an imposition. It was hard to describe my relationship with him. He never made a big issue out of anything. He had his own quiet but dependable way about him. He hardly ever told me that he loved me, but he always managed to show me. When I was little, he helped me with my homework and listened attentively to the stories I brought home from school. Every day when he came home from work I would be waiting by the front window. As soon as he walked in, I would run to greet him. I was always glad to see him. He reminded me of Bing Crosby with his soulful eyes. And he always had a pipe clamped in his teeth. When I needed support, I always felt that I could anchor myself in him. He was a port of calm.

My mother was different. She was outgoing and she had a wonderful sense of humor. She always had the meals on the table at the right times, the kids were always well taken care of, the house was always clean and tidy, but she carried a gathering storm inside her. I didn't notice it when I was younger. For most of my childhood and even now, she appeared to be the perfect mother: silky brown hair neatly in place, blue eyes sparkling. I always felt a little bit in awe of her well-organized life. She was smart. I could never manage to put anything past her. She always seemed to know what I was up to. I felt close to her, too, even though during my childhood there were times that she made me feel uncomfortable. Shopping for clothes was one such time. Until I was about twelve, my mother had me convinced that my body was less than perfect. She didn't intend to make me feel that way; it just sort of happened. Whenever we went shopping she would mention my short waist to the saleslady, whispering that it was slightly out of proportion and asking the woman for any outfits that might camouflage my deficiency—from the father's side of the family. "They're not bad-looking people, you understand," she would say, "it's just that the women are on the stocky side." I would cringe with embarrassment.

She was raised by the old school: get married, set up a nice home, raise children. She was distant in ways, perhaps because her own mother had been. My grandmother was strict, religious, and concerned with form. She rarely demonstrated affection, even later in life when I knew a little more about her. Perhaps that was why my mother had her other side, the side that wrote poetry and believed in metaphysics: reincarnation, auras, and out-of-body experiences. Perhaps this was her rebellion against her own mother, if not her escape. My father didn't believe in mysticism. "When you're dead, you're dead," he'd say. She didn't talk about it much with him.

I knew that my mother and sister would come through the door at any time. They would be a comfort to me. I was feeling more and more insecure. Just like during my childhood, I wanted to hide.

10.

The Vision

Los Angeles
1976

Silence was all that remained. The room was not mine. How I arrived, I did not know. God, God, God, protect me from whatever this is, wherever I am. One presence, one power. One presence, one power. God. All there is is God. I felt incapable of action. As if to test myself, I tried to sit up. I could hardly lift my head. I tried again to no avail. I was paralyzed. I concentrated all my efforts. I must not panic. Whatever the force that bound me, I would not escape it with desperation. I searched my head for other alternatives, but found no way to free myself.

A vibration ran through my body. I hovered, suspended. My heart was pounding. I felt like I was having a heart attack. I couldn't breathe. There was air all around me but I couldn't breathe. My limbs and trunk lay stiff, extended, wands for the divinity whose energy transformed me. My body was not mine. I tried to look around, but my head would not move. I could only move my eyes.

The room was long, tall and narrow. Bookshelves filled with worn volumes and manuscripts lined the right wall. I could discern titles, but I could not read them. They blurred. The library stretched from floor to ceiling. But the floor was not really a floor. It was made of earth, earth packed down hard. Contoured by the weight of feet, it shined. The glow of use. A slow-paced pilgrimage had passed this place over years, decades, centuries. The ritual began before recorded time. I floated three feet above the floor. It was cool. Cool and dark. I began to rise. The vibration coursed through me. Its energy lifted me. The floor receded.

I was moved above a refectory table. Glancing down, I could see that it was marred and gouged. Wide and long. It nearly filled the room. My body stretched out above it. The edge projected out. There were things on the table. I sensed shapes and forms below me, outlines, rough hewn wood.

A mumbling and muttering began. Before me stood a figure, elevated as if on a pulpit. It towered, insurmountable. A long dark robe swooped around the body; swathes of cloth covered the face. Eyes, arms, and legs hid inside the draping curves. Only a voice emerged. "Truth and beauty lie within." The voice spoke to me, but low as if to itself, repeating the sentence over and over. "Truth and beauty lie within." It was a woman. I could not see her, but I knew her face was disfigured. Her head hung down, turned to the ground. The hood dropped over and cloaked her scars. Her words echoed. "Look within. Look within. Truth and beauty lie within." Her hand moved up and down, then side to side. Up and down. Side to side. The robe swayed. She was crossing herself. Murmuring and crossing herself again and again.

The force moved me again. Gently, but firmly, I was lowered. The vibration kept me rigid, held in midair above the floor. Across from me was a wooden cot. On top of it lay a man turned on his side with his back to me. He had shaggy brown hair, broad shoulders, and long legs. His body curled in a fetal position, asking for comfort, but offering no surrender. He was dressed in a dark blue jogging suit. His face was turned away, but I had seen this silhouette before. Then the understanding came to me. I knew this man. This was Fritz.

I concentrated. If only by force of will, I had to make him turn around. Look at me, look at me. I'm here. I see you. My thoughts brushed him lightly like moth wings. He stirred but didn't turn.

Fritz, turn over. Open your eyes. See that I am here. Know that I am here. Help me to help you. Help me. I pleaded to no avail. Deep in sleep, the figure remained turned toward the wall, turned away from me.

I scanned the room. Only cobwebs filled the corners. There was nothing more. This was all: the floor, the bookshelves, the table, the cot, the woman. She murmured with unceasing diligence: "Truth and beauty lie within. Truth and beauty lie within."

I tried to move. I knew I could not, but I tried. I focused all my energy on my arm. If only I could reach out. If only I could touch him, he would see me, and know I was here. My arm felt heavy. I was so weak. Only space lay between us, only air. Move. Move! I screamed in my head. No one heard. The murmuring continued. My arm stayed by my side. Fritz lay curled, facing the wall.

I felt a cold blast of air. In my mind's eye, I saw a door open behind me. I could see the chasm. A black void. Cold. Dark. Limitless. A chasm of nothing: without space, or time. The door slid on its hinges, slowly, silently. I would soon be gone, taken back, through the opening. I had to make Fritz hear me, this was my only chance.

I had to move my arm. My being flowed into it. I watched my hand rise: I waved good-bye. My hand seemed distorted; the motion, exaggerated. The air hung thick like water. The body in blue did not respond.

The force dragged me back. It possessed my body. I wanted to stay. I tried to resist. Fritz was here. Here was where I belonged. I could not leave. As if in response, the power increased, insistently drawing me back. I was sucked out the door and thrust into a vacuum. My body traveled. I surrendered. I had no choice. My spinal cord relaxed, a taut string let slack. The world went black.

11.

The Phone Call

Los Angeles
1976

T he night's occurrence hung over me, casting shadows. I'd never had an experience like this before, although I had other metaphysical episodes and visitations, as a child. My parents called them dreams. Sometimes I'd wake up standing out on the lawn. They would find me there.

The encounters would start with a scanning. Paralyzing beams of light and vibrations would fill my body. The air would thicken. An energy would focus on my forehead, then move over my limbs. After a while, I learned not to be afraid. I would fight the energy, try to escape it. I knew that I would have to wake up alone, sweating, exhausted. I did not want to face the disbelief, the raised eyebrows. Then, one day, as suddenly as the visitations had begun, they stopped. Until Fritz disappeared. Then they began again. Slowly. Once, twice. The paralysis. The thickening air. The vibration. And now this experience. I contemplated the implications of what I was told. Do not look without, look within. Truth and beauty lie within. It seemed so simple, and yet so infinitely complicated, like a riddle. I knew that the important things in life were intangible, internal.

The phone rang. I picked it up.

"Hello, hello!" a voice said quickly.

"Hello," I said cautiously.

"Is this Janice Pennington?"

"Yes, it is. . . . Who is this?"

"I just received an urgent message that I was to call Janice Pennington. The message said there was an emergency."

An emergency? "What emergency?" I asked.

"The message said to call this number. It said to call Janice Pennington immediately. You are Janice Pennington, aren't you?" he questioned.

I felt as though I was failing an important test.

"This is Janice Pennington, isn't it? I know I dialed the number on the message. Is this 784-6843?"

"Yes, that's my number, but I didn't leave a message," I told him.

"Where might I know you from?" he queried.

"What was your name again?" I asked. He still had not told me.

"Hillman. Mike Hillman," he said, sounding annoyed. "I'm a producer. I did *Rich Man, Poor Man*."

"Oh, I work at CBS," I informed him, "on *The Price Is Right*."

"Maybe you know someone that I know?" he suggested.

He listed a few names, but there seemed to be no one we both knew.

I was puzzled. "You know, my number is unlisted. Where did you get my number and that message?"

"It was left with my service," he replied brusquely, as if the answer were obvious. "The message said it was an emergency. It was urgent that I call you. Maybe we've met socially."

If the circumstances had been different I would have hung up, but I was desperate.

"Well, I spend most of my time in Aspen, actually, not in L.A. My husband and I live in Aspen." The last sentence sounded strange to my ears as I said it. It was no longer true.

"Aspen!" he exclaimed. "I live in Aspen part of the year. I have a home there. . . . What's your husband's name?"

"Fritz," I replied slowly. "Fritz Stammberger."

"Oh, yes, I've heard of him. He had a business or something."

"He owns a print shop." Many people knew of Fritz through his work.

"Maybe he left the message."

I was silent for a moment. "I don't think so," I finally said. "My husband's disappeared."

"Disappeared! Maybe the person who left this message had some information for you."

A torrent of questions stormed down: Where did Fritz disappear? When had he left? What had been his plans? The questions fell in rapid succession. I hardly had time to answer one question before Mike Hillman had asked another. His interest was peculiar.

His voice droned on. "That must have been difficult. Has anyone contacted you about him? Did your husband say anything that would lead you to think he wouldn't be coming back?"

"There was this talk we had . . . about trust." I trailed off, again uncertain whether I wanted to say anything. Since Conway's failed attempt, I felt like my chances of finding Fritz were very slim. I needed help. "He asked me this strange question, wanted to know about my past, whether there was anything he should know. But . . . he knew everything."

"Go on," Hillman prompted.

"It wasn't so much what he said as how he said it. 'You know someday you may hear something about me, and I trust you know me well enough to know it wouldn't be true?'"

Mike Hillman responded, suddenly matter-of-fact and businesslike, "Well, I suppose anything's possible. . . . Here, let me give you a number where you can reach me. I happen to know a few people who might be able to help. . . . If you call this line, I'll know that it could only be you."

Hillman began reeling off the number. I scrambled to grab a pad of paper and a pen.

"These people are very influential and politically powerful. I'll contact them and get back to you."

I hardly had a chance to say good-bye before he hung up. What a strange man. The longer I thought about it, the stranger the conversation seemed.

He mentioned being a producer. Maybe his interest in the business explained his interest in me. Hillman had said he worked on the Universal lot. A friend of mine, Pete Terranova, was an executive at Universal. Maybe he could tell me more about Hillman.

As the Universal operator directed my call, I thought of how little

Hillman had said about himself. It sounded as if he was the one volunteering information and offering ways to help, but in reality he had gotten me to do all the talking.

When Pete answered the phone, I asked him immediately, "Who produced *Rich Man, Poor Man?*"

"Whoa, whoa. Baby, I haven't talked to you in weeks. Why don't we save the TV trivia for later," Pete said.

I realized that Pete had no idea what the situation was. I explained. Cynical by nature, he became immediately suspicious.

"Listen, baby, Mike Hillman didn't produce *Rich Man, Poor Man,*" he said. "Never heard of him. Let me look into this guy's background and see what I can find out."

"I'd appreciate anything," I replied.

"Okay. Hold on a second and I'll check."

If Hillman had nothing to do with this television series or with Universal, then who is he?

"Janice, are you there?" asked Pete when he returned.

"Yes, I'm still here."

"I'm sorry that took so long. From the looks of it, your Mike Hillman had nothing to do with *Rich Man, Poor Man.* He sure as hell wasn't the producer. I'll see if I can find out anything else and get back to you, but, personally, baby, sounds like he was trying to con you. I think that you are a little too trusting, a little too gullible, if you don't mind me saying so," Pete stated. I felt foolish.

"The whole thing went so fast. . . . I didn't have a clue. Well, thanks for everything," I said.

"No trouble. You know that. Take care of yourself, baby. Hang in there."

"Yeah."

I spent the rest of the day writing letters to the CIA, the FBI, and any other government office I could think of. The whole time I kept thinking about Mike Hillman and his mysterious phone call. And the phone number he gave me; I was almost afraid to try it. I didn't know who would answer. I didn't know what I would say. I called. The phone rang.

It was strange that he would know I was trying to reach him. I couldn't be the only person calling him. There was no answer. I hung up.

I finished the letter I'd been writing, then took out the typewriter. Formal correspondence usually received more respect. I straightened out the paper and checked the ribbon. The phone rang.

"Hello," I answered eagerly.

"Hi, baby. It's me, Pete. Well, we checked this Hillman guy out as best we could and came up with absolutely nothing. He's never been on the Universal lot. I took the liberty of calling the main office and having them run a check. I don't know where this guy came from, but I'd bet my ass that he didn't call to help. Can I ask you a personal question?"

"Sure."

"Was there any shady business that Fritz was involved in? Smuggling? He wasn't into drugs, was he? Because Hillman sounds pretty shady to me, and it sounds like he called you to find out what you knew about Fritz."

"No, Fritz wasn't into anything like that. He wouldn't have anything to do with that."

"Sorry . . . I had to ask. Look, I'll talk to you later."

I was taken aback, a little shaken and beginning to worry about the circumstances surrounding Fritz's disappearance. The thought that he was involved in the intrigue around it had never crossed my mind. The pieces of the puzzle were getting more scrambled: Jim MacGeyver's visit in Aspen, Mike Hillman's call this morning, the letters Fritz had, his connections with royalty in the Far East. These seemed to corroborate my central feeling that Fritz was alive, but doing what?

I thought about his climbing trips, from Argentina to the Himalayas. Did Hillman know something? Did Conway? Even Pete seemed to sense something.

What had Fritz done?

I sealed my house. I turned off the lights and the television in the bedroom. Darkness encroached. I did not know who would come here. I did not know who to trust or who to believe. I had to keep this quiet, to myself. That was the safest way. I shut and locked the door.

12.

The Wanderer

Los Angeles
1976

I stopped at the mailbox and shuffled through the mail. There were some bills and one big fat envelope. I hurried inside to open it. It was a package from Pakistan from Jim MacGeyver. Inside there was page after page in Jim's cramped handwriting. I was anxious to know what he had discovered:

> . . . There was a man wandering in the Kalash Valley in Pakistan believed to be Fritz. One of my guides knew about Fritz and had been impressed with his skills. He agreed that with his capabilities, Fritz could have climbed Tirich Mir alone and then hiked into some remote area of Pakistan or even another country. Another guide said that he had seen a man, very tall, skinny, rather mad-looking, a foreigner wearing Pakistani clothes, about thirty miles from where we were.
>
> As you know, I never accepted the fact that Fritz was dead on Tirich Mir. By this time I really felt eighty percent sure that this tall man was Fritz. I decided that one way or another I would go to the Kalash Valley to try and find him.
>
> On the morning of October 6, we were prepared to search and find this tall, crazy-looking man and departed from Rawalpindi via Peshawar on Pakistan Airlines flight 603 for Chitral.
>
> Arriving in Chitral, we dropped our luggage off at the Tirich Mir Hotel. Immediately we went to the superintendent of police

to register for our climb. This process took about two hours so during this time I talked to the registering agent about missing foreigners. Finally, he started talking about "Stammberger." I tried not to show too much interest. I didn't want the agent to know that I was searching for Fritz in case he had anything to hide, so I asked vague questions. His answers were curt and, if not directly evasive, it was clear from their brevity that he didn't really want to go into the matter further.

Our papers and passports, which had been taken from us, were returned shortly thereafter, and we went to the district commissioner to get permission to go into the Kalash Valley. We got this permission without any trouble from the assistant D.C., who reminded me of Snidely Whiplash from the Bullwinkle cartoon. Even in this relatively routine situation, the assistant could not conceal a barely restrained hostility. This man would later prove to be a very unnerving character.

Back at the hotel, we decided that we had to return to the office to question them in a more direct manner. This would necessitate leveling with them about our mission and risking any defensive reaction on their part. The next day we met with the D.C., the assistant D.C., and the superintendent of police. We told them that we had come from the U.S.A. As soon as I said it, I knew we were in for a rough ride.

"Do you have any police report on the search for Fritz Stammberger?" I asked them.

"Yes," the D.C. said with some effort. He picked up a file that looked to be about two inches thick and started reading excerpts to us:

"'Stammberger was last seen in Chitral on September 27, 1975. Two porters had accompanied him toward base camp. The first was Usman Kahn. The second and last man known to be with Stammberger was Sher Barang. These men were both questioned but nothing that they said shed any new light on the matter. The district commissioner asked the police to conduct the search in November of 1975; the report was filed with the district commissioner in May of 1976.'" The D.C. shut the file with finality. "In our mind this man was a fool."

I asked if I might have a copy of the report to give you, Janice. They took this very offensively.

"Why are you interrogating us?" the assistant district commissioner barked. "What right do you have to be asking these questions?" The man was furious. He told us to get out of the office immediately. Soon they were all shouting at us. "Out! Out! You have no right to be here."

I left the room. My head was pounding. Why wouldn't they let me read that file?

Having no time to waste, we hired a Jeep, loaded our luggage and departed to the Kalash region where the wanderer had been reported seen. Upon our arrival we were told that there was a festival going on to honor the death of a prominent leader of the Kalash people.

We checked into the Kalash View Inn and started to mingle among the people. The Kalash of Karfiristan are a dying tribe. They speak their own language and trace their ancestors back to Alexander the Great. They have no religion whatsoever, though the recent completion of a road to the valley has had its effect on them from the Moslems. They drink wine, wear black clothes, and are exceedingly filthy, never bathing in an entire year and only replacing their clothes when they rot off. They bury their dead in coffins above the ground, even though the government has tried to stop this practice. When one of their leaders dies, all the men dance up a frenzy, and whoever is the last one left standing is the next leader. All in all, I would call them, as a group or tribe, an anthropologist's dream for study.

When we arrived, the dancing had begun. Drums were pounding loudly; the crowd swelled all around us. The people were caught up in a rhythmic chant. Every now and then a scream would pierce through the night air. Many of the dancers appeared to have their own boosters. The din was indescribable. To a Westerner, the scene sure qualified as colorful—straight out of a movie about Genghis Khan. To me, even though I grew up in Pakistan and am very familiar with the practices of the people, the experience began to get claustrophobic. With all the chaos, I wondered how we would be able to see anything.

All of a sudden, one guide grabbed my shoulder. "Jim, look quickly!" he said.

I turned around and saw nothing at first but the continued swirling of bodies. "Where?"

"Over there," he shouted, pointing.

"I don't . . . ," I began. And then I saw him—for a split second. From the shoulders up, a profile, a mane of long hair. A tall man who towered over the Kalash. An instant later he disappeared behind a hut.

"Come on!" I said. We gave chase, forcing ourselves through the thick crowds, the cavorting revelers, down impossibly narrow alleys. We had no idea where we were going, no sense of direction; we didn't even know if we were on the man's track— we could have been just rushing blindly.

Finally, we turned a corner and there was a man, standing some hundred yards away, a tall man, just over six feet. With him was a big dog. My pulse was racing. He had his back to us, but it definitely seemed like he could have been the man of the guide's description. I slowed my pace somewhat, wanting to appear calm so as to not frighten him off. Then, as I approached, I began to get incredibly nervous. What would I say to him if it were Fritz? "Remember me?" What kind of state would he be in? Would he resent the fact that we had been able to find him? I even started to slow down, trying to figure out what to say and feeling terrified all of a sudden that I would blow it.

Then the man began to walk away. I had to do something. "Wait," I called, and began running. The man stopped and turned around. The guide's description was right on the money. Even from where he was I could see the wildness in his eyes. As I got closer, words were still failing me. I found myself wondering if I would even recognize him if he were Fritz—it had been such a long time since I'd seen him. A minute later I was standing directly in front of him . . . and I still didn't know! I stammered out an introduction for myself.

Then he spoke, and it was immediately obvious—this was not Fritz. I did not even hear half of the words he said at first. All I could think of was that Fritz had seemed so close, and now he was just as far away as ever. Fritz had escaped once more.

The tall man—six feet-two inches to be exact—was a Jamaican by the name of Ted Noble. He was not crazy at all, as it turned out, but was quite sane. As a matter of fact, we stayed in Kalash two more nights and became rather good friends with Ted Noble. We questioned him and he gave us a great deal of valuable information about the Chitral area. We also took the time to question other people in the village, trying to find out if any other tall men had been seen. There were no additional clues. Ted Noble was almost definitely the man we had been looking for all along. We left bitterly disappointed.

In conclusion, Jim's letter went on to say:

We decided the only other possible route we could take in our search would be to go to Gilgit via Parpish, Mustuch and Sandur Pass and question people along the way, but we were unable to do so after a heavy snowfall. Finally, we called off our search and I departed for Rawalpindi. I had done everything I could do to try to find out anything about Fritz and felt dismayed once again when I realized there wasn't any more concrete proof to give you, Janice.

It is very obvious in my mind that Fritz didn't want anyone to know what he planned to do. He didn't have permission from the Ministry of Tourism in Pakistan to climb. He didn't even say hello to his old friend in Chitral, Prince Burchanadin. He climbed late in the year to avoid contact with any other would-be climbers on the mountain. And more important than all these above factors, he never told you or any other of his friends. The question is why?

I personally feel Fritz did it because he had something much bigger in mind than Tirich Mir.

Yours sincerely,

Jim MacGeyver

I threw the papers on the floor. They flew apart, drifted, then settled. First Harry Conway and now Jim MacGeyver—both had failed. Fritz Stammberger was nowhere to be found.

13.

Political Prisoners

Los Angeles
1976

A fter a while they disconnected the wire from his finger and connected it to his ear. Immediately, he felt a horrifying surge of electricity, like a nail driven underneath the ball of his eye, coursing through his head. His body shook uncontrollably. His front teeth started breaking.

Some fool with a maniacal grin held a mirror in front of his face. It looked like a grotesque parody of a jack-o'-lantern. His eyes were filled with blood.

'Look what's happening to your lovely green eyes. Soon you will not be able to see at all. You will lose your mind. You see, you have already started bleeding in your mouth.'

A sickening glob of red tissue dribbled from the side of his mouth. The flow increased. He began to gag. He could not close his lips; the torrent gushed down his chin, splashing all over him. He collapsed into the pool of dirty water at his feet. After another electric shock he was writhing in blood. His captors set about beating him with truncheons. They kicked him again and again, in the stomach, in the groin, in the head. An unearthly moan rose from his throat, as if his chest was slowly being crushed. After an excruciating minute of this ungodly wail, it was clear that he was trying to form a word. He said it again, and this time I recognized it. He was calling my name.

I sat up, drenched in sweat. The darkness before me could not erase the vision. The pictures flashed before my eyes. I had to move, to get away from them. I turned on the light and stared at the brochures lying on the nightstand.

I could not stop looking at the prisoner of conscience plastered on the cover. Every time I glanced at this image I could not look away. This man had become a mannequin, hiding his feelings behind a mask of scarred indifference. A poster boy of torture. I didn't know who had exploited him. Somewhere along the line he became damaged goods. He was released from prison, but there was no joy on his face. He would never be whole. I did not want to think of what Fritz might be like now. This faceless, nameless man on the brochure had survived eight months in captivity. How long could Fritz survive?

I had considered all along that he could be in prison. Ever since the call from "Mike Hillman," I could not shake the thought that Fritz might have been arrested for espionage. I called the number he gave me incessantly, day and night, at all hours. No one ever answered. I was slowly becoming more and more certain that Fritz was, like this man, a prisoner of conscience.

Unfortunately, Amnesty International did not agree with me. I went into the kitchen and sat down. The letter I received with the brochure lay on the table. It was barely more than a form letter. The organization was besieged with thousands of requests for aid. Apparently, countless individuals have fallen into the gears of international politics. Amnesty International limited itself to helping individuals imprisoned in their own countries, and Fritz was a German national lost in Pakistan. The letter ended with condolences and good wishes. I had my fill of empty empathy.

I found out that the CIA installation in Pakistan was second in size and importance only to the main headquarters in Langley, Virginia. The CIA's electronic intercept station, the U-2 spy program, and other operations were centered in Pakistan. And the area around Tirich Mir was especially volatile. Tirich Mir lies near the borders of five countries: Russia, China, India, Pakistan, and Afghanistan.

Two years after Fritz disappeared, the Soviet Union supported a communist coup in Afghanistan, and now the U.S.S.R. was trying to shore up the pro-Russian government against the country's mountain guerrillas, the mujahadin. Fritz had talked of these men with deep admiration. I could not rule out the possibility that he had gotten mixed up in running arms from Pakistan to the rebels.

Knowing Fritz's strong idealistic beliefs, I started feeling more than ever that he may have been involved in some master plan, or caught up in the middle of one. The mission could have been for Afghanistan, Pakistan, Tibet, or even the CIA. Any number of things could have happened to Fritz and no one would have said a word.

When I began to suspect that Fritz was involved in political espionage, I withdrew. Was he a spy? Was our marriage a sham? Did anyone else close to us know or suspect? Why didn't he trust me enough to tell me? Is he dead or alive? Fear had taken over. Fear of what had happened to Fritz. Fear of what might happen to me. Only my family was allowed in. There were days when I even hid from them. My mother and my sister kept prodding me. They wanted me to abandon my shell. They said it was not healthy. They didn't like the way it looked, the way I looked. Crazy. They never said it out loud, but they probably thought it. I was afraid of losing the world I had created with Fritz. I was afraid they would take it away from me. I was afraid I would give it away. I didn't trust myself. Sometimes I hurt so much. I would have given away anything just to end the pain, but I was determined not to need anyone.

Then the dreams started.

The metaphysical experiences were one thing. I knew what to expect. The vibration, the air thickening, the paralysis.

The dreams were different. They came without warning, sudden as electrical storms. Mental terror. They were rational, almost. My worst fears fragmented, distorted. The mind shorted out. Memories blurred. I saw Fritz mangled. I could not escape them, could not predict them. And I began to have them every night. I could no longer retreat into my mind, my house, the world I had created. It was turning on me, turning me out.

* * *

His name was Bob Peloquin. The person who told me about him was Larry Dubois, a writer friend of mine. He described him as a scary man, someone I'd want to keep on my side. Peloquin was very powerful in the intelligence world. In a word, he was uncanny. His mind did not miss a trick. If anyone could help me, he could.

Peloquin had started out working for the government. He worked for naval intelligence during the Fifties, then for the National Security Agency and later for the Justice Department. In all three positions, he developed a reputation for brilliance and fearlessness. It was Peloquin who brought down Jimmy Hoffa, president of the Teamsters. Hoffa was indicted many times, but had always slipped away. Peloquin, however, was able to come up with an airtight jury-tampering case, and pinned the rap on Jimmy Hoffa for the first time.

As the head of the Justice Department's first strike force against the Mob, beginning in 1966, Peloquin's ability to infiltrate the Magaddino family, once one of the most impenetrable Mafia clans, was unheard of. Due to his success, the strike force became established firmly as a valuable means of investigating organized crime.

After sixteen years in government service, Peloquin formed Intertel, one of the most powerful private investigating firms in the world. When Howard Hughes discovered that McGraw-Hill was about to publish an "authorized" autobiography of him, which he'd never heard of, he contacted Intertel. Intertel investigated. The scam looked foolproof. McGraw-Hill had issued two checks totaling $650,000 to Hughes as an advance and the checks had been cashed. Everybody began to accuse everybody else of lying. A McGraw-Hill executive appeared on *The Today Show* with the canceled checks; he showed them on the air, made out to and endorsed by "H. R. Hughes." The case seemed closed.

Then Peloquin was brought in. The first thing he did was to get a videotape of *The Today Show*. He stopped the tape when the McGraw-Hill exec held up the checks, and took a photo of the screen. Then, he enlarged the photos until he could read the endorsements. The checks had been deposited at a branch of Credit Suisse in Zurich. In Zurich, Peloquin learned that the H. R. Hughes who deposited the checks was actually a woman. Acting on a hunch, Peloquin called his Washington office and had them wire a photo of the "authorized" author's wife. The woman in the photo was positively identified as "H. R. Hughes."

Peloquin solved the case in two days.

I was about to meet him. I had to convince Bob Peloquin to take my case. I had tried taking on the system alone, and I had failed; but with Peloquin investigating, things would change.

14.

Super Sleuth

Los Angeles
1976-77

As soon as I walked into the lobby of the Century Plaza Hotel in Los Angeles, I spotted them. Three serious-looking men in identical gray suits stood together, hands crossed at their waists. Their coats were buttoned in the heat. As I walked toward them, wondering which of the three was my man, they studied me with a cool, professional scrutiny. Finally, one of them stepped forward.

"Miss Pennington?" he questioned.

"Yes . . . ," I answered, hesitantly.

"I'm Bob Peloquin," he introduced himself.

Awkwardly shaking his hand, I replied, "Nice to meet you."

"This is Vadja Kolombatovic," he continued, pointing to one of the men who stood a short distance away, "and Richard Weller. Two of my colleagues."

Trying to act nonchalant, I suggested, "Well, shall we sit down somewhere? . . . perhaps, the bar?"

"No, I think it would be best if we met in one of the rooms. We'll have more privacy there."

I hesitated, then agreed. I watched people pass us as we walked toward the elevator. They knew so little of what was going on. They saw three businessmen and a woman. Nothing unusual about that. We could be anyone. The elevator door slid open and we walked in. There were no other passengers. As the doors closed, I realized that I knew little of what was going on myself. These three men had nothing more than their manner as credentials, yet here I was trusting them. I did not know where they were taking me. If anything should happen, I was on my own. I should have insisted on remaining in the lobby, where there were other people around.

The ride was silent. The last time I rode up one of these elevators I was nineteen. The Nina Blanchard modeling agency had arranged an interview with Jonathan Winters. He needed someone for his television special. That time no one met me in the lobby. I phoned up to his room. His business manager answered. They were doing interviews up there he said, telling me the floor and room number. I went up, holding my portfolio of pictures, expecting to see a suite or something. The two men were sitting in a regular hotel room. One bed, one table. That was it. Right after I arrived, the business manager left. A meeting, he said. That was when I began to feel uncomfortable, sitting on the bed, my pictures spread around me. But Jonathan Winters was a perfect gentleman.

I scanned the faces of Peloquin and his men, looking for some kind of connection. They gave up nothing. Their eyes, even in the confines of the elevator, restlessly scrutinized everything in sight. I steeled myself. Every floor we ascended added pressure, yet we kept rising. Finally, we reached the top floor. The doors opened.

In the room, we got right down to business.

"Why do you want to hire Intertel?" Peloquin asked.

I explained, keeping my voice as steady as possible, why I believed there was more to Fritz's disappearance than met the eye. "As you already know, my husband disappeared about a year ago. I've spent the past twelve months trying to find him on my own, but I haven't had much success. The government refuses to answer my letters. No one will confirm whether Fritz is alive or dead or even whether they know what's happened to him. But he couldn't have just disappeared into thin air. Someone must know something."

"What makes you so sure that you haven't found everything there is to know? Your husband was climbing alone, am I correct?"

"Well, I think he was doing more than just climbing in the area." As I talked, Peloquin continued to study me intently, as if I were under investigation. His eyes were penetrating, frightening, very difficult to look at. I had no idea what he thought of the things I was telling him.

"I don't want to be presumptuous," he said, "but were you and your husband happily married?"

I wondered how many people thought this question but didn't ask it. "Yes, we were very happy," I answered.

"And you loved him?"

"Very much."

"You weren't having any trouble then?"

"No."

"How about financial troubles?"

"No."

"What about drugs? Was Fritz involved with drugs in any way?"

"No, not at all." I held his gaze. I had to convince him to take this case.

"Do you think it is possible Fritz was working for the American government?" he asked finally.

"Yes. He was fervently interested in the people and politics of the region."

"Many people have an interest in that region," Peloquin said dismissively.

"But there were some things Fritz said to me, like 'One day you may hear that I'm a Russian spy.' He said that I shouldn't believe it. And he said that I might have to go away with him to an island where there was no one else. He said that I wouldn't have a choice, I'd have to go. Also he'd often speak in riddles. 'What would you do if you had a very difficult situation, a difficult thing to figure out? How would you go about solving this problem?' he'd asked. 'I think I would take it to its simplest form, the lowest common denominator, and start from there,'" I'd answered. "Fritz had also asked me, 'Are you ready for the revolution?' 'Could you feed people in the streets?' I didn't know what he was talking about specifically." Peloquin's face was utterly unreadable. I told him of Fritz's letters, of his international contacts, of the case where CIA agents had posed as climbers. Peloquin still did not respond. I went on. I catalogued the people involved: Harry Conway, Jim MacGeyver, Mike Hillman.

When I reached the point of the mysterious Mike Hillman phone call,

Peloquin perked up. His companions exchanged a glance.

"I've tried the number dozens of times, at all hours, and no one's ever answered."

"That number might tell us something. Someone wants to know what you know," Peloquin said. "It's impossible to say who, or whether it means anything. Why don't you write it down for me, and I'll see what I can find."

Excited, I wrote down the information and continued. "I figured that call was important. Something just wasn't right about it; it didn't feel right. I brought this letter, one of the last ones Fritz mailed to me." I hadn't noticed it at first, but when I'd gone back through Fritz's things I'd found it. I pulled it out of my bag. "It was misdirected. Doesn't that seem odd? Fritz wrote it in Pakistan, but it's postmarked Osaka, Japan. How would it have gotten there?" I asked, then turned the letter over. Not only was the postmark different, but on the back of the letter Fritz had drawn a crude map of the area. I showed it to Peloquin, and pointed out an airplane in the center of the picture.

"And then there's this plane. It's going in the wrong direction. If he was heading to Tirich Mir, it should be turned around. Fritz wouldn't make this mistake by accident. Do you think it could mean anything?"

Peloquin seemed genuinely perplexed. "Anything's possible. It could have been misrouted, but that's highly unlikely. It is odd, isn't it?"

He made a few notes as I was finishing up. "Janice," he said finally, "I'm going to be straight with you. There are any number of possibilities other than the obvious one for Fritz's disappearance. He may have been working for the government. He may have simply had an accident. I can tell you two things: First, I think it's a long shot that we will find out very much, if anything. Secondly, this operation is very expensive. It takes a lot of operatives and a lot of travel. We already have some men in that area working on another case, so you could avoid the start-up cost, but the expenses could still be substantial. Is this financially possible for you?"

I would cover it somehow. "Money's not my main concern. I have to know what happened to my husband."

He began gathering up the papers I had brought. "Here's how it

71

works. I'll take this information back to my people in Washington and we'll discuss the details of how to proceed. We certainly would not want to waste your money or our time. From the things that you've told me, it does seem like there's much more to this than meets the eye. It sounds like your husband may have been involved in things you weren't aware of. What I need you to do now is to compile information, anything you think might help. It would be a good idea to go to Aspen. We'll have one of our men meet you there so they could interview the people Fritz talked to before he left. . . . Does he have any family in this country?"

"No. His father lives in Munich."

"Did he see his father before he left?"

"Well, his flight stopped in Munich, but I don't know for how long."

"What airline did he take?"

"Pan Am."

"Have you checked to see if the other half of his ticket has been used?"

"Yes. I did. I asked his travel agent to check it for me. It was never used or refunded," I answered.

He thought for a second. "Have you seen Fritz's father since the disappearance? What was his name?"

"Wolfgang . . . I usually call him Opa. No, I haven't, but he's planning to come to Aspen. He never saw where his son lived. If he doesn't come out here, I may go there and visit."

"That might be a good idea."

We were on our feet, shaking hands. "The man who'll probably work with you is Vadja Kolombatovic," he said with a slight smile. All of a sudden, Peloquin was radiating warmth. Maybe it was just a relative thaw, but there was no denying that behind his cool demeanor, there was charm. "It was nice to meet you, Janice," he concluded as he led me to the door.

I felt I passed some monumental test. I had feared I would fail. I convinced these men that finding Fritz Stammberger was a mission worthy of their involvement. I had never quite had the courage to go up the mountain with him, but now, in some way, I felt as if I had.

15.

Murder on Tirich Mir

Aspen
1977

V adja Kolombatovic and I agreed to meet at noon for lunch. There were several people he wanted to interview in town, most importantly Harry Conway. Vadja wanted to be sure he knew everything there was to know regarding Harry's search. In the meeting with Peloquin, I might have left out some small detail of vital importance, something subtle, hidden.

As I turned into the street that led into town, I checked my watch. It was early. I still had three-quarters of an hour. I hadn't yet chosen the gift I planned to buy for my niece Jessica. I wanted it to be something special. Christmas was such an exciting holiday for children. Since I had no children of my own, Jessica was the closest thing I had to a daughter. I walked in and out of a toy store, then a children's clothing shop. I didn't want to buy another game that would be shelved, and I didn't think Jessica really needed or wanted another doll. I wanted to give her something that would make her feel special, even grown up. When I was a child I would have done anything to feel more grown up. Age symbolized so many things: freedom, romance, pretty clothes and trinkets. I entered a boutique.

These kinds of specialty stores didn't exist when I was a child. At least, they didn't exist in Seattle. No one thought to devote an entire shop to fancy and dreams. The closest I came to such things was in the local department store. With my mother's hand latched onto mine, I ran along behind her: her steps were twice mine. We were headed for the children's clothing and shoes. I dreaded the semiannual ritual. No ifs, ands or buts were allowed once we began. I'd have to try on the same old sensible, ugly shoes. They were sturdy, practical. Tan. The big decision revolved around which shoe size to purchase. How fast would I grow was the question. My inconsistent rate of change caused my mother endless frustration. The sole choice she left me involved color. But well-soled shoes rarely came in any colors besides white, black, and tan. This dull rainbow did not exactly provide a palette with which to paint a child's imagination. I wanted red. It wasn't very practical for school, she'd say.

We took the usual journey to the customary store, same department. I was expecting the usual choices and had almost resigned myself to the process. The tan shoes were bought again. I held the package as my mother paid, carefully counting the bills out from her wallet. As we walked through the store, I wanted to drop the shoes, abandon them. I longed for the day I would receive a pair of patent leather Mary Jane's: shiny, new, tied with grosgrain ribbons. Reality conflicted with fantasy, or fancy, yet again.

I looked around the boutique again. The saleslady approached.

"Here are a few things your niece might like," she said pointing out several items. They shone like jewels in the light of my childhood memories. What I would have done to own one of these things when I was young! A smooth pair of pink ballet slippers, soft as gloves, laced with satin ribbons. An other-worldly tutu complete with shimmering top and fluffy taffeta skirt. A pair of shiny black tap shoes that could tinkle out a melody on any wood floor. I bought them all, perfect gifts, and arranged to have them wrapped and delivered. Fortified by this success, I plunged back out onto the street. I was ready to meet Vadja.

As I walked into the restaurant, I looked around. By the window there was Vadja reading the paper. He hardly looked the type to be in international intelligence. He looked up. I waved. Vadja reminded me of someone's European uncle.

"So," I asked as I approached, "is there any news?"

"Yes, there is," he said, pulling my chair out for me. "The phone number you gave to Bob Peloquin was traced to an apartment in Marina del Rey. A safe house." Before I could ask him what that was, he continued. "No one lives there. All there is is a telephone. The number is listed to a woman. Whoever it was who called you, I'm sure his name was not Mike Hillman. He was probably checking to see what you knew about Fritz or his plans. It's possible that he may have wanted to know if anyone contacted you about Fritz. Or he may have wanted to find out whether Fritz himself called. We have no way of determining exactly who set up this safe house, but they are usually run by agencies like the CIA, the FBI and other intelligence agencies."

"What do you think of this?" I asked Vadja.

"I don't know yet. I don't want to speculate," he said. "In addition, it's important for us to note that the Swiss couple who disappeared in the Himalayas have been found not far from where Fritz vanished."

Peloquin mentioned these people when he described other searches happening concurrently in the area. Ernst and Marianne Zeller, both twenty-six years old, had been on a long journey that began in Turkey and was to take them through Pakistan, Iran, Afghanistan, India, and farther on to Australia. They were last heard from in October of the preceding year; a letter was postmarked Garam Chasma, a village forty-five kilometers northwest of Chitral. Their next destination was unknown, but they promised to get in touch a month later with the Swiss embassy in Delhi, India. No word was ever heard from them. Like Fritz, they disappeared without a trace.

Zeller's father flew to Pakistan to begin his own investigation. In trying to track his son and daughter-in-law, he faced the same blank wall of silence that I had found. Last I'd heard, he left and gave up. But evidently, he returned.

"As you know," Vadja went on, "Mr. Zeller's first attempt ended in failure, but the second time he found the truth. I have the report. I was going to wait, but if you'd like to see it . . ."

I took the report Vadja held out to me, and began to read quickly through it, looking for material relevant to my own search.

"On October 14, 1977, Ernst and Marianne were led on a false track by some inhabitants of the region who offered to take them over the Birir mountain pass to Bumburet—a tour recommended in a travel prospectus—and there, at the height of four thousand meters, they were robbed and murdered." A list of useless facts followed, documentation that tried to project some semblance of order, of control, on the tragic event.

"Extremely depressing is the fact that the whole valley knew about the murder from the very first day. It was neither possible for the four culprits to act without being noticed, nor could strange objects remain unidentified; for their evaluation a fence is needed. Even the authorities of Chitral must have known of the deed. Some of their declarations subsequently turned against themselves, and the diversions they used to hush up the distressing affair were all too obvious. After all, in 1975 the German, Stammberger, disappeared while climbing the Tirich Mir, and Kronberger vanished on the Pagram Pass. In 1976, Charles Kitchings, an American traveling in the Kalash region, also disappeared without leaving a trace. In these cases, the success of the investigations undertaken was foiled by a curtain of silence and the tactic of doing nothing."

The report ended: "In our grief for our beloved dead we have a deep feeling of thankfulness for having discovered with certitude their tragic fate, and we are consoled by knowing that they both lie at rest in the beautiful cemetery of their homeland."

The last sentence hit full force. Mr. Zeller was able to find out the truth. What I would do for the peace of any sure truth!

"The man charged with the Zellers' murders had a number of watches in addition to theirs," Vadja said. He was quiet for a moment, then asked, "Do you know of any watch that Fritz may have had with him?"

"Yes." His watch with the Zellers, the thought of it. I had given it to him. On the back I had it inscribed, "To my darling" signed "Janice." I could picture Fritz opening the box, taking it out.

The world refracted through the flawed prism of anger. Some bastard had killed that poor couple, dropping their bodies on the mountainside. I could just picture him reading the inscription. I told Vadja about the watch.

"Running a check on this information could take anywhere from several weeks to several months," he informed me. "I will have to make an inquiry through the Pakistani prison authorities."

I did not know if I could wait a few months. There was little ambiguity as to what finding Fritz's watch would mean. "Vadja, I've been thinking: maybe I should talk to the people over there myself. I feel like I should be there."

"Janice," he said gently, "we have men checking on that information. Trust me, they know what they're doing. And they'll be able to do what needs to be done much more quickly than you could. Besides, there's always an element of risk."

I knew there was an element of risk. My fear of what might happen was what had kept me here so long. Paralyzed. But the Zellers got answers. "I could talk to people. They might listen to me. Vadja, I just don't know anymore. I don't know if I'm doing the right thing."

Vadja thought for a second. "I realize the news is unsettling," he said, "but there will be many bulletins like this. Most will lead nowhere."

I knew what he was saying, but I felt guilty.

Vadja looked at his watch. "Janice, it's time for us to go to the dentist's office to get Fritz's records. Ready to go?"

I said yes and stood. After leaving the restaurant, we walked along in silence. We had just a short way to go.

We crossed the street and ascended the stairs to the dentist's office. "Retrieving these records, you understand, is a mere formality. We gather this kind of information in every case we undertake," Vadja said gently. I knew what that meant. There was only one reason for dental records . . . to identify bodies. A person's teeth and skull provided a unique record. I felt sick as I entered the office.

"Come, Janice. We'll do this as quickly as possible."

I walked up to the wavy glass window designed to screen the staff from the patients. A certain amount of distance kept up the professional veneer. I was glad Vadja was with me.

"Yes?" asked the receptionist as she slid the partition halfway open.

"I . . . I'm here to retrieve my husband's records," I finally said.

Her mouth puckered, and she let out a small breath of annoyance. "Just a minute," she said, and opened an overstuffed file drawer. "I'll need to see some identification and you'll have to fill these out," she said handing me several forms.

Vadja took my hand and led me to a couch. I could not believe that

I was doing this. Name. Date of birth. Signature of patient or next-of-kin.

I signed at the bottom of each page, pressing the pen down hard. After I finished, Vadja took the clipboard from my hands.

I watched him walk to the window. His back turned to me as he waited for the receptionist to come and take the forms.

"Was everything all right?" I asked as he sat down.

"Yes. She said it will take a few minutes to find the X-rays," he answered. I nodded in understanding and swallowed down the stone in my throat. It went down, then bobbed back up.

"So," I began. Conversation would make the time pass faster. "You mentioned something about fliers as we left the cafe. I didn't quite catch what you were saying."

"I had men put up missing person fliers in English and Urdu around the area where Fritz disappeared. Since word of mouth is the main way news gets around, these fliers might stir some interest. They'll give people something to talk about. A reward was offered. The odds that we'll get any response are about fifty-fifty. The population is rather tightly knit."

"What will you do if no one comes forth?"

"That is a possibility, but if there's anyone willing to talk, we'll find them. We've placed ads with pictures of Fritz in the local papers and we have someone interviewing people in the area. He's going to try and find the porter who went up to base camp with Fritz. Now that some time has passed, he might be willing to say more, maybe tell us something he wasn't willing to confide to the local police. And, of course, I've been in touch with the Pakistani authorities, the German embassy, and our own embassy. If they find out anything, we'll be the first to know."

"Ms. Pennington."

The dentist was standing in the doorway that led into the inner sanctums. He held a large manila envelope. He motioned us inside.

"I wanted to explain a few things about these particular X-rays to you," the dentist said, unsheathing the black-and-white prints. There were Fritz's bones, the barest outlines of his being. Underneath his lips, his smooth cheeks, lay these cavities, this hollowness empty of warmth, life. The stark white glared up at me out of the darkness.

"Yes, yes," I mumbled. "Please, just tell Vadja." I wanted to leave the dim back room decorated with lighted panels and hung with garish pictures. From a distance the blacks and whites looked interchangeable. How could they tell one person from another stripped down to the bone? No skin, no flesh. Just these hard markers. Each person was separable, alone, in exactly the same way. In the end we would all end up looking like these pictures.

In the waiting room, two patients arrived. They glanced up briefly before returning to the magazines in their hands. I sat down to wait for Vadja.

"Everything all right?" he asked as he returned.

"Yes, fine."

We left. At the hotel, I said good-bye. He was to leave for Los Angeles the next day. He promised to contact me if he had questions or information. As I walked the few blocks home, I replayed the encounter with the dentist. Sometimes it seemed as if an entire story could be told in a few instants. There I was, attempting to do something about Fritz's disappearance. But I could not face the most basic details, like his X-rays. I became dependent on Vadja, who seemed to know more, partly because he had been trained and partly because he was a man.

It had been this way from the beginning. When I first stopped hearing from Fritz, I wanted to go to Pakistan and start searching for him immediately. But I didn't. Harry Conway discouraged me. Now Vadja had. I wanted so desperately to know the truth, but it seemed that each time I neared it, I turned away. I had to operate by proxy.

16.

Times Make the Man

Aspen
1977-78

I felt as though I was walking to the principal's office, passing through the corridors of Lake Forest Park Elementary School with that horrible feeling of dread in the pit of my stomach. Everyone was looking at me as if I was separate, tainted, as though I no longer belonged.

Since Fritz's disappearance I barely kept our finances going, writing check after check for the condominium payments, for the utility bills, for Fritz's accounts at the mountaineering store. I didn't know how long I could keep it up. I tried not to think about it as I headed for Fritz's office. I was going to talk to Harry Conway. Fritz's company, a printing and magazine business, was still running as usual, and I figured Conway could advance me some of Fritz's profits. As I entered the hall that served as the office, the secretary asked if she could help me. I told her that I wanted to speak with Harry. She said that he had stepped out for a minute. As I waited for him to return, I walked through the main room. The man running the presses glanced up at me, then looked down. The machines were doing their work.

While flipping through some magazines that were lying on a nearby counter, I saw the latest issue of *The Climber,* Fritz's magazine. It had a new format. The cover seemed dull without the color and graphics he liked. I skimmed some of the articles. They were basically the same.

It seemed as if the same writers were still working on the magazine. That was a good sign. Not that much would have changed when Fritz got back.

It was a while since I had been around these offices. I used to come by every Friday to meet Fritz for lunch. He would come into the office, with his hands darkened with ink. I'd sit at his desk while he cleaned himself off. Now the outer room looked worn and unfamiliar. Someone had cleared the top of his desk since the last time I'd been here. It seemed cold and spare. Functional.

Harry walked back in.

"Hello, Janice," he greeted me. "How are you enjoying your stay in Aspen?"

"Fine, thanks." There was an odd formality to his manner. He seemed uncomfortable with my presence. I told him why I needed to see him.

"Well, there isn't much in the account," he said. "I might be able to advance you a hundred dollars or so."

Not much in the account? There should be plenty. Fritz and I used to withdraw his salary from it. We used to pay all our expenses with money from the business, and not a dime was taken out in months; there had to be something. "How could the balance be so low?" I asked. "I only wanted to take out a few hundred. There must be at least enough to cover that."

"I don't know what to tell you, Janice."

But Harry was Fritz's partner. He had to know. "There's probably an error or something," I said. Harry sat behind his desk. Thinking that Fritz would return and everything would go back to normal, I had been ignoring the issue of the business, praying I wouldn't have to deal with it. But he hadn't returned, and nothing was normal anymore. I had to face it. There was no reason to avoid Harry; this didn't have to be a confrontation, merely a discussion.

"I also want to talk to you about the business," I said.

He leaned back in his chair. "What about it?"

"Well, we haven't discussed it, but I want to continue running it the same way Fritz did with the same arrangement you had with him. I'll continue renting the space from you."

"Janice," he interrupted, "you know nothing about running a printing business. Besides, Fritz didn't have a lease, and we shook hands over this arrangement. . . . I really feel the right thing, the only thing, is for me to run the business, to run it the way it needs to be run."

"But Harry, the manager always took care of the business when Fritz was away before. He does such a great job of it, I thought I would offer him a percentage to work here full time." I could see that Harry wasn't receptive to the idea.

"Janice, why don't we talk about this later. I have a deadline to meet. Maybe I could stop by the condo tonight, early, uh, on my way home. . . . By the way, about the condo . . . do you intend to keep it?"

This question came out of the blue. "Of course I'm going to keep it." I was angry.

He shifted in his chair, taking a minute before he spoke. "Well if you change your mind . . . I thought if it was becoming too much of a burden I could take it off your hands. That way you wouldn't have those extra payments every month. I heard about the Bank of Aspen putting pressure on you. I could offer you twenty-five thousand dollars."

I felt the knot tighten in my stomach and travel up to my chest, making it hard to breathe. He didn't think Fritz would ever be back. He wanted the business and he wanted the condo.

"Harry, it's just that these last few months have been difficult with the lawyers' fees and a lot of unpaid bills that Fritz left. I'll find a way to catch up on the payment . . . and with the business. Fritz spent eleven years building it, building his accounts. . . ."

Harry was irritated. He stood up, letting me know that there was nothing more to be said. "Janice, I really have to get back to the story I'm working on, if you'll excuse me. We'll talk more about this later."

I could feel the heat through my cheeks as I was dismissed. I felt gutted, skinned. I would get a lawyer when I returned to Los Angeles.

Now that Fritz was gone, his friends no longer felt responsible for helping. It was as if, after his disappearance, their bonds with me disappeared as well. I was on my own.

17.

Parapsychology

Los Angeles
1977

S hadows filled the barren courtyard. Students sat, read, studied, scattered about like pawns on a chessboard. I passed them and looked for the building I'd visited the week before. It reminded me of a mausoleum with its functional architecture and stone steps. I walked up apprehensively and pulled open the door.

The hallways intersected like chutes in a maze. The corridors echoed with my footsteps. The farther I walked, the farther the lab seemed. The sound resounded off the linoleum, then bounced back from institutionally cheerful yellow walls. Offices, bathrooms. An old ceramic water fountain.

I entered the room at the end of the hall. The musty air smelled of rat pellets. The door to the office was ajar. I knocked lightly, then entered. There was no one inside. Harshly lit and windowless, the room looked like a cell. I took a seat. A magazine on parapsychology lay on the table. I nervously flipped through the pages, riffling back and forth.

After I started having the dreams and the out-of-body experiences, my mother suggested I go to the University of California, Los Angeles, (UCLA) to see if there were any resources I could use to unravel the paradoxical messages. She heard about their new parapsychology department, the brainchild of Dr. Thelma Moss. My mother had read all of Dr. Moss's articles about past life regression. A woman of about fifty, dignified and professional, Dr. Moss was a forerunner in her field, and famous for her studies in metaphysics. I found her calm academic manner reassuring.

During my last visit, I gave Dr. Moss a paper bag full of Fritz's things: the cartoon-print shirt he wore when we met, a carved figurine he brought back from a climb, a chain attached to the cap of a pen he wore around his neck so he could jot down thoughts whenever they struck him. These were the things closest to him.

As I opened another magazine, Barry Taft entered, followed by two people I hadn't met. Barry worked with Dr. Moss on telepathic experiments. He was a graduate student. When we met, he struck me immediately as a curious, intense person. His small stature, with expressive hands and quick, darting eyes resembled nothing so much as an elf. I soon learned that he had a quick mind, too.

The people he was with were talking animatedly. They were probably members of the research team that went through Fritz's things. I was anxious to hear what they found. They were all students of parapsychology. They sat themselves at the table in the center of the room. Barry bounced into his chair, a head shorter than everyone else. He produced a tape recorder.

"This is some of what we found. I think you'll be interested in what people have started to pick up on." After a few more words of preparation, he started the tape.

A low hushed voice began detailing impressions. "Carl, the name Carl . . . important . . . stomach cramps . . ." They were just short, disjointed thoughts. I immediately took out a pen and started making notes. "A blow to the left side . . . there's more to this than meets the eye . . . money problems . . . an address, 19604 . . . no fear . . . small boat." More to this than meets the eye. Peloquin and Nellie had said the same thing. " Get away, have to get away, don't know how. . . Hermie knows where he is . . . March of this year relates to what has happened to him . . . break out, break free . . . He is in San Francisco, or near San Francisco . . . left ear struck, left side of his face . . . ran from something." Again, I was hearing that he was injured.

The tape player clicked off. Barry quickly replaced the tape with another. I looked around the table to see if I could catch a glimpse of what this meant; every eye was fixed on the tape machine.

Another voice began speaking. "There's an undercurrent of violence

. . . feels drugged . . . pressure in chest . . . bubonic plague . . . sinking sensation . . . Vicky comes to mind . . . stomach, maybe appendix." Stomach again. And Vicky. These people knew something. "Short of breath . . . staccato . . . money problems . . . head hurts . . . Boston, Rhode Island . . . can't turn head . . . Silver or Stanley . . . Bennington, Vermont." All these places and names. I looked at Barry to see if he could piece them together. He said that they did their readings separately.

He waited for me to finish writing before starting a new tape. "Roller-coaster feeling . . . someone mean, clear image . . . weak feeling, hot violent temperature, virus . . . crying, eyes watering, sad."

Next and last, Barry put his tape in place. "Pain in face . . . pressure, chest pressure . . . curled up, near a wall." My out-of-body experience. Fritz lying on the cot. "Starving . . . pain left arm . . . friend, dark blond hair, knows something . . . Kubrick . . . confusion, many places he shouldn't have been . . . location twenty-eight degrees northwest magnetic fourteen or forty-one miles from starting point . . . badly injured . . . involved in many things you weren't aware of . . . two other people with him . . . Capri or Catree, the name Falstaff or Falstad or Volstad . . . voices, 'Stop telling me that,' 'I already know,' 'Leave me alone, stop!' . . . headstrong, lost orientation . . . dark-haired woman in her thirties, Russian looking, thin nose, blue eyes, large heavy clothing . . . her name starts with an A or L . . . the words Declee or Diktlee or Tecklee . . . dizzy feeling . . . left clavicle."

The tape ended. Barry looked spent but satisfied. The same thing cropped up time and again. Fritz was involved in much that I didn't know about. The researchers began to leave their seats. "I hope we helped in some way," one man said as he left the room.

"Did anything strike a chord?" Barry asked.

"Yes, the name Vicky . . . the man lying down . . . but . . ."

"Anything else?" he demanded.

"I don't know. A lot of things I've heard before. It's hard to know what's important."

"The numbers?"

"No, no, the numbers didn't mean anything . . ."

"It could be a zip code," he mused. "Maybe the places . . . were any of them places you've been with Fritz, places either of you have been before?"

"Possibly. It's hard to say. I hoped you'd be able to tell me."

He looked at me quizzically as if he didn't understand what I was asking him for. "Think about the tapes. Why don't I give them to you. Maybe if you go home and play them over. . . . See if something comes to you."

I already knew what I knew. I wanted to know what he could tell me. There had to be more. Something. Anything.

I shifted in my seat. He scraped his chair back and tilted it.

"Barry . . ." He was immersed in thought, tapping a pencil on his forehead.

"Barry," I repeated.

The front legs of his chair solidly hit the cement floor as he sat forward. "Say that again," he said, then continued, as if to himself. "It was difficult for some members of our group to tune into the items. It's been some time since your husband disappeared."

There was a pause. "Well," he said, "there are some solid things for you to go on." Solid? I felt as though I was standing on a bed of shifting ground, quicksand ready to swallow me when I fall.

I simply looked at him as he got up and began to push chairs back into place. "I have to meet Dr. Moss in the lab," he said.

I wasn't ready to leave yet. There had to be something more, something he had forgotten. "Isn't there more that you could do with the tapes here, find some pattern, some correlation? What does twenty-eight degrees northwest magnetic mean; where would that be?"

He stood uncomfortably by the door. I felt the tears welling up as I bent down to pick up the box and my bag. I was coming away with less than I thought I would. "I was not the only one who had been seeing things," I mumbled almost to myself.

"Are you going to be okay?"

I held the tears back. I couldn't break down in front of him.

"Janice?" he said more gently.

"I . . . I . . ." It was too difficult to continue.

"Why don't you sit down for a minute?" He led me to a chair. "Don't think this is the end of what we'll do to help you. We're very interested in this case. This is all we can do today, but . . . I need some time to think about what to do next."

The tears were streaming down my face. I turned away. "I know, I know, Barry," I managed to stammer. "It's just that I'm not the only one who's been seeing Fritz."

"What do you mean?" he asked.

"Some of my friends, they've been coming to me with stories. Things have been happening that they can't explain. It's almost as if they don't want to tell me these things."

"Be more specific," he prompted.

"Last Wednesday my friend Jeff Stone called me. He was supposed to be in Aspen, staying at the condo. I knew that something was wrong, that something must have happened."

"Really . . ."

"He didn't know what to say to me, where to begin. I started to get the feeling that he didn't want to tell me something.

"Jeff had been staying at the condominium with a friend when it happened. It was their first night there. His friend was watching some TV. Jeff decided to take a shower. While he was in the shower, his friend fell asleep. Neither one of them knew exactly what happened. When his friend woke up an hour later, the shower was still running. He went in to check on Jeff and found him lying on the floor of the shower stall. There was a huge gash in the side of his face; blood was running down the drain. In the hospital, when Jeff regained consciousness, he didn't remember any of it.

"When Jeff phoned me, I remembered an incident that happened last September. A friend of Fritz's and mine, Kurt Frings, called.

"'I didn't know whether to tell you this or not,' he'd said. 'I had a dream about Fritz. It was about a week ago now. Fritz and I were in some mental institution, like an insane asylum. I don't know how I knew that, I just had that impression, the way you do in dreams. Anyway, we were talking. All I remember is that he was telling me that he was coming back, but he didn't want me to tell you. He wanted to surprise you. He said he would be coming home at Christmas.'

"I always felt that Fritz would come back at Christmas. The last thing I said to him was that I couldn't wait until Christmas."

"Wasn't he supposed to come back in October?"

"Yes. . . . I never understood why I said Christmas."

"Hmm," Barry mused to himself.

"And," I told him, "Kurt was just the beginning. A couple of weeks after that my friend Jelinda DeVorzon approached me with a dream about Fritz. He'd called her on the phone to say that he was home, that he had gotten into some trouble in Pakistan, but that everything had been worked out and he was fine. It was an extremely vivid dream she said."

Barry sat back, squinting in concentration. It seemed he kept listening long after I stopped talking. He rocked back on his chair.

"I don't know how you'd feel about this," he drawled, speaking at an unusually slow pace, "but I was thinking . . . How would you feel about having the group come to your home? It would be easier for us to connect with your husband if we were in a place where he had lived. Maybe we could have a meditation or a seance, something to focus the energy of the group. I've led a few projects like this." He explained the details.

I hardly had anyone visit my house anymore. I liked to keep to myself. But if he thought that having the research group over would help, I'd do it. Maybe then I'd find out something concrete. A place. A name. An answer.

The story was unraveling, coming apart, and I didn't know how the clues would weave together. Like Nancy Drew, I kept accumulating information. So far there was no logical pattern.

18.

The King

Los Angeles
1977

I pulled up the long winding drive that led to the house. This private road seemed to have a life of its own, undulating like a snake beneath my wheels. The gravel landing forked into two arcs like fanged jaws. And there was the house—fastidious, white—at the top of the driveway.

I dusted some powder on my nose and put on lipstick. Over the months, I learned how to disguise the pain. I learned how to look well for short periods of time. It is the way any wounded animal conceals its hurt, protects itself. No one wanted to witness my experience. The night before, I went to a dinner party at my sister Ann's apartment. I barely managed to stay for an hour. I could not sustain the charade. Everyone knew I was hurt, but they didn't want to see it anymore. Although they asked me to stay longer, they were relieved when I went home early; then the good times could continue without the awkwardness. They wanted to forget that tragedy could hit them as well.

Elvis Presley was kinder than most. He knew loss. We met when I was a young fan keeping vigilant guard in the lobby of the Knickerbocker Hotel, where Elvis had stayed when he was in Los Angeles. Through the benevolence of a friendly doorman, I was smuggled into Elvis's suite and got his autograph. At the time, this felt like the fulfillment of my dream, my highest aspiration. I was fourteen.

At our next encounter, years later, I was already working on *The Price Is Right*. We ended up going to the same dentist's office, talked and became friends.

As I was shown in, I wondered what Elvis wanted to give me. His message had said only that he had something for me concerning Fritz.

"He'll be in in just a moment," his housekeeper informed me.

I sank into a leather sofa and listened to her footsteps recede, sounding louder on the wood floors, softer on the carpets. I settled in to wait. In some strange way all the experiences I'd been hearing about— Jeff's, Jelinda's, and others'—began to make sense. The presences felt, the messages sent.

From the moment I met Fritz, I experienced a strange connection, a feeling reminiscent of my metaphysical experiences. Especially when I looked into his eyes. I was drawn to his eyes. I didn't really know what to make of it. Sometimes when I thought about it or tried to communicate my knowledge, the words wouldn't come out right. I felt as though I was speaking a language that no one could understand, describing a sensation that no one had felt before. But the connection was there and I knew Fritz experienced it, was drawn in by it as much as I was.

Elvis's entrance broke into my reverie. "Janice. How are you?" he beamed as he stepped into the study. He glanced at me searchingly and gave me a hug. "I am really sorry to hear about Fritz," he began. "You haven't found out anything more?"

"No," I said.

"Listen, I know some people in Washington. I'd like to help you. Maybe I could make some inquiries through them."

"I would appreciate that," I said.

"I'll see what I can do," he answered. "I came across a letter that Fritz had written asking me to help sponsor the Makalu expedition. I thought you'd want to see it," he said, and handed me a sheet of the stationery Fritz had made up for the trip. I could still see him at the kitchen table working on the project.

Dear Elvis,

I am sure that nobody has ever come up to you with an idea which he did not present as the most terrific, fantastic, and unique. I do that and go a step further. I gamble. If you do not agree that the idea is fascinating, I will let you come to my next climb with your helicopter and cut my rope . . .

As I read the letter, Elvis could see that I was upset.

"It's okay," he comforted me. "It'll be okay . . . " He didn't know how to continue.

I smiled wanly. "I know . . ."

He picked up a book from the table. "Here . . . this is what I wanted to give you. It's something that's helped me a lot . . . and I'd like you to have it."

I turned it over in my hands and looked at the cover. *The Impersonal Life*. It was a book on spirituality, metaphysics. Few people were this sensitive. He knew that this was what I needed now, something to keep me going. I had always believed in a spiritual reality underlying what appeared to be. I read from a page in the middle. "Everything outward is but the shadow of reality."

After we finished our visit, Elvis put his arm around my shoulders and walked with me to the car. I left his house and wound down through the streets of Beverly Hills. "Everything outward is but the shadow of reality" repeated in my head. It was certainly true for me. Lately in my life, it seemed that the world of dreams had begun to merge with what was real.

Elvis was one of my heroes. By marrying Fritz I thought I had achieved my dream. I had married my own hero. With his loss I had my future taken away.

19.

The Diaries

Los Angeles
1978

Fritz's father, Opa, asked me to come to Germany, but I didn't have time to go until now. There was a break in shooting *The Price Is Right*. I had a few weeks to myself. Vadja and I were meeting one last time before I went.

I opened the door and welcomed in the man on whom I came to depend. One of the few people I still allowed myself to trust.

"How have you been, Janice?" Vadja asked, warmly grasping my hand.

"As well as can be expected," I replied.

"I have some news," he said as he sat down, placing his attaché case on the coffee table and clicking open the locks. He pulled out some papers. "Fritz had a selective service number. He was in the army."

Vadja handed me a computer printout. A list of names. Parts of it were blacked out. I looked down the page. There it was. Friedrich Ludwig Stammberger. Fritz was German. Why would he enlist in the U.S. Army?

Vadja filled me in on what he knew. "As far as we can find, he signed on in 1965, but was never activated. As you can see, he registered in Monterey, California."

Sixty-five. That was nearly a decade before I met him.

"Do you think there's any connection between this and the fact that it was the Pakistani army that provided Harry with a helicopter for the search?"

"It's hard to say," Vadja replied. "I received this information the other day and I haven't had time to check on it. I wanted to let you know before you left for Germany, because Fritz may have mentioned this to his father. He might be able to tell us something. . . . Clues turn up in the most unlikely places," he added, almost to himself.

"Opa mentioned finding some old diaries that Fritz kept years ago," I said. "They were written in the Sixties. There might be something in them. . . ."

"There might," Vadja assented. "I'll arrange for you to meet with Bob Peloquin after you return from Germany," he added, closing his briefcase. "Unfortunately, I won't be able to attend the meeting. We've had several new cases open and they need me in Washington."

"So when should I get in touch with you?"

He considered my question. "I'm sorry to have to tell you this, Janice," he began, "but I'm no longer going to be able to work on the case. Of course, if you need to talk, please call. I wish you the very best."

"Vadja, why?" I asked.

"Well, when you return from Germany, Bob Peloquin will explain everything to you," Vadja replied. He shook my hand one last time. "I wish things could have been different," he said. I couldn't understand it. What did he mean that I could call him but that he no longer would be working on the case?

There was a look of sadness on his face as he turned to leave.

* * *

Munich, Germany
1978

I stood in the cattle call of customs awaiting my turn. The last time I had been in Munich it was when Fritz and I visited Germany on our honeymoon in 1973. I did not notice much then. The line moved as rapidly as an earthworm squeezing along segment by segment. The expressionless customs inspectors rummaged through suitcases. They dispensed only the barest nods of acknowledgment. Mechanical. Impersonal. I wondered if I would recognize Opa. We first met on that honeymoon trip. I only saw him once since then.

The bodies pressed in behind me. Finally, it was my turn. After a cursory inspection, I was allowed to pass. I stuffed my passport back into my handbag and walked down the carpeted hallway that led away from the desk. A trickle of passengers moved down the corridor. As I neared the end, I heard the buzz, the voices getting louder. Friends. Families. Harsh consonants and deep vowels blended into a hum of German.

I scanned the eager faces in the airport waiting room. This was the crowd that met all international flights. Wives, mothers, sisters, daughters. Husbands, fathers, brothers, sons. The close ones. The colors changed, the dress, the smells, but the expectancy was the same in every airport. Energy ran through the air.

I made out Opa's face in the crowd. Once it had been chiseled, sharp; now the skin hung loosely. His eyes were ringed. Weathered. He looked lost, peering at the newly arrived passengers. It was almost as if he had been let down one too many times, first losing most of his family, now his son. I remembered him as somewhat taller. He'd acquired a slight stoop.

He saw me and waved, then waved again, as if unsure. I reached him and put my hand out between the arms waving in front of him, around him. We connected, our fingers clasping in the semblance of a handshake.

We drove through narrow, repaved streets as we left the airport. Darkness had fallen and I could not see what lay on either side of the road. The headlights illuminated shrubs and the edges of sidewalks. Our sparse conversation provided little relief from the lack of scenery. As we arrived at his house, I noticed that the front lawn needed tending. Tall grass and weeds covered the yard. The gate creaked as Opa drew it back and motioned me through. I walked down the rough brick walkway, broken where the grass had pushed up between the cracks. In the house, Opa took my bags to the guest room. Like his son, Opa had a penchant for doing things correctly.

The house hadn't changed much. A few knickknacks sat on the

mantel, covered with dust. The same prints hung on the walls, hiding clean squares of paint. A thinly padded sofa still stood beneath the window. This was the house of a man who lived alone.

I hadn't noticed Opa's age the first time we met. He'd reminded me of his son: vibrant, good-natured, and full of life. This time, as he stepped into the doorway, I noticed that his hair had turned white. His clothes spoke of another era, as did his eyes. I accepted his offer of a late dinner.

He brought out some dark bread that smelled nutty, sweet, and fresh. On a small glass plate he arranged some thinly sliced, pungent hard cheese. Olives, pickles, cherry tomatoes, and cucumber rounds filled small bowls. The metal tray rattled as he set it down. He left again returning with fluted glasses and a bottle of sparkling wine. He did not have much, but he knew how to present what he did have. There was something in his gracious unhurried gestures, the simple food, that helped to pace life. He poured us some wine, and encouraged me to eat. After dinner, I climbed the steep staircase leading to my room. It was the same room I stayed in with Fritz on our honeymoon. I opened the narrow door and hesitantly stepped in. It felt familiar, comfortable, the stark furniture, the bed covered with a sumptuous comforter. I changed quickly and dropped onto the soft down. There was a comfort in being in his father's house. I passed into a sound sleep.

It was early; mellifluous yellow streamed through the window. I went over and pushed back the curtain. The street below was empty, deceptively calm. Noise from the main thoroughfare a few streets over drifted up as I untied the sash and let the morning air in. I could picture the early bustle: a few commuters hurrying along the damp pavement, an occasional car honking. At this hour the traffic had just begun to flow. I pulled on some jeans and a sweater and left quietly, trying not to disturb Opa. I was heading to one of the cafes for coffee, maybe a roll.

On the street, a nearby cafe was emitting a warm, soft aroma: the smell of freshly baked bread. As I neared the cafe, coffee overpowered the smell of bread. The strong, brown beans had been ground, pounded. The spice of caffeine tinged the air. After coffee and a roll, I continued down the street.

The stores were just beginning to open. The modern shop windows clashed with the older walnut paneling and heavy, impenetrable doors. The hand-painted merchandise seemed out-of-date. Bavarian steins. Cuckoo clocks. Wooden dolls. Teddy bears. They reminded me of Christmas.

There was a sense of relief in walking around alone. No one knew me. I turned into a narrow cobbled lane where the walls seemed to reach out on either side, leaning toward each other. I walked down the road until it twisted into a loop, a cul-de-sac. There was a church at the end.

A gold and jewel-encrusted crucifix stood above the archway. Stained-glass windows portrayed Jesus and the Apostles in lead. Leaving the morning behind, I entered. Candles and the scent of burnt incense filled the cavernous hall. This was a Catholic church, an aged one. Rows of hand-carved pews lined up on both sides of the center aisle. Beyond the last pew stood the altar. Brocade draped over the corners. The cloth rested in curves.

My grandmother had always told me that there was only one way to receive God, and that was to be true to Him above all else. As I was going to sleep, she used to ask, "Have you said your prayers?" She'd make me get out of bed, and we'd kneel on the cold, hard floor. "Now I lay me down to sleep, I pray the Lord my soul to keep. If I should die before I wake, I pray the Lord my soul to take." As she turned out the light, she stood for a moment in the doorway. I remembered her shape, tall and dark, filling the doorway. Stoic. "You have to love God above everything else in your life," she'd say. "Even more than Mommy and Daddy?" I asked. "Yes, even more than your mother and father," she said.

On the side of the altar lay a table filled with candles. I lit one for Fritz and set it in a holder. My donation clinked into the glass. Outside, the sky was vast. I walked toward a park filled with trees. I wanted to see the leaves turn color the way they did at this time of the year. I felt a powerful connection to Fritz in the outdoors. It was where he belonged, uncaged, unfettered by the inanities of civilization.

The days of my visit went quickly. Too quickly. Day after day for two weeks, Opa and I went over documents and notes of all kinds. He knew nothing about Fritz having enlisted in the U.S. Army as Vadja claimed. I met with many of Fritz's friends and even went to Austria to meet with one of them who climbed with him on Makalu in 1974. Meetings were arranged with German officials. Everybody had their own theories on what might have happened to Fritz, but I came away with no facts or definite leads. Only maybes.

Opa had a chance to share many memories with me. If a wife can't let go of a missing husband, how can a father let go of a missing son?

Now it was already time to go to the airport. I helped Opa put my luggage in the car. I went in and got my last small bag. Opa followed me up to the room.

"This is everything, I think," I said to him.

"No, it is not everything," he said and handed me a parcel. "Some *Bunte* magazines and some of Fritz's books." The diaries. He was giving me the diaries. I knew what a sacrifice this was. He was giving me the innermost secrets of his son. What was recorded on those pages? Why hadn't he sent them to me before? Why now? I wondered. All the writing was in German. I couldn't wait to get back to Los Angeles to have them translated. Three thousand pages of information. Years of Fritz's life documented by his own hand.

Opa told me that he never read them. I asked him why and he responded by saying that it was out of respect for his son's privacy. Now, he felt that I, as Fritz's wife, should have them. Opa patted my hand. It'll be all right, he seemed to be saying.

He helped me carry the journals to the car and put them in the trunk. I watched him go back to lock the door. He was old. This was the last time I saw him.

20.

At Work

Los Angeles
1978

W
e filed into the Green Room at Studio 33 at CBS Television City. I took my usual chair in the corner. An ugly brown recliner next to the coffeepot. The doughnuts and bagels were across the room. One of the stage managers came in with scrambled eggs and greasy hash browns from the commissary. The room smelled like bad overcooked food. It was too early and too soon after my trip. A ten-hour flight. I landed in Los Angeles the evening before, and awoke with rush-hour traffic and the long drive through Laurel Canyon that morning.

"Well," the director began, "I hate to have to start the meeting this way, but I'm afraid we're probably going to run late in rehearsal. We have new cameramen on camera two and camera four, and we'll have to run through some of the games."

Then he turned to me. "Janice, I don't know if you were aware of it or not, but the last time we played the Poker Game you were late on bringing out the tags. What was wrong?"

"I took my usual cue. Camera three wasn't on."

"I really think you were late. That's why I like to rehearse everything. Also the crew has been too noisy backstage during the show. Next time it happens we are going to stop tape."

The stage manager looked down. He was the backstage clown. He kept the crew's spirits up, and we loved him for it. The crew worked hard. It was true that sometimes things got a little out of hand backstage, with either the tension or the laughter. Ten-hour days would wear anyone down.

The director continued on. "In the first act, Holly, you show the refrigerator/freezer, and then hold up the 409 kitchen cleanser. Make sure to hold it straight to camera . . . last week, I don't know which one of you it was, but someone held a product upside down, then turned it around. You know the sponsor isn't too thrilled about those kinds of things."

He went through the first four acts of the show in minute detail. "Janice, you show the car behind door two. Holly, you're on the sailboat. By the way, after the last rehearsal there'll be pizza in the Green Room for everyone. Something to keep you going and let you know how much I appreciate all of your hard work. We'll start rehearsal in ten minutes."

I picked up my bag to leave. Ten minutes until rehearsal. I went to prepare. Marcelle, the wardrobe woman, was already in my dressing room.

"There's not too much today," she said as I walked in. "We're going to use the Martian costumes and then we'll have fittings after the first show." The costume was about four feet around. I liked the character roles better.

The P.A. crackled. "Okay, girls, on stage. We're starting." The stage manager's voice emanated from the public-address system. My ten minutes were up.

21.

The Body

Los Angeles
1978

Ever since I returned from Germany, my sleep had been off. I napped at odd hours. It was almost as if my body reached some unseen stress level, and shut down automatically. I was scanning through the first translated pages from Fritz's journals. I'd sent them to the Berlitz School of Language the day after I returned. Going through these early writings made me realize how much I was coming to know and understand the man I loved, only after he'd vanished from my life. When we were together I tried to spend as much time as possible with him, thinking that I was getting to know him better, that we were creating memories. But that was not the case. I only saw the sides of him that he wanted me to see. And while I shared things that I didn't tell anyone else, there were many things that he omitted, intentionally and unintentionally.

I propped myself up and rubbed my eyes. The early evening evaporated. It was nearly six o'clock. I walked outside to see the last of the sunset. As I sat on the stoop, a delivery truck pulled up and a man stepped out, looking at the numbers on the houses before he came up the walk.

"Yes?" I asked inquisitively.

"Package here for a Ms. Janice Pennington," the man said.

"I'm Ms. Pennington," I answered. He passed a clipboard to me.

"Please sign near the X," he instructed.

I did and was handed an envelope in urgent yellow. Holding onto it, I had the premonition that perhaps this was something I didn't want to know. Taking a deep breath, I tore it open; it was from the State Department.

Ms. Pennington,

We are forwarding a telegram received by our office. Our office will be contacting you to confirm the identification. We offer our condolences in your time of grief.

> Bill Smith
> Department of State

And then the other page.

SUBJECT: MOUNTAINEERING ACCIDENT

1. WE UNDERSTAND THAT A PROMINENT GERMAN MOUNTAIN CLIMBER, FRITZ LUDWIG STAMMBERGER DISAPPEARED WHILE CLIMBING TIRICH MIR IN SEPTEMBER 1975. HIS BODY WAS NOT FOUND AT THE TIME. ACCORDING TO RECENT INFORMATION A POLISH MOUNTAINEERING GROUP FOUND HIS BODY WHILE CLIMBING TIRICH MIR LAST YEAR.

2. COULD YOU CONFIRM THIS INFORMATION. WHILE THE ACCIDENT TOOK PLACE IN PAKISTAN, THE INFORMATION WE ARE TRYING TO CONFIRM WAS OBTAINED IN NEW DELHI, INDIA.

I put the paper down on the coffee table. I did not want to touch it. All prior searches, including Elvis Presley's attempts, led me nowhere. Now I was faced with the possibility of Fritz's death. Immediately I called Bob Peloquin's office in Washington, D.C. He was not in. His secretary assured me that she would give him the message. I asked for Vadja, and I was told that he was unable to take my call. I was frantic.

I needed to talk to someone who could give me more information.

Why had the information been given in New Delhi, India, instead of Pakistan? Who had given that information?

Deep inside me, I still felt that Fritz was alive.

22.

Enough

Los Angeles
April 1978

I had made up my mind. A friend suggested that I contact Neil Griffin, an international attorney who had offices in Los Angeles. Neil agreed to pursue my rights regarding both the print shop and Fritz's magazine.

The Price Is Right salary wasn't sufficient. My career outside of the show had been on hold, so no additional income was being generated. It was a financial drain to support both houses in addition to fulfilling Fritz's personal commitments prior to his disappearance.

Harry Conway left me no option. I hadn't heard from him in more than a year. I learned that he moved the shop to another location, and that he took down the hand-carved wooden sign with Fritz's name as proprietor. Also, he changed the name of the business. Earlier I felt no urgency in resolving the business situation with Harry. I expected him to be fair, and if not for me, at least out of respect for his long-standing friendship with Fritz. Now I knew otherwise. I was outraged. I called him and asked for Fritz's sign back and he said that he didn't know where it was, that it might be out in the alley behind some boxes. This type of excuse sounded all too familiar.

"I want that sign. Have somebody find it and hold it for me at the shop. I'm coming to town and I will pick it up then. Don't let the same thing happen that happened with the books and knapsack in Pakistan!" I shouted. There was silence on the other end. I hung up. Why was he in such a hurry to get rid of Fritz's things? Was it greed, or something else?

* * *

Neil Griffin was a heavyset man in his late thirties, always impeccably dressed in handmade suits. A mover. After our initial meeting to discuss Fritz's business in Aspen, Neil also offered to assist me in my search for Fritz. He let me know that he had contacts in high places around the world, people with access. I welcomed his interest and told him to go ahead to see what he could find out. He promised to contact General Phillips, the director of intelligence for the U.S. Air Force in Honolulu, Hawaii. He believed that in the complex machinery of the government, especially in matters of foreign affairs, a man with the general's background and inside connections was invaluable. His knowledge and access were extensive. The general traveled several times a year to Pakistan and to other countries in the region. He was friends with the defense attachés in Islamabad, Pakistan. I carried with me every hope that he would bring me the news that I was longing for. Having Neil working with me was comforting, and the first bright spot I had had in a long time.

The first thing Neil did was to get in touch with Harry in Aspen. Harry told him that there was no binding agreement, that all of his business deals with Fritz had been agreed upon with a handshake, nothing in writing. He was not obligated to me, he said, and he reiterated that I didn't know anything about running a printing business.

Neil informed me that, as the guardian of Fritz's estate, I was entitled to Fritz's business and if Harry wanted it, he should compensate me for it. I gave Neil the go-ahead to pursue the case as he saw fit. Neil sent Harry a demand letter informing him that, after his thorough review and analysis, based on the law, that Harry had totally and effectively taken over the business operations without the benefit of a sale or buy-out to the Stammberger estate in any way. Therefore, we told Harry that I expected the sum of one hundred thousand dollars for Fritz's business. He was given ten days to respond.

I was being forced to experience all the things that I had been taught were wrong. Among others, dishonesty and betrayal. One of the persons

I had relied on and trusted the most, because he was Fritz's closest friend, was the one who was pulling the rug out from under me now. My ally became my adversary. I questioned everything that he had told me in the past. Did he have a hidden agenda? And if so, what was it?

23.

The Seance

Los Angeles
1978

I tied the sash on my robe as I stepped out of the bathroom. Barry Taft of UCLA was due to arrive any minute. The date we'd set all those months before had finally arrived: tonight there was to be a seance. I brushed the wet mass of hair away as I maneuvered into a blouse.

Ivy leaves slapped up against the window, then made a hissing sound as they swept across. The vines, which blanketed the house, crept down over the windows as if they meant to inch their way inside when I wasn't looking.

After I finished dressing, I went to arrange the refreshments. Cheese and crackers. Wine. I straightened the piles of books and magazines on the coffee table.

Barry arrived first with two women and a man whose faces I recognized, but whose names I forgot. I showed them in while Barry charged ahead, consumed by the event at hand.

"I was thinking things over as we drove here," he said, after a cursory greeting. "It would probably help if we could walk around and get a feel for the house before the seance. Would that be all right with you?"

"Certainly," I answered. As they walked off, I called after them, "Feel free to look around."

I went over to the fireplace and dragged a new log off of the stack next to it. I heaved it onto the few pieces of already burnt wood, then sat back on my heels and began balling up newspaper for kindling. I could hear the people walking around the house. In the bedroom, dresser drawers opened and then closed. I could see the silky garments, lingerie, underwear I had just chosen from. I heard toiletries being moved in the bathroom. Fritz's things were still there, behind the cabinet mirror. His silver shaving brush and razor. His after-shave. In the kitchen, someone bumped the antique high chair, rattling the dish and spoon I kept on its tray. I had bought the high chair when I'd thought I could still have children. Dark oak with wheels on the bottom and carved legs. I had envisioned motherhood: feeding, diapering, strolling, sleeping. Now an old abused teddy filled the chair. I leaned back and peered through the arched doorway. Whoever had made the sound had left. It always amazed me how quickly people can come and go.

I focused on building the fire again. These people were looking through my home with my permission. I had consented to it. If I asked them to stop they would. It was all perfectly within my control. But it did not feel that way. It did not feel like I had a choice. I struck the match. As I set it in the center of the pile, there was a muffled knock at the door. More people. My mother and my sister Ann entered full of energy, eyes sparkling with anticipation.

"Janice, you know I would have been here earlier," my mother bubbled, "but Ann was late. She had to get Jessica into bed. Is everybody here?" she whispered. She was dressed for the occasion. She wore a long purple sweater, gold shoes, and a big jeweled ring with an amethyst, the soul stone. Her clothes were all in purple and gold, spiritual colors.

I hugged them both. "If you want to take a few minutes and walk around the house, go ahead. Barry thought it might be a good idea," I said.

Awkward as kindergartners, we convened in a circle before the fire. Barry walked around adjusting the positions of various members, evening out the circle. He placed me at the head of the group, my back to the fire, then lit a candle. It was time to begin.

A hush settled over us. The carpet glowed a deep red, darkened by shadow. A pool of blood for sacrifice. We were here to appease the gods. Our shadows danced across the walls, although no one moved. I felt the warmth of the flames behind me.

"Focus on the candle," Barry's voice instructed. I concentrated, striving to join my energy with the others. I wanted a connection.

"Now join hands," Barry interjected. Outstretched fingers reached for mine. The skin of Mom's hand contrasted with the smooth parchment of Ann's. Mom held my hand delicately as if it were fragile, while Ann knew. Her fine bones gripped mine firmly, supportively. This was about strength, her hand said to me. I pressed it, thankful. I was glad that she was sitting next to me. I felt disconnected, distant from the rest.

Beyond the group I could see the pictures of Fritz on my antique table. They were obscured by the bodies, the shadows. I knew them by heart. I had picked them up so many times, fondled and caressed the frames, traced my fingers lightly about the outlines of his face, his physique. This was my private dungeon, my private hell.

Barry rang a bell. The crystalline sound returned me to the gathering. I concentrated on the love I felt for Fritz. We could do this. We would do this. I felt calm inside. I was ready to receive.

I imagined Aspen. Fritz. The feeling of his arm cloaking my shoulders. I thought I heard the bell ring again but I was not sure. It sounded faint, tinkling in the distance. A shallow sound. I felt his presence for an instant, but it withdrew. I could feel it leaving; then, it pulled away.

I opened my eyes and looked at the circle around me. Some of the others' eyes were open, some closed, but all the faces looked spent. The eyes I met returned glazed stares. They were not seeing me. I stared at the wall across from me. The hardwood paneling, the bricks, the hanging copper pots.

After a few moments, Barry spoke, acknowledging what we all knew. These realities beyond reality needed no recognition, no second voice. They were simply there, they spoke with their presence. Or with their absence. We would not reach Fritz. Barry spoke quietly, succinctly.

"I think that's all we can do tonight," he said. Hands dropped to sides. People shook their arms out. We were glad to be released. Conversation began softly again. Legs sprawled forward on the carpet. There was not much else to be done.

I thanked each person at the door. The group ushered itself out as if still linked. The seance was a disappointment. I expected more.

"Are you sure you don't want me to stay? Would you like to come over and spend the night with us?" my mother asked. She felt hesitant about leaving.

"No, I feel like being alone," I replied. After they left, I went to the oak wine rack in the kitchen and pulled out a bottle of wine. I grabbed a glass and the corkscrew and walked back to my bedroom, locking the door behind me.

24.

Trust

Aspen
1978

I hesitated briefly before opening the door to the shop. It looked modern and bright with plate glass windows facing the street. I rehearsed in my head dozens of times what I would say to Harry as I crisscrossed through town looking for their new location. As soon as I stepped inside the shop, my mind drew a blank. A blond girl with a fresh scrubbed face and an open smile asked if I needed help. I explained to her that I had come to pick up the sign that had hung on the old print shop owned by Fritz Stammberger. She stated that she knew nothing about Fritz Stammberger or any sign. She got up and told me to follow her into the printing room.

The heavy smell of ink mixed with chemicals permeated the air as the big oily monsters spit out the printed pages into neat little piles. I heard Harry's voice over the roar of the machines. When he saw me, he waved his hand in my direction and started walking toward me.

"Janice, I didn't know you were coming. Why didn't you call and let me know?" he asked.

"I told you I would come to pick up Fritz's sign when I spoke with you last," I answered. He shifted slightly from one foot to the other; his expression turned more serious.

"We've looked everywhere. . . no one has been able to locate it." He hesitated. "Somehow it must have been misplaced during the move."

"Misplaced? How could it be misplaced?" I snapped back. Another stupid excuse, just like the one with the knapsack and Fritz's books. By now I knew that this argument would take me nowhere. He didn't give a damn. The business was flourishing and that was all he cared about. I had become an annoyance he wanted to be rid of. He was benefiting from the eleven years it took Fritz to build up the business. I wished that Fritz were standing in front of Harry instead of me.

I turned on my heels and stormed out of the room. I was enraged. Under my breath I muttered, "Greedy son of a bitch." At that moment I hated Harry Conway.

* * *

Los Angeles
1978

It was late and I was dead tired. I had just arrived home from my trip to Aspen. I played back the messages on my machine: Neil Griffin called, and General Phillips came up empty-handed. The general had contacted several sources in Pakistan, at different levels of government, but none of them could shed any light on the case. The only information that he was able to get was that Fritz was last seen in Chitral, Pakistan, in late September of 1975.

As soon as the message ended, I called Neil.

"Neil, I'm sorry to call you so late. . . I just got in and heard your message. Also, I need you to put more pressure on Conway. I. . . "

Neil interrupted. "Janice, I'm sorry the general couldn't help much. I'll do my best to help you. You sound too distraught to be alone; I'm concerned about you. Let me come over. . . you need company," he offered.

"Thank you, I'll manage," I answered.

"I'll be right over," he persisted.

"Please, Neil, don't. I just want to go to sleep. We can talk in the morning," I replied. He wouldn't take no for an answer.

"With all the bad news. . . the general not being able to help and the problem with Conway. . . I don't think that you should be alone right now. . . ." He went on and on. I told him no once more and after wishing him a good night, I hung up. I locked the doors around the house and got ready for bed. I pulled the comforter up to my neck and curled into a ball. I just wanted to forget everything.

I was wounded. Harry Conway's actions made a dent in my psychological fiber. I always gave people the benefit of the doubt. I wanted to see only the good in them. He had gone too far. As much as I wanted to, I wasn't able to fall into a deep sleep. In my grogginess I could hear the faint ticking of the antique clock in the living room. Then I heard a rustling sound. I rolled on my side and listened, holding my breath. I was trying to identify what type of sound it was. It sounded like footsteps sliding on the carpet in the hallway outside my door. I cocked my head. Another sound, another footstep. Was it my imagination or was someone in my house? I squinted and tried to adjust my eyes to the darkness. I couldn't see anything, but I felt that there was someone in my room. I bolted up only to see the shadow of a man lowering himself down next to me. He was lifting the comforter and sliding in next to me. I screamed.

His strong hands reached out, groping for my shoulders.

"Shh . . . it's me, Janice—Neil," he whispered.

"What?" I yelled. "How did you get in here?" I asked, while pushing him away as he advanced even more toward me. He was still in his three-piece suit; only his shoes had been removed.

"Get out of here, how dare you . . . how did you get in?" I snapped furiously at him again.

"With a credit card. I forced the lock. I can get into anyplace," he answered smugly.

"You broke in, Neil," I said, shocked, while I struggled with him. He was on his feet and I was flying at him, pushing him into the hall toward the front door.

"You don't understand. . . I was just here to help you," he sputtered.

"Just get the hell out of here before I call the police," I replied. I opened the front door and pushed him as hard as I could. He stumbled out holding his shoes in his hands. My heartbeat was out of control. Tears streamed down my cheeks. I ran into the bathroom, snapped on the light, and threw up.

25.

The End

Beverly Hills
1978

I couldn't get the cable off of my mind as I made my way to the restaurant where I was going to meet with Peloquin. Pips in Beverly Hills. He was my last chance. I wove my way among the tables, edging between chairs pressed nearly back-to-back. Bob Peloquin was seated at a table strategically placed, as always, with a good vantage point. From where he sat, he could watch everything without being noticed. He had probably seen me making my way in.

I slowed my pace as I approached him.

"Hello, Janice," he began. His face, as usual, revealed nothing. It was practiced at revealing nothing.

During the usual polite exchanges, I smiled and tried to give the impression of being at ease. I picked up the menu and scanned the choices. I wondered if I wanted to hear what he had to say.

Peloquin was watching me, waiting for me to finish. He was studying me. I closed the menu deliberately and set it down. After the waiter came over to take our orders, Peloquin started talking. He recounted the details of the case.

"As you well know, our first step was putting up posters throughout the region where your husband disappeared. The response to the posters was about what we expected. We interviewed several people who claimed to have definitive information, but, unfortunately, their stories contained serious discrepancies."

He continued, discussing probable explanations. He reviewed the information received by the FBI, mentioning the contacts Intertel had also made with other intelligence agencies. The catalogue of leads led to dead ends. I had lived through the entire search. I knew the story.

"As you know, the place you were calling was actually a safe house in Marina del Rey. Hillman obviously wanted to know what you knew. At the moment that is all we can tell you."

He stopped and cut into the steak he'd ordered, firmly slicing a morsel of flesh, dipping it into the sauce and raising it neatly, precisely to his mouth. I watched him, waiting. He took another bite. He was done: that was all he was going to say. He did not mention the body. I put down my fork and looked at him. His eyes took me in, neither cruelly nor with compassion; I was a specimen.

"What about the State Department cable referring to a body found on Tirich Mir?" I asked.

He looked up at me and paused while cutting the food on his plate. Then he answered me:

"We began to receive information about the sighting, but the implications were not definite. I instructed Vadja to wait until we had something concrete to tell you. A Canadian alpine group discovered the corpse while climbing Tirich Mir last autumn. It had lodged in a crevasse between glaciers. Since it was out of reach, the climbers were unable to take any clothing samples. They photographed it, then left to get assistance. A storm hit before they could return with more sophisticated equipment. The body was lost. The picture was all that remained in the form of evidence. It first passed through the international climbing circles. The Canadian team sent it off to the Polish Alpine Club in Gdansk, which had lost a member in the region a few months earlier. Initially, the Poles believed that this was their man, but a few weeks later, their team member was uncovered in a completely different location, so the picture was sent back to the Canadians who put it back in circulation within the climbing community. It was not until a member of the Polish Alpine Club mentioned the picture to an American embassy official in Warsaw that anyone thought of connecting the body with Fritz. Since the identification was not conclusive, you were not notified."

I swallowed some wine. The cable had unnerved me, but somehow Peloquin's explanation was worse. He delivered the details so matter-of-factly, as if this were simply a newspaper story that bore no connection to real people, real lives. I stared at my hands, at the crinkled skin on my knuckles. No evidence survived but a bad photograph of a man in a crevasse. A crevasse is the point of separation between an old glacier and a new one. A crack. It looked still, but it was a place of constant motion, an ice fall like the bottom of a slow river. It moved bit by bit except when a larger chunk dislodged. A climber trapped in a crevasse had little hope of surviving. I pushed my food around on my plate, then asked the question that had been plaguing me.

"How likely do you think it is . . . that this body is my husband's?"

Peloquin sat very still for a moment, then leaned forward and clasped his hands together, elbows on the table. "Personally, I don't think it is. I've seen the photograph and a more detailed report. The man in the picture was between five-ten and five-eleven. Fritz, you've told me, is six-foot-two." He stopped for a second and sat back, assessing my response. "The other identifications, as you know, were very tentative. Mistakes have already been made. Of course, the most certain way to identify the body would be to have a relative look at it," he said neutrally.

I stared at him. He was suggesting that I look at the picture. The prospect of staring at a mutilated body was too real. I crumpled back into my chair.

"But," Peloquin said, returning to my question, "it's highly unlikely that this is Fritz."

I nodded. "Is it possible to have Vadja still working on the case?" I asked.

"No, it isn't," he replied.

"If there's any way he could continue working with me, I would much prefer it. There's some new information I'd like to discuss with him." We had a rapport, a connection. I didn't want to lose it. Even if someone else was as efficient, it wouldn't be the same. They wouldn't have the same concern. "I don't know if this will help at all, but I found out some things when I was going through Fritz's diaries." Peloquin was silent. He'd finished his food. Something inside me shrank into a small hard point, turning in, turning away from this blockade of indifference.

"Janice," he said gravely, "even if we do find out what happened to Fritz, maybe it would be better that you not know."

He couldn't mean it. Better that I not know? "I have to know whatever you find out, no matter what it is. I have to know the truth. Regardless of what it is. For all I care he can have a new family in Russia, he can be involved in whatever, but I must know: is he dead, alive or in jail? You must promise me that you will tell me, no matter what it is."

He stared back, cold as stone. "I'm sorry, Janice, but Intertel will no longer be able to assist you in this matter. We've done all we can." He was dropping the case. There was no sympathy, no recognition. His mind was made up.

I got up in silence. I was angry. How in the hell could he walk away from this case? His company was hired to find Fritz. As far as I was concerned he had no right to decide when to give up looking. What did he know that he didn't want to reveal to me? Who told him to stop, and why? Bob Peloquin's decision was the last blow.

I let Neil Griffin go and, after much thought, I decided not to get another attorney and file a lawsuit against Harry Conway. Not because I didn't want to, but because I no longer had the energy to keep fighting. I was depleted and disappointed.

If Harry was that greedy, I would let him have it. He would have to live with the guilt of it for the rest of his life.

Friendship and trust were violated. I had reached the end of my rope.

26.

Fated

Beverly Hills
1977-80

I n September 1977, while shopping in Beverly Hills, I met Carlos de
Abreu. A week earlier I had been in Gucci's store and had fixed my
attention on a painting hanging behind the counter: a silk scarf in a
frame, a tawny lioness. I could not justify buying it, so I didn't. But I
kept thinking about it, and I returned to buy it. It's strange that the first
time we met, I did not notice him, at least not right away, even though
he was extremely handsome. Carlos told me later that when he saw me
running across Rodeo Drive toward Gucci's, he turned to a friend of his
and said, "That's my woman, and someday she is going to be my wife."
He approached me in the store and introduced himself. He handed me
his business card and invited me to attend the opening of a jewelry store
that he was opening in Palm Springs. I never went to the desert or called
him. Since Fritz's disappearance, I kept every man at arm's length. I
didn't want to start a relationship that I knew I couldn't handle
emotionally.

Working at *The Price Is Right* filled the void. It allowed me to present
an image. "The girl who shows the prizes"—that was how people saw
me. Always smiling, pointing at refrigerators, a facade like a mistress of
illusion. But in reality my life was all too different from what it seemed.
No longer was I the idealistic, always happy person that I once was. My
inability to find Fritz, plus all that I had learned through the process,
made me mature in a way I didn't like, I hadn't wanted.

The Harry Conway and Neil Griffin experiences took a toll. I loved

117

life, truth, honesty, and happiness; but my experience in the world clouded all those positive feelings. Disappointment took over. For a long time, the idea of becoming close to another person, taking another chance, made me apprehensive. Since the disappearance, intimacy meant pain. I thought that if I got close to someone, I would lose them.

Two and a half years went by before I saw Carlos again. As if by fate, we ran into each other in Beverly Hills. He was having lunch at La Scala Boutique restaurant with one of his friends. When I entered the room, he got up from his table, rushed to the front door, and invited me to join him. I was caught off guard. He explained how we had met a few years earlier at Gucci's. I barely remembered it. He was excited to see me. He had become the director of Cartier International and he had moved back to Los Angeles. I joined his table.

* * *

Carlos drove over the pass into the San Fernando Valley to pick me up. He had called me several times over the past month to ask me out to dinner. I finally accepted. He wouldn't hear of my meeting him halfway, even though we lived about the same distance from the heart of Los Angeles.

"Indian food?" he asked.

"That sounds good," I replied.

"You're going to love this place," he said. "It reminds me of an Indian restaurant I used to go to in Mozambique." Carlos grew up in Mozambique, a former Portuguese colony in Africa. "The food is hot, though . . . do you like spicy food?"

"Only every other day," I teased him.

We turned off of La Cienega Boulevard, home to what was called "restaurant row." The street was lined with choice establishments; many of the best places to dine in the city were collected there. The valet opened my door, then gave Carlos a ticket for the car. Carlos held out his arm and I linked mine with his.

Inside, the restaurant was richly appointed. Brass samovars rested on marble pedestals. Carved mahogany partitions and tapestries separated groups of patrons. Near the register were gilded statuettes of a goddess with arms like a spider. Almond eyes and rounded breasts.

"Table for dinner?" the hostess asked.

Carlos nodded. He seemed perfectly at home here. He told me that a close friend of his in high school had been from India. Before the revolution in Mozambique, there had been many immigrants from Pakistan and India, he said. Whole communities.

The sitar music in the background reminded me of the tapes I had listened to just after Fritz disappeared. Quiet music that incorporated a certain discord, the hint of cacophony. The busboy set water glasses in front of us. Carlos smiled at me and opened the menu. I glanced away from his eyes. I almost felt shy. The way he looked at me was unsettling.

After dinner we drove out along the Pacific Coast Highway, following the curve of the ocean. It was a humid summer night, but near the water, there was a breeze. The moon came out. As we walked down to the edge of the surf, he told me that the California beach reminded him of his home, of Africa. There, too, there were cliffs by the water, huge stretches of sand.

"But I can never go back there. Never," he said firmly. A look of anger flickered over his face. As we walked along the sand, he described how he had lost his home, how he'd been forced into exile.

"It started with a coup d'état in Portugal. A communist faction of the Portuguese armed forces overthrew the dictatorship on April 25, 1974. The takeover happened within twenty-four hours. The tanks rolled into Lisbon and the revolution of the 'Carnations' was over. After the new government had been established in power, they released the Portuguese colonies—Angola, Guinea, Mozambique, East Timor, and Macau. After five hundred years of colonial rule, the native Africans could finally reverse their roles and regain independence. It seemed there would be no more slavery, tyranny, or racism."

A sea gull dropped down and skimmed along the water's surface, disappearing into the night.

Right after the coup in Lisbon, Carlos left Portugal and went to Madrid, Spain. He abandoned the Portuguese air force, and he knew there was no way back. His fight would go on, not in the cafe-lined esplanades of Europe, but on the continent that he knew best: Africa. I wondered how much discord Carlos had had in his life. Leaving Mozambique, then Portugal. He had been to so many places that I knew so little about. He had traveled the world.

The Frelimo (Front of Liberation of Mozambique) was his enemy— for ten years its guerrilla tactics had tormented Carlos and his family. They had already been in Africa for three generations. Two of those generations had been born on the continent. They, too, were Africans. But the Frelimo's ideology of communism would try to take away the colonialists' way of life. "They would kill, maim, rape . . . and destroy," Carlos told me.

As we walked back to the car, Carlos put his arm around me. I shivered.

"Are you cold?" he asked, solicitous.

"A little," I said. The weather along the sea was always cooler than inland. He took off his jacket and draped it around my shoulders. He was kind. Thoughtful. It had been a long time since someone had taken care of me this way.

It was true, in some ways he reminded me of Fritz, but not entirely. Fritz chose to be an adventurer. Carlos, like me, had stumbled into a life on the edge.

27.

The African Domino

Mozambique
1975

A frica. It was July 1975. The sun had barely risen, the windshield of the red Ford Capri was covered with mud. The driver and Carlos traveled all night on the dirt roads of the southern African continent. The sooner he arrived at his destination, the sooner he would know how much he had been betrayed. Their trip from Johannesburg, South Africa, to Lourenço Marques, the capital of the former Portuguese colony of Mozambique, had taken them close to eight hours. The cover of night lessened the risk of being stoned to death. As they approached the capital city, the remote noises from the suburbs could be faintly heard, like a soft murmur. Carlos straightened his body and lit up another cigarette. Neither he nor the driver uttered a word.

The "African domino theory" was becoming a reality—a communist takeover in one country leading to another in a neighboring country—first the Portuguese colonies, next Rhodesia, and later South Africa. Russia would be vindicated and compensated. Its support of the guerrilla movements, with arms, training, and money, had paid off. The Frelimo leadership would keep its promises to the Soviet Union. The United States, on the other hand, had backed out. Senator Frank Church and others wanted easy victories. Hard work, risk, was not for them. They did not want to fight to create a democracy. No more Vietnams, they said. In the stroke of a few months, the decision of these few men would change the history of the world, the history of Portugal, the history of Africa.

As they entered the city, they smelled the exhaust from the public buses—"machimbombos," which were jammed with people hanging from their doors. They felt uneasy. Carlos was born in this city twenty-one years before, and for eighteen years he had spent his life in it. But now everything seemed different. The air, the smells, even the buildings—everything was different. People who were once familiar looked like strangers. It was as though they were imported, dropped by a spaceship.

As they drove into the city's bowels, there wasn't a single nerve in Carlos's body that wasn't tense. To be white and to drive a car through the streets was dangerous. The rage and anger accumulated through the centuries could be unleashed at any moment. A car accident, the wrong look, anything could spark the fuse. There were no police, no Portuguese armed forces. It was God, the whites, and the blacks. No rules, no laws. Just raw feelings and blind actions without regard for being just or right.

The Avenida Pinheiro Chagas was only too familiar to Carlos. He had driven it many times before, to school, to parties, to visits with friends. Suddenly, his car was forced to the side of the street by a military Jeep with four communist black Frelimo guerrillas armed with Kalashnikov machine guns.

Time stopped. His cigarette dropped in his lap; the driver looked at Carlos as if to say good-bye. The car went over to the curb and came to a complete stop. They didn't dare move. The guerrillas stopped their Jeep and spread themselves in a semicircle. Guns ready. The smell of something burning came from Carlos's left pant leg where his cigarette butt had dropped a few seconds before. Speaking with a heavy accent, one of the guerrillas told them to move out of the car.

As Carlos and the driver got out, they were told to lie face down on the pavement. A small crowd started to gather. Two of the guerrillas got inside the Capri and started tearing apart the seats and everything that might conceal something. The jeering from the crowd grew louder. Carlos's life passed through his mind like a movie spinning on a fast-forward reel. A piece of metal was thrown at them. More people gathered at the edge of the crowd. Someone started spitting. The crowd shouted: "Justice! Beat them! Do to them what they have been doing to us all these years!"

The leader of the guerrillas approached Carlos and asked him where he was going. Where did he live? Before he could answer, the crowd tried to move closer, the guerrillas became agitated, one of the guerrillas discharged a volley of gunfire. The crowd dispersed, running. Shouts were heard from every direction.

"Where were you going?" the guerrilla leader yelled into Carlos's ear.

With only an instant of hesitation, Carlos responded, "To Frelimo headquarters."

The guerrilla leader ordered Carlos and the driver into their car. As the Jeep with four soldiers escorted the red Capri, Carlos could no longer contain his pain. The enemy was protecting him. The communist Frelimo guerrillas defending him. It made no sense. Life seemed upside down. He cried. His fate was about to be sealed. In a few minutes, he would be face to face with the head of Frelimo's secret services— Jacinto Soares Veloso.

The military Jeep made its way through one neighborhood, then another, heading out toward the bluffs that overlooked the ocean. The city became a disaster area when the Portuguese government withdrew.

As they neared the guerrilla headquarters, Carlos could smell the sea breeze. A scent of freshness and freedom. Nature and water, symbols of purity. The headquarters were located in the same historical buildings, in the Polana residential area, that had been the command center for the colony's governors through the centuries. It sat at the top of a cliff overlooking downtown and the bay. It was a place where plots of annihilation had been conceived, where the might of colonialism worked day and night devising strategies to protect the "elite," the ruling class.

The stark-white seven-foot wall surrounding the compound became visible. The driver slowed down and stopped the car in front of a heavy metal gate where an armed guerrilla asked what they wanted. They had come to see Comrade Jacinto. The sentry stepped back respectfully and signaled somebody inside to open the gates.

Carlos couldn't stop the thoughts, the memories. His Lourenço

Marques, the city kissed by the bay, the warm Indian Ocean. The same ocean that covered miles and miles of the country's coastline. A country with a quarter of a million whites and eight million blacks. Wildlife, tourist resorts, beaches, nightlife. A paradise on earth. But the spoils of victory only went to those who conquered, who won, regardless of the price.

As Carlos walked from his car to the second floor of the colonial structure, he noticed that there were armed guerrillas everywhere. Strange, very strange. He was in the middle of the enemy, a few feet away; there were so many of them. He proceeded to a hallway where an officer sat at a desk blocking a door behind him. Carlos identified himself and the man got up and asked Carlos to follow him. There, in a small room, no bigger than ten by twenty feet, resided the answer to Carlos's future. As he walked in, he was greeted by a balding, six-foot man whose gentle manner was nothing more than a mask, the mask of deceit and of hidden evil. Jacinto Soares Veloso was a former second lieutenant and pilot of the Portuguese air force who had deserted to the Frelimo. He was the head of the dreaded Frelimo secret services. The most dangerous white man inside the Liberation Movement. Jacinto asked Carlos to have a seat and introduced him to a short, stocky black man, a Frelimo general.

History, what a farce, Carlos thought. Here were two Portuguese men in Africa—one a former air force pilot, a deserter, a communist; the other, Carlos, also a former air force pilot, a capitalist—trying to negotiate, to carve out their futures. Carlos thought about how his path had crossed Jacinto's in the past. Carlos's mother, Maria, had known Jacinto since he was six years old. Jacinto's father had been a policeman for the Portuguese government. Carlos's grandfather had also been a policeman. Maria had grown up playing with Jacinto. Even today, she still called him "Bebe," meaning "Baby." There were too many affinities between him and this man.

With a heavy accent, Jacinto started speaking: "What we need now is that all Mozambicans come back to the Motherland. Now that we have defeated the foreigners, we want to start rebuilding our country. We don't want officers or people who were part of the Special Forces of

Portugal: they were brainwashed and they are dangerous." He continued in a monotone. "We are not going to have an air force. We need to build the infrastructure. We want technicians, people at sergeant level." Carlos continued listening. What infrastructures was he talking about? What qualified people did he want? At sergeant level only?

Finally, Carlos asked him: "Jacinto, what is going to happen to people like my parents; what about our properties, our businesses?"

"Well," he said, "before there were twenty people without any shoes, and one with twenty pairs. Now everybody is going to have a pair." Carlos felt a chill shoot up his spine. All the hard work that his family, his grandfather and father had done to build and accumulate over years would be gone. The words had been said. This marked the end of his "secured future."

"Go back to Portugal and travel through the different air bases. Recruit Mozambicans, tell them to come back. That's all you can do for us now," Jacinto said in closing.

Recruit Mozambicans. Those words would stick in Carlos's memory for many years. Life had played a trick on him. It had turned one hundred eighty degrees. Back to zero.

He smiled faintly at Jacinto, thanked him for the meeting, and left with a gentle shake of hands and the faint promise to go back to Europe and recruit "Mozambicans."

As he got in the car, Carlos asked the driver to leave the compound. "Foreigners" Jacinto had said. He was referring to the Portuguese people. His parents, his family. My God, how history, borders, ideology would create divisions, false barriers, concepts, lies. All lies. Carlos felt numb. He needed to go by his house, to see it for a last time. The driver followed Carlos's directions. Carlos was oblivious to the noise of the city waking up as they passed through it. He wanted out, as fast as possible. Back to South Africa to Johannesburg. There were decisions to be made. The process wouldn't wait. He, too, could make a difference. Communism would have to die.

As he arrived at the front of his three-story house, he saw his mother watching through a second-floor window. The metal bars in the windows made it look like she was in jail. A few months earlier no protection seemed necessary; it seemed so free, so peaceful, even innocent, and now it was a matter of life and death. Them versus us. No selected enemy, just random hate. Black against white. Did people know that one of their leaders was white? and Portuguese? The head of their secret services.

People were drunk with thoughts of hope, freedom, and power. How things could change in life, so fast.

A smile came to his mother's face when she saw her son approaching. She was only forty-eight, but she looked older. There was a tumult inside her heart. She was torn between her love for her husband and her love for her new country.

Carlos's father was three years older than his mother. His background was different. A self-made man. He had worked since age twelve. He had started from nothing and studied to become an electrical engineer. He knew how to work hard, seven days a week, fourteen hours a day. Looking for a better life, a better future, he had emigrated to Mozambique. Now the country was in a state of disarray.

Carlos hurried to hug his mother and father and asked them to prepare to leave with him, to go to South Africa. After a few minutes his mother told him, she had been born in Mozambique and she wanted to stay; she wanted to contribute to the good of the country. His father, with tears in his eyes, tried to plead with her to be reasonable, to understand that the situation was more serious than she thought. But to no avail. She refused to leave, to budge—after all, her friend "Bebe" would protect her. The fight between Carlos's parents showed him that the political process was like a wildfire burning out of control. Burning everyone and everything that would stand in its path. He felt sorry for his father but he couldn't do more. He decided to stay and sleep until dark, at which time he could escape under the cover of night.

When Carlos told me that he'd cried the last time he was in his home, I was touched. Even though Carlos seemed to be angry, he was very sensitive. One could hurt his feelings easily. He was like a wounded animal. He had been betrayed: his future, had been taken away from him. That dream was gone. In a different way, I felt the same. With Fritz gone, I was hurt. When I married Fritz, I believed that I had fulfilled my cycle in life, that we would happily grow old together. With his disappearance I was forced to learn things that I never thought existed or were even possible. How small the world really was. How human rights had been disregarded. How much what happened somewhere else on the globe could affect us here at home. I'd trusted and believed in our leaders, blindly. My priorities had been my career in Hollywood, my family, and my friends. Fate tore my naiveté apart. Like Carlos I felt betrayed, and above all my magic future—my fantasy that had become reality—was gone.

28.

Freedom at Last

South Africa/Brazil
1976-77

S oon after Carlos left Mozambique, his parents had to flee the country, and they were placed in a refugee camp inside South Africa. During their escape, they were stoned and almost burned alive in their car, but they made it across the border.

The two superpowers had a game to play in Africa, and Angola and Mozambique were at stake. Angola was a bigger prize, because it had gold, diamonds, and, above all, oil. The communists wanted to ensure that Angola stayed communist. The Soviet Union had already provided weapons and training to the Angolan MPLA, the communist Popular Movement for the Liberation of Angola. The United States and the People's Republic of China decided to back the FNLA, the National Front for the Liberation of Angola and the UNITA, the National Union for Total Independence of Angola, led by Jonas Savimbi.

In 1975, the CIA and the South African government initiated a recruiting operation. Once again in southern Africa, communism would meet democracy. Unfortunately, as the forces for democracy were rallying in Angola and Mozambique, they were failing elsewhere in the world. In the spring of 1975, Saigon had just fallen, the U.S. had been beaten in Southeast Asia by the communists and our government didn't want to get into another Vietnam. The House of Representatives, the Senate, the Church Committee, and the Rockefeller Commission were holding hearings on the CIA's activities. It was bad timing for those fighting communism in Africa.

Carlos told me how the Special Commandos, backed by the South African armed forces and the CIA, had arrived within a few miles of the Angolan capital, Luanda, when he and his colleagues received the news. The CIA was backing out. They could no longer support the initiative against the communist MPLA troops. Not even Henry Kissinger could change the minds of our senators and congressmen.

The pain of losing to the communists was almost worse than losing his country, he'd said, because he hadn't trusted the whole operation from the beginning. He'd been uncomfortable knowing that Red China was helping the democratic forces in Africa. He felt that the U.S. alliance with China was a bad marriage, even though its main objective was to destroy the Soviet Union. For Carlos, a communist was a communist, no matter what uniform he wore. Carlos felt that we should be fighting Red China as well as the Soviet Union.

After the CIA withdrew its support, Carlos was offered a group of two hundred soldiers to lead inside Angola. He did not accept. Soon after, he was threatened by the South African intelligence services. The South Africans were ready to send him back to Portugal. There he would be considered a deserter and a confirmed anticommunist; the Portuguese government was fringe communist at that time. Carlos's safety was in jeopardy. In Portugal, jail would be his welcome mat.

After evaluating his options, in 1976, at age twenty-two, he said good-bye to his parents one last time, and fled to Brazil.

* * *

As the TWA flight approached the Galeao Airport in Rio de Janeiro, Carlos could see through the plane's small window the famous statue of Jesus with opened arms, the Corcovado. Brazil had been a Portuguese colony. Its independence was declared by the Portuguese king, Dom Pedro, who was exiled in the early eighteen hundreds because the Spaniards had invaded and occupied Portugal for thirty years.

On leaving the African continent, Carlos set out to build a new life for himself. The Americas had always been a place for rebirth and opportunity.

The beginning was rough. To make ends meet, he had to work two jobs: one during the day in public relations at the well-known H. Stern jewelry chain, and another at night as an English teacher. The sunny beaches during the day and the glitter of Rio's nightlife were no more than temptations for him to look at, not to partake in. There was neither time nor money. Carlos told me of his adventures looking for better opportunities and higher salaries in the Amazon, the bowels of Brazil. He left Rio and traveled to the city of Manaus in the heart of the Amazon forest. He witnessed misery, exploitation, and the monopolization of power by the elite. Indians, women, and children were the victims of oppression and abuse, both physical and mental. He couldn't stomach it. He felt that the socioeconomic injustices in the fiber of Brazilian society were a time bomb waiting to blow up, and he didn't want to be a part of any more revolutions. He was right. The Corcovado statue that received him with its open arms had never closed those same arms of welcome. The promise was never delivered. In July 1977, he arrived in Los Angeles. The United States of America at last, the bastion of freedom and opportunity. This would be Carlos's last stop on his long journey for liberty.

In the games of world politics, the same pattern surfaced time and again. Be it in Vietnam, Afghanistan, Angola, or Mozambique, the same players were always involved: the United States, the Soviet Union, and the People's Republic of China. Three countries that toyed with the world. One round of the game had played out in Carlos's homeland, Portuguese Africa. There the Soviet Union had beaten the United States. Communism had won.

29.

Courtship

Los Angeles
1982

In the window I could see his reflection, dilute, pencil-drawn, bent over a pot. He closed his eyes and concentrated. The aroma reached me clearly: cream and butter melding. Spice flecks jittered into the sauce while he stirred. I stared out past this shadow etching to the tree outside. It had grown with me through the years. It had bowed and twisted, dodging and jockeying for the light. The branches of this tree had gnarled and spotted.

Outside, the leaves whispered communion, the sky deepened. Carlos was slicing potatoes. He turned around and glanced at me, flashed a smile, then returned to his work. His hands ably cut and chopped the translucent ovals. The eyes were still on the potatoes, even though the skins had been removed. "They have more character this way," he'd answered when I'd pointed this out to him once before. Character. I liked watching his hands. Long tapered fingers. They were strong; young, but experienced.

"So, what was your day like?" I asked.

"Pretty good, it was pretty good," he answered. "I had a few things to do. There were some things I needed to buy for tonight." Probably the lobsters. He'd just taken them out of the bag and laid them on the counter, split in half, feelers and claws outstretched stiffly. The white flesh needed butter. He slathered it on, rubbing it in. His hands pressed in slow circles, reaching out every once in a while to scoop some spice and add it in. Then came the Tabasco, liberally doused over the seasoned flesh. The hot juice ran a diluted red, almost orange, the color of flames. He flipped the lobsters into the pan. This was Carlos's unconventional custom: pan-frying them before tossing them into the broiler. It sealed the flavors in, he said. He was so attentive to detail. The small things had won me over. The way he conducted his life. If he was to court me, he would do it correctly. He knew what he wanted from life, how he wanted his life, and he went about attaining his goals. In some sense, I was one of them.

I got up and moved to the breakfast table. From here I could look at Carlos while he finished the potatoes. I drew a knee up and rested my chin. I liked watching him.

"You want your lobster spicy?" Carlos's voice broke in. He held his hands out as if they were an offering. They were covered with butter and spices. "Um, yes, spicy sounds good," I smiled back at him.

I went to help, laying a hand on his back as I opened the refrigerator. Lettuce, tomatoes, red onions. I gathered these up, then unloaded them onto the counter. Carlos moved aside intuitively. I nudged into the space between him and the sink, then turned on the water, splattering the vegetables. I turned them, rubbing gently with my thumbs to remove dirt.

"So what happened with that letter you sent to the State Department?" Carlos began. He knew all about Fritz and my efforts to find him. We had been friends for so long before we ever went out that he knew all the details. Several years' worth of facts, trivia, hunches.

"They haven't responded yet," I answered. I didn't expect much of a response. I'd sent the letter a long time ago when I still felt Fritz was out there somewhere. My hopes for bridging the distance diminished with time. The odds dictated failure. But part of me still wanted the peace of mind that came with a definite answer. I ripped the lettuce.

"Well," Carlos offered. "Your letter may have gotten lost among others. People disappear all the time, unfortunately."

I winced. Carlos was simply stating a fact. After his own escape from a country in revolution, he knew of unexplained vanishings. Disappearances. Historical forces, dictators, volunteered few explanations. He was twenty-nine, but he had seen a lot. He was a resilient man. A fighter.

"What's on your mind?" Carlos asked, interrupting my mental monologue. He had a way of doing this, knowing when to step in.

"Oh, not much. I'm fine. Really," I said. He stared at me for a moment while I tossed the salad, then grabbed a towel and wiped off his hands.

"You know, we forgot something important," he stated.

"We did?" I'd thought we had all the ingredients we needed. I ran through what we needed to complete the meal: wine, bread, olive oil, red wine vinegar.

"Music," Carlos announced. "What do you feel like hearing?"

"Oh, anything. Something melodic, guitar. Segovia might be nice."

"Just one moment, madame," he joked.

I set the table, thinking over how many times I had done this. There had been Fritz. Now there was Carlos. It was not often that I took a man into my home. There were not many men who could really hold their own. I was independent. I gave Carlos a hard time sometimes. I didn't allow him into my head, or my heart, unconditionally, which was not quite fair. I had complete access to his thoughts, his feelings. He'd told me that once, and I believed him. But I could not offer him the same. He understood. If he didn't understand, he accepted the differences between us. Difference did not intimidate him.

I laid down the placemats, cloth with fluted edging and some embroidery, then reached for the plates. Thick crockery. Solid blue glaze. The blond wood table had been sanded smooth, soft as petals. I finished folding the napkins into flowers which floated in the middle of the dishes, lilies on makeshift ponds.

Carlos walked up behind me with some candles. The light in the room was just beginning to fade. He handed me the matches. I leaned over to the center of the table and put the flaring match to the candle. It took a second, then caught, sizzling a little. The joy of being consumed. He put his arm around my waist and drew me close. His chest pressed up against my back: it was a solid, firm support.

After dinner, we went into the living room. At this moment, I could not read him. He was standing edgily near the window. I sank back into the cushions and watched the light play in his dark hair. His arm rested on the window siding, on the narrow white border. The vulnerable part of the house. As I contemplated him, he turned toward me and watched me watching. We had an understanding. Between us this distance was allowed: it was the other side of intimacy. He studied me for a moment and then came over.

He stood before me for an instant, it seemed. Then he eased himself down beside me and took my hand. He kissed me. I kissed him back. I was falling in love with him and I didn't want to. I didn't want to risk ever being hurt the way I had been with Fritz. I gently pushed him away and asked him if he would like an after-dinner drink.

"No, thank you. I just want you here next to me," he said. I got up and walked to the kitchen. I knew that I was about to sabotage my own happiness.

30.

Las Vegas

Las Vegas
1982

L as Vegas amplified and distorted nature's push and pull. Sex
ruled everything. I didn't usually think of sex as a principle, but
in this city it was. The floor shows, the hookers on the street, the
plush bedroom suites all suggested sex; the whole feel of the place was
lusty. The impulse to gamble, the yearning for power, the desire to
control money, men, women—those longings all came from the same
place: a need for primacy, for propagation. There was no way to avoid
sex here, now. I had not wanted to feel so assaulted. And at the same
time, I had wanted to feel this. I had wanted to feel the contact, the
forced intimacy that all this struggling produced.

Ever since I accepted Carlos's invitation to go with him to Las Vegas
I had been a nervous wreck. I was excited but filled with anxiety and
second thoughts all at the same time. Packing took hours. I went back
and forth, filling my suitcase, then taking clothes out. I had put in one
outfit, replaced it with another one, then decided to take neither, then
decided to take both. Finally I sat myself down on the edge of my bed
and decided to leave. Carlos and I had been spending more time
together. The more he pursued me, the more I resisted and pulled away.
I knew I had pushed him to the limit. I didn't want that to happen. I
wanted to be with him, but I was afraid. I had to force my life forward,
make a change, even if it was difficult or painful. Even if it was a
mistake.

The Vegas ballroom was full. I turned from the curtain and glanced at Carlos once again. I twisted my fingers together in my lap, then took a sip of my drink.

The showgirls began parading on the catwalk. Strands of faux jewels and sequins woven into the mesh barely cupping their breasts. These didn't move as they turned and pirouetted, lifting arms, legs, bending at the waist. These girls seemed to control every motion, every movement of their bodies. Carlos turned to me and smiled, white teeth catching what light there was. I adjusted uncomfortably in my chair, trying to find a position that was less tense. His eyes smiled, too, and then he turned to watch the show again. I felt butterflies in my stomach in anticipation.

After the women exited the stage through the invisible slits on either side of the curtain, we got up and began to leave. The casino lobby spilled out into the night through rows of revolving glass doors. Gaudy neon matched the bulbs flashing on the slot machines. The stars and the moon were hidden in the backdrop of black spread flat and opaque behind the shining marquees.

We stood outside, commenting on the spectacle we had just seen inside the showroom as we waited for our limousine to take us to our hotel. The accoutrements of glamour were so easily acquired in Las Vegas that I would have almost preferred to walk. The symbols meant nothing.

As the conversation dropped off, I turned away from the glitz and faced the desert, a blank space behind the chaos.

Years before, I had lived in the desert, in a car. My first real boyfriend, Glenn, and I had landed in Las Vegas after driving across the United States. We had no money and there was work here. The Desert Inn had offered me a job as a dancer. I never danced before, but I learned; I learned in a hurry. Two hundred fifty dollars a week was what they paid. The first month we weren't able to afford an apartment, so we'd lived out of an old Nash Ambassador and slept under the stars. The cold would wake us up in the morning. I preferred sleeping outdoors for a month rather than ask my parents for money. Sleeping in a car was a small price to pay for freedom. Now I was spending the night at Caesar's Palace. Things had changed.

I turned back toward the rows of hotels, the wide boulevards filled with oversized American cars, the signs flashing patterns on and off like Morse code. Flesh here, food there, money everywhere. This was a place of forgetting, a place where people left real life and joined a collective fairy tale. Carlos's hand lightly touched my arm as he brushed past. He stood by the opened limousine door and waited for me to enter before him. I climbed in and sat back for the ride.

The end of the evening finally arrived. We stood in the elevator feeling the floors drop away below us. As the elevator climbed higher and higher, my tension rose with it. My stomach cramped up with nerves. Carlos seemed excited. I sighed heavily. The elevator doors slid open.

When we got to the room, Carlos headed for the wet bar in the corner. I just stood awkwardly. I didn't know quite where to put myself in this room. Earlier, I had just rushed in to leave my bags and change before we left for the evening. Now I meandered toward the love seat and dropped my purse down.

I picked up the scent of Carlos's cologne. He sat down next to me. He held my gaze, then spoke in a voice thickened with a Portuguese undertow. "You are going to sleep with me," he said. His piercing brown eyes held no question. This was a statement: there was no other place for me but in his bed.

He used the bathroom first, then I went in. I turned on the water in the sink. I looked into the bedroom. The bed was across the room. Carlos was turned on his side facing me. I walked to the edge of the bed and stood there for a second. I lifted the covers gently and slid beneath them.

The dresser came into focus. I was being hugged. Carlos's arm curled around my waist. His hand caressed my stomach. The warmth of his touch radiated outward each time his fingers brushed my skin. It was as if he was passing on his own emotion. He could no longer contain it. His hands charged my body. It had been so long since I had felt like this.

As if sensing my question, he pressed me closer, then turned my body around gently until I faced him. I could not meet his eyes, yet I did not want to look away. I closed my eyes. He cupped my face in his hands and raised it. I opened my eyes. He was looking straight into them. He was looking at me.

I had known this before. I had known this with Fritz. After a second of silence, he curled around me from behind, cradling me in his body. I eased back into his arms, although the tension at my core did not fully dissolve. I still felt it there, waiting to explode and consume the smaller, gentler explosions his touch created. I didn't want to tense up. I didn't want to fight this.

With one motion there was no thought. Our bodies rolled together. Flesh on flesh. We joined, we rocked. The tide inside me pulled him. Our bodies intertwined. Each curve folded into another—natural, urgent, raw. My legs wrapped around his back and held tightly. I wanted more of him, all of him. I wanted to consume him, envelope him with my being, take him whole.

He breathed me in, taking my breath, then released me. A sigh escaped. I heard the sound as if it were not my own. It resounded through my chest and found release again. I moaned.

His hands molded to my shoulder blades, the wings behind my back, as if urging me to fly. Holding me firmly, he let me down. Then he moved down himself. His tongue slid across my abdomen, stopping, then continuing on until he reached my belly. His mouth cascaded down the side of my stomach, pausing in the gap where my waist gave way. He rested there and then began again, teasing. He drank it in with the night air, the intangible elixir which brought this madness on, this need to consume.

I looked up above his head. The ceiling was mirrored. There we were. I watched. A voyeur. I met my eyes. The two bodies moved in time. I closed my eyes and let myself rock. Back and forth until the motion stopped. And the comfort was gone.

I twisted in Carlos's arms. We kissed again. The bed, the man, the rumpled sheets; it all seemed disconnected. What were we doing? Fritz's face stirred in my memory. What had I done?

I looked at Carlos and he looked back at me with a smile. He reached into the dresser next to the bed.

"Janice," he began, "I have something for you. I want you to know what my intentions are." He held a velvet box. He placed it in my hand. I opened it; inside was a ring. Seven diamonds in a row. A lucky number seven was, sometimes. In the Bible, in Egypt, the people had seven years of bad luck, then seven years of good. Famine, harvest.

Since Fritz's disappearance I had not thought that I would ever accept a ring from another man. But the present time had overtaken me. My body moved forward even as my mind clung to the past. Carlos slipped the ring on my finger.

31.

Resurrection

Los Angeles
September 1982

I considered the enormity of what I had just done. I felt detached from the events that had transpired. The receptionist at the Aspen courthouse was as helpful as I could have expected. Her bureaucratic function did not hinder her tact. When I requested a court date to declare Fritz dead, she responded with complete aplomb. She arranged the details. She could not have doubted who I was. Fritz's disappearance still circulated around the town's gossip mills, though the story had been ground to a fine powder. Seven years had passed. Seven years. I found that hard to believe.

Carlos had asked me to marry him and I accepted. I could no longer postpone my decision to let Fritz go, to declare him dead.

I didn't like the idea of going to court. I had dealt with lawyers and judges before. Legal judgments. The process somehow did not seem applicable to the matter at hand. I pictured the courtroom: empty seats, my counsel and I behind a table, the judge up on a platform.

The secretary had said that I would need a copy of our marriage license. I had it, somewhere. It was going to take some doing to find it, though. It had been a while since I looked through Fritz's things.

I opened the desk drawers and started riffling through their contents. Notes to myself, Fritz's letters, Aspen snapshots. Not to mention cobwebs and spiders. An ecosystem. There were things in here I had not looked at in years.

Funny how most of life came down to paper. A memo. Scraggly

sheets of notebook paper. Journals. Messages. These things made it difficult to forget, let go. I squeamishly moved a few items around. Blank stationery. A letter underneath. It was addressed to Opa in Fritz's hand. Never sent. Forgotten. I took it in my hand and smoothed the dented edges.

So much had accumulated. Shelves full of records that I never finished sorting. Random information. Boxes filled with books. *The Autobiography of a Yogi. How to Ascend the Highest Peaks.* I went back to the drawers. I would need trash bags. I had to start throwing some of this stuff out.

I started sorting through the papers, looking them over one by one. A dark blue scrap fell from between the sheets. Half a ticket stub. I inspected it. Recycled paper. Specks of dirt. I could hardly make out the words. The Way We. *The Way We Were.* It had been a dusty, windblown night when we'd seen it. The Santa Ana winds had been raging through Los Angeles. I remembered that. The wind. Dry. Hot. Moving.

Garbage. I could not be hanging on to scraps like this, old pieces of nonsense. I threw the ticket away. The green trash bag slid out of my hand and fell to the floor between my legs. A bag full of refuse, slippery and smooth like an embryo.

I gathered it up and took it outside. It was so full, heavy. There was so much more to go through.

The dingy light inside was mixed in shades of gray. A room filled with shadows, silent ghosts. Dead time, dead years, dead life. A dead relationship. My life died in this room when Fritz disappeared. It had been all I could do to keep the job I had. My ambition dried up. I retreated.

I looked at the pile in the middle of the room. Confrontation after confrontation. Each time I started in again, I had to face off with it. I took out some empty boxes. I would keep one. A small one. Everything else had to go. A little pain now would prevent more later.

More loose sheets of paper, print shop type samples, newspaper clippings. I wanted to drop the whole mess into the black hole which memory could be. Without looking, I crammed things into bags, extra boxes, whatever I could find. Pictures, dried flowers, love notes. No mercy. I pulled my hand across my forehead and wiped the sweat. A reel of film. Mountain climbing footage. A novel both he and I had read. A love story. The boarding passes from our honeymoon trip. And, at last, the marriage license.

The Stammbergers. Our marriage had represented something to me, a meeting, a perfection. Now I questioned it; I no longer knew what it had been. I'd lived off the memories until I started to recycle them. Remembering changed memories. They faded. They'd worn through, worn out. The original was gone.

I picked up the boarding passes, which belonged in the garbage, and put them in the box. I got up off the floor and brushed the dust from my shorts. My knees hurt from sitting in one position. I strapped tape across the box. The remains of my life with Fritz. Mementos in flimsy coffins. I took the boxes outside to the car and put them in the trunk.

When I returned to the house, the phone was ringing. Maybe it was Carlos. I wanted to tell him what I had done.

"Hello," I answered.

"Janice? . . . Janice, this is Jim. Jim MacGeyver."

"Jim, where are you?" I had not heard from him since I had received the package by mail describing his search for Fritz. He'd vanished without a word six years before.

"I'm calling from Pakistan and can't talk long. But I have some news for you."

"Yes?" I said, trying to suppress anxiety.

"I've talked to three separate groups of people and found out that Fritz is alive in a high-security prison near Chitral. . . . I'll have him home by Christmas."

"Alive!" I cut in. "What people? How did you find . . ."

"I can't talk long. All I can tell you is that three people confirmed that he's alive and in prison."

"How? I mean . . ."

"It's dangerous for me to talk from here. I'm going to Munich. I'll call you from there in a few days. Bye." That was all he said, then there was a click and we were disconnected.

The pieces of the puzzle were shifting. Nellie, the psychic, had told me back in 1975 that "there's more to this than meets the eye . . . he's alive," the mysterious Mike Hillman trying to probe how much I knew about Fritz and his whereabouts and also Bob Peloquin's final statement, ". . . if we find something more than this, perhaps it's better that you not know." Could I trust what Jim MacGeyver told me?

Fritz was alive. Why was he in jail? What crime had he committed? Why hadn't our consular services informed me of his capture? What were they hiding?

I replaced the receiver and entered the room, the study. The shelves were half-empty. Boxes were strewn about. The desk drawers hung open. The place looked ransacked. In my frenzy, I went through every book, every folder, every drawer, every filing cabinet. I left no shelf undisturbed. Carnage filled the corners. Lumpy plastic bags lay about. Body bags. I thought that it was over. That was why I was doing this. That was why I could do this.

I had buried this man, buried him. Fritz was rising from the dead.

32.

Splash

Malibu
1982

T he Whale Watch restaurant, which later became Splash, was a hangout for celebrities and stars living along the shore in exclusive Westward Beach, a few miles from famous Broad Beach and Malibu. It was an out-of-the-way, cozy stop where people could share an intimate dinner without being bothered. It was a favorite of Johnny Carson.

Carlos selected this restaurant. Due to his job at Cartier, he traveled quite a lot, and when he was back in Los Angeles, he wanted to spend as much time with me as possible. Somewhere quiet. He was a romantic at heart and he was looking forward to our wedding. I didn't know what to do. Cancel the date? Tell him over the phone? Have the dinner, and not tell him about the call from MacGeyver?

I met Carlos as planned. The maître d' greeted me with a warm smile when I arrived and walked me to my table next to the window. The view from the dining room was breathtaking at sunset. The pungent smell of garlic and mixed spices filled the air. He summoned the waiter and told him to bring me an appetizer, something new on the menu, just to sample until Carlos arrived. A bottle of red wine was opened and poured with a flourish, then he returned to the front of the restaurant to greet a party of four that stepped off the elevator. Carlos stepped out behind them.

He looked happy as he caught my eye across the room. He was tan, with a white, flashing smile full of life. That was what drew me to him

144

more than anything else: his enthusiasm for ideas and fulfilling his dreams, his ambitions, whether in business or in his personal life. He saw things through, no matter how difficult; he wouldn't give up. There was a purity in that.

He gave me a kiss and pulled his chair back as he sat down across from me, taking my hand.

"I have very good news. It looks like I may be going to Switzerland. Phillippe Charriol, the ex-president of Cartier wants to make me an offer to start a new international distribution company. He wants to offer me a partnership," Carlos said. He was very excited. He came to the United States in July 1977, and five years later had his first chance at being his own boss. I knew that that was what he always wanted. Independence, and control of his destiny. He picked up his glass of red wine and toasted to us. The waiter came by to let us know what the specials were. Carlos was anxious to continue sharing his news.

"Where would the company be based?" I asked.

The waiter took our orders and dashed to another table.

"At the beginning, it will be in New York, but we would open our headquarters in Geneva, Switzerland, and a subsidiary in Hong Kong. I think this is a very good move for me. Phillippe will give me twenty-five percent of the company stock." He smiled and had another sip of our red wine.

"We'll still go ahead as we planned and look for a house out here; it won't change anything, except for one year or so we would have to do some commuting. We don't have to make any decisions tonight, though; I want us to enjoy the evening. As a matter of fact, I have a surprise for you," he said with pride.

"What is it?" I asked eagerly.

"No, you have to wait until after the dinner." He smiled again.

I picked up my fork. How could I tell him about Jim MacGeyver's call telling me that he had found out Fritz was in a high-security prison and that he would have Fritz home by Christmas? How could I tell him that we had to cancel our wedding?

"What is it, babe?" He jarred my thoughts. I looked up at him and smiled.

"Nothing. I'm just thinking. I'm very happy that we are here together. I love you," I answered.

After dinner, we walked on the beach. Carlos was talking about his plans for the future, for us.

"We can finally start our life together," he concluded happily, pressing my hand in his. We continued to walk along the water in silence. I watched the waves cascading in, one at a time, then a series.

"So," he said, "what do you think?"

He had asked me a question that I hadn't heard.

"I'm sorry, babe . . . " I started to apologize, but he continued excitedly. "What do you think about looking for a house, a place of our own?"

"Well . . . ," I began hesitantly. I had to tell him sometime, but it just wasn't easy. I couldn't seem to get the words out.

"I know . . . you have a place already . . . but we should start anew," he affirmed.

To leave all those memories behind, my house . . . I hadn't thought about that. We stood still for a moment. Carlos folded his arms around me from behind, holding me close. "Well, you don't have to decide now," he said. "It's a lot to think about all at once—jobs, houses . . . getting married." He slid his arm around my waist and hugged me.

My body stiffened. I didn't know what to say. I turned to look at the ocean, the last light shimmering on the waves. Carlos was a little disconcerted, but then a smile crossed his face. "Guess what?" he whispered in my ear flirtatiously.

"What?" I whispered back, momentarily drawn into his mood, his exuberance.

"I still have a surprise for you," he hinted. I felt a twinge of pain, of conscience. My eyes clouded over. He stopped and hugged me again. "Hey, don't worry. You know that inn you like . . . I reserved a room for us."

The Malibu Colony Inn, I thought warmly. "Carlos . . . but—"

"But, what?" he laughed.

We checked in at the inn. As soon as we got to our room, Carlos started kissing the back of my neck, then my ear. I tried to respond to him, to forget my tension, but I could only feel tenderness toward him. Tenderness, not passion. I can't keep this pretense up, I thought as I traced the lines of his body with my fingers. He kissed me lightly on my mouth and drew back.

He stroked my hair. I couldn't tell him now. It wasn't the right time. I could feel his breath moving from my lips, down my neck . . . over my body. I could feel him, but . . .

I pulled away from him, just a little. He noticed.

"What's wrong?" he questioned.

I didn't say anything.

"Look," he said more firmly, "what's going on? All night long you've been tuning out on me."

"I . . . I . . ." My voice died away leaving the sentence unfinished.

"Babe, talk to me," he insisted.

"This afternoon . . . I got a phone call," I managed to get out.

"Yes . . . ?" he prompted.

". . . from Pakistan." I wavered, then added, "It was from Jim MacGeyver."

"MacGeyver!" Carlos exploded. "What's he doing calling you? After all these years," he spit out. "Janice, MacGeyver is a loser. You know that and I know that. He never delivered and he never will. Period."

I hated when Carlos yelled at me. Slowly, quietly, the tears were sliding down my cheeks. He moved next to me.

"What did he say?"

I turned toward him. "Carlos . . . you know that I love you?"

He stared at me without response.

"MacGeyver told me that Fritz is in prison . . . he's alive."

I felt Carlos's arm tighten around me. He looked shell-shocked; his face was pale and empty, hardened. A stone mask.

I didn't know what to say or do. I put my head against his shoulder and lay still.

33.

Death Sentence

Aspen
1983

After being postponed twice, the day in court arrived. MacGeyver's phone call disconcerted me, left me uncertain. I wasn't able to do it, to declare Fritz legally deceased. But months passed and MacGeyver disappeared again. Just that one phone call and then nothing. I chose not to wait any longer. Carlos and I set our wedding date for April 20, 1984.

I sat back on the bench and watched the clerks race through the hall. They carried memos, contracts. Possibly even a death sentence or a reprieve.

Occasionally, high heels sounded in the corridor. A woman was somewhat of a rarity in this hall. Although one or two female attorneys passed by, most of the women sat by open doors, behind desks, near typewriters. They worked from nine to five.

I looked up at the woman as she drew near. She was hiding behind her hair. It concealed her face so that I could not make out her expression. As she walked by the courtroom to my left, I saw that she was in her own world. She was holding her hand like a visor before her eyes, as if it could help her see better, clear the glare. Her other hand was held, clenching and unclenching, by her side. Her body was curved like a shield. It looked like she'd been crying. I watched her walk down the hallway and disappear around the corner.

I glanced at the doors to my left. No movement stirred behind them. They were not about to open soon. I headed for the bathroom around the same corner, following the imaginary path blazed in my head by the unhappy woman. I leaned into the carved wooden door that led into the bathroom. The buildings in Aspen were not as old as they seemed. The handmade quality of the place and its accoutrements gave it an age it had not lived through.

I turned on the brass faucet and watched the water stream down. As I rubbed my hands together, I heard a faint whimper emerge through the hiss of water. In the mirror I saw that one of the stalls was closed. I gently shut off the water and heard the crying subside. There would not be one without the other. I reached for a paper towel as I kept listening for another sound, any sound. It seemed this woman wanted to be alone, yet I had been alone enough to know how little comfort there was in solitude.

I crumpled the paper towel and walked toward the door. I knew she was listening to me as intently as I was listening to her. I put on some lipstick, then went out. I had been the one behind the locked door before, half wishing for someone to intervene.

As I walked back toward the courtroom, I saw the others rise. My lawyer and the new court clerk were filing in as I neared. It had been more than ten years since I last saw the inside of a courtroom and the last one had looked different than this. It was antiseptic, bare metal and plastic interspersed with token wood. The judge was in a hurry. He called the room to order. The gavel struck. One sound, able to destroy the distance of years: wood resounding on wood, metal on metal. The last time I was in a courtroom the judge had handed me a sentence: three days at the Sybil Brand Institute for Women.

The nightmare began in Judge Davenport's courtroom in Van Nuys, California. Judge Davenport. His name seemed innocuous enough, but he was not. He felt imprisoned behind the bench and took his anger out on others, especially young women. He threw me in prison because I was two days late on a ticket. He felt I was being deviant, questioning his authority, and said that he was going to teach me about responsibility. My freedom must have insulted him.

After the bailiff led me out of the courtroom, I was marched onto a black-and-white bus with barred windows. The seats were modified.

Each prisoner was placed in a separate cage. People whose crimes ranged from petty theft to murder rode side by side. I was allowed one phone call. When my family discovered where I was being sent, they were told that the sentence could not be revoked without Judge Davenport's approval.

It was one in the morning when they brought me in. I was stripped, deloused, and led to my cell. The guard shined her flashlight into the cell and pointed me to the upper bunk. A huge woman occupied the lower one. As I moved past, the woman's snore startled me and I jumped. The guard laughed, and walked away. I lay down and curled up, and waited for morning.

I remembered the precise screech when a cell door slid shut, metal scraping against itself. It was like fingernails on a blackboard. The days in L.A.'s downtown county jail scratched against my memory. I shivered.

At least Aspen was a small town, unlike Los Angeles. It was unlikely that I'd encounter the same kind of impersonal, dehumanizing screwup here. The judge called my name. I stood, and nodded at his words. In the eight years since Fritz disappeared, I wondered if he had been in a courtroom like this, if he was put on trial, judged. Laws were made to help people live together. But sometimes they make the group more important than the individual, and there is something intrinsically wrong in that, flattening individuals into caricatures, generic humanity. Prison brings people down to the lowest common denominator of existence: eating and sleeping.

The proceedings for declaring Fritz dead were nearly over. My lawyer returned to my side and put his hand on my shoulder as he sat down. The judge was motioning me to the bench.

I approached the judicial pedestal. The man behind it was older, more kindly. He wanted to help. Help was a hindrance sometimes, but I could not tell him that.

He leaned forward over his hands, which were folded together, clasped in prayer. I hoped that this wouldn't last too long. He asked me a few questions, then nodded his head and sat back, pensive. He peaked his fingers, and rested his chin on top. This seemed to say this was a delicate matter. I waited for his decision.

150

"Would you please come with me to my chambers?" he asked, then announced a brief recess. I followed him through a short hallway. We pushed past a heavy door into the office, with walls filled with ledger-sized volumes. No windows. Dark leather furniture and a massive desk completed the gloom. He turned around to face me. He was shorter than I, and his robe hung like an ill-fitted child's costume. He no longer seemed as imposing. I sat down. He sat in the high-backed chair behind the desk.

He resumed the thinking position he had held in the other room. His eyes peered out, enlarged by thick glasses, as he attempted to scrutinize my expression, plumb my sincerity. I knew that he was a nice man, probably a grandfather. However, his attempt to discover my reasons for declaring my husband dead offended me. He was presuming a knowl-edge which he simply did not have. All of his education and all of his years in the legal profession could not teach him who I was. He did not know me.

He began to explain the gravity, the severity of having someone declared dead. He reviewed the difficulties, the consequences, if the person should ever be found alive. He spoke of actions which once done could never be undone. He told me that he knew I had already thought of all these things, but that he wanted me to think of them again, one last time, to make certain this was the right thing for me to do. The state would not suffer for mistakenly declaring a man dead.

But I was here to put an end to the endless thoughts, and the cycles of possibilities that had been playing over in my head for months, days, years, like a broken record. I was the only one in this room whose feelings, life, time, energy, spirit, were tied to today's outcome. When MacGeyver called, I canceled the original court date. I waited until Christmas, but it had passed. There had been no word. I was here to validate the only answer I knew, the only resolution I had available to me. That was why, how, I managed to respond calmly. No one else could help me through this. This day was about me, me alone.

The judge's monologue was winding to a close as I nodded my head to shake away the thoughts he flung out at me. He thought I was agreeing with him and in a sense I was. I knew all of what he said by heart.

"I have just one more question for you," he said. I nodded once more. "In your heart of hearts, do you honestly believe that Fritz Stammberger, your husband, is dead?" This question was in earnest. Silence would not be enough. I had to answer.

I slid my hand beneath my thigh. "Yes. Yes, I do," I responded.

"Very well then," he said.

I uncrossed my fingers, slid my hand out from underneath my leg, got up, and walked out to the courtroom. The gavel slammed down as the judge called for order once again.

"This is for the court record," he said to the court reporter. "By the power vested in me by the state of Colorado, I hereby do declare Fritz Stammberger, former resident of Aspen, officially deceased." I watched the gavel in slow motion as, with one stroke, it sealed Fritz's fate. The mallet hung suspended for a moment, half its weight projected up on top, half hanging from the cylinder on the bottom. It was a moment of balance, of opposition. Then gravity took over and the hammer gathered momentum, becoming heavier, more weighty with each descending inch, until it struck. Like a thunderbolt, the sound shattered the silence. Chairs scraped back, pens retracted. Life resumed.

34.

New Beginning

Encino
1985

I leaned up against a wooden column and watched the carpenter leave. It was six o'clock and the workday, which began at seven that morning, was over. The construction crew had been working on our new house for a week. Oak and palm trees shrouded the tile roof of the Spanish hacienda. Since 1920, when George Arliss, the English actor, had owned it, the house in Encino, California, was a sanctuary for the Hollywood crowd—actors, actresses, musicians, and producers.

It didn't seem as though more than one year had already passed since the court had declared Fritz dead. The court didn't do it, I did, I reminded myself, as I stood upright and brushed dust off my pants. There was not an inch of this house that was not speckled with dust. Former walls, floors, ceilings. The day we moved in, Carlos and I were knocking out false walls, letting in space and light. The place had been a nightmare: pea green carpets with patches of dirt pounded in, large reddish-brown spots where wine had spilled, holes in the plaster. A family with teenagers lived here before us.

It was hard for me to live at home as a teenager. So much energy and so many rules. That's why I left at fourteen. I sensed that there was nothing left for me to learn from school or from my family. I wouldn't have learned at that time, anyway. I had wanted to find things out on my own, to travel. And I did. Now I was in my own house, and I was remodeling it.

The first thing I did was to rip out the carpets. Carlos had helped me pull back long swathes to reveal the floor, raw wood that had been covered over for years. We had wanted to let it breathe. There had been something disturbing about the wilted green carpets. Their color had been drained, as if its life was beaten out of it, flattened, trampled. The house smelled of neglect: the carpets, the fireplaces, and the wood, chunks missing from posts and scratches raked into the paneling. Outside, huge black birds filled the trees with raucous calling. Crows, the real estate agent had said. I liked them, their darkness. Carlos said they were omens of death. To me, they were not so much omens of death as omens of change, of the passage of time. They stayed around to witness the transitions.

I climbed into the area under construction to see what had changed. I did this every day after most of the workmen had left. It was the way I kept in touch with the place, made it mine. Home implies a certain knowledge, a certain intimacy with a place.

My walk began in the living room. Tremendous beams extended across the ceiling, a rough wood floor stretched from wall to glass door. One whole side of the room opened onto the courtyard in the middle of the house. A large open space. Trees and flowers grew where the sun poured in. Air coursed through the windows into the room. The space inside created a feeling of freedom. It was like the space I carried around inside myself, the space where I meditated, the space where I knew there were things I would never know. This was a place I needed. Without it I could not grow.

Back in the house, I ran my hand over the fireplace that covered one of the inner walls. The stone was raw, sharp from the sandblasting the day before. There were seven fireplaces in the house. Seven. When Carlos and I first walked around the house I silently counted the number of fireplaces, because I had a premonition. I knew there were seven.

I looked at the fireplace. To think what it had looked like before: matte black with white graffiti scrawled across it. Some form of internal art, external expression. Black, white. I wandered out the doors that led to the courtyard.

It boggled my mind to think that people, who are only a part of nature, had come to rival it, to compete with it. People always have a purpose, need a purpose. Something to give their lives form. Work. Boundaries. Guidelines. Routine.

This house was going to be the product of our labors. We needed to do this, to build something ourselves, together. It was a solid fortress against my past, a past that never really passed on its own. Sometimes, in my mind, not a day had passed since Fritz had disappeared. Not a day.

I did not want Carlos to marry me. I thought he deserved more. I was older than he and I couldn't have children. It had taken him years to convince me differently. And he was right. There were things we could build: a house, a relationship, a new life. We knew how to work hard.

Even our wedding fit in between our schedules. The rehearsal dinner was Thursday. I tried to eat as little as possible. My gown was white, long, beaded and pencil thin. I could just imagine my stomach poking out, rounding itself as if to suggest that one last detail had been overlooked. I worked out religiously.

Friday. I took the whole day to prepare. And then the wedding. In the evening. Candles down the aisle. Warmth, fire, wax. A heart-shaped wreath of flowers. And the ceremony. Then the celebration. For a while it had seemed to go on around me, flowing in waves, as if I was not a part of it, as though I was being washed around in the ocean. But now I was caught up in the flow. The days took on their own rhythm, and I liked it. Living with Carlos was my chance for a new beginning.

35.

Betrayal

Encino
1985-86

It was early on one of those crisp November mornings. The seven-foot wooden gate swung open as the gold Mercedes pulled up to the front of the house. Carlos got out of his car and walked to the front door. Gently he tried to open it, to no avail; it was locked. Irritated, he went around to the kitchen on the side of the house. The back door was open. He forgot his keys. He hurriedly went from room to room looking for them. As he passed the basement door he noticed that it was slightly ajar. There was no sound coming from inside, but something didn't seem quite right.

I was going through some boxes when I heard his footsteps in the house. Then silence. Only a few seconds had passed when I looked up and saw a pair of legs descending the basement stairs. I froze in silence. Carlos looked down at me and saw photos and letters from Fritz spread across the floor. Carlos's face was expressionless; his eyes, blank. He kicked at the papers, scattering the photos and the letters across the floor.

"I can't believe this. I thought you got rid of all of that! I thought we were done with this guy," Carlos yelled.

As if in slow motion, I watched him turn and disappear.

After a few minutes, he came back.

"Look, I've tried to be understanding, I've tried to be patient, but this is too much. I can't go on living with a ghost, with your past. I'm tired of it. You refuse to go forward," Carlos said.

"That's not fair. I was just going through these boxes to put them away. It's no big deal," I replied.

"It is a big deal. You told me you burned his things," he continued.

"I did burn most of them," I said.

"Then what is the stuff you were looking through? Why is it still around?" he asked.

"They're his journals. They're not really mine. It wouldn't be right!" I answered.

"I don't care if you don't think it's right. I don't want them here. This is my house, our house. I thought we were building something together here. You're working your ass off, I'm working my ass off, trying to pay for this thing, having it redone, and then you go and invite this ex-husband of yours back in. I thought we had an understanding. It's been eleven years now. Can't you see that? Can't you see that you're living in the past? The man is dead!" he said, nearly screaming.

Carlos stared at me furiously, silent, seething. I opened my mouth to speak, but he held up his hand.

"No, don't. I'm too angry. I don't want to talk. Words, just words. They mean nothing. It's what you do that counts," he said as he paced the room, gesticulating, talking to himself. I caged him. I surrounded him with my memories. That was no way to live. I didn't know what to say to him. I was stunned and ashamed.

Carlos turned around, leaving as quickly as he had arrived. I could hear him upstairs in our bedroom. And then a few minutes later I heard him leave. I had pushed him too far. I was afraid that I lost him.

I turned off Wilshire Boulevard onto Ocean Avenue. The ocean was to my right as I drove, looking for the Pacific Coast Hotel on the corner of Pico Boulevard and Ocean Avenue in Santa Monica. My stomach was in knots. Carlos left. He stormed out of the house. Hours later I received a call, he had checked into a hotel. I hadn't fooled him any more than I'd fooled myself, and I needed to face it if I wanted our marriage to work. I hoped to get away with it, to keep pushing the line, that invisible line where tolerance ends. I figured Carlos loved me enough that I could get away with keeping my emotional involvement with Fritz. Carlos not only gave up other women to be with me, he changed his whole life. He moved from New York. He waited years until I was ready. I was being selfish, and now it might be too late to go back. The damage was done.

I was reluctant to knock. I didn't know what to say. Carlos was mad, and hurt. I tapped on the door. "Who is it?" Carlos asked. "It's me, Janice," I replied. He opened the door, but didn't wait for me to come in; he went directly to his bed and continued watching the TV. I walked in and closed the door behind me. I was hoping that everything would go back to normal by itself. It didn't. Carlos stared straight through me with his dark eyes. I felt like I was with a stranger, not my husband.

"Carlos, what are you doing here? Why don't you come back to the house?" I asked.

"I want you to know that I'm not going back. There's no place for me there. It's not my home any longer," he stated.

I felt sick. I knew he meant it.

"This isn't the solution," I softly said.

"It is for me," he shot back. "I've tried everything else . . . let me ask you something," he went on. "What was it about this guy, what was so great? He sure didn't sound so great to me; he didn't even look out for you. He wasn't honest." He looked up for my reaction to what he had said, then walked over and increased the volume on the TV. He continued almost to himself, then suddenly started a second verbal assault.

"He put you in jeopardy by not letting you know what his plans were. Does that sound like a man who loves his wife? Not to me, it doesn't," he said.

"You don't know what we shared, Carlos," I replied.

"What do you mean I don't know—then tell me, what was it? Was it sex? Was he so great?" he screamed.

"That's not fair. That wasn't what our relationship was," I said.

"Oh please, I don't think you even know what it was. If you do, then tell me. All I see is a guy who was selfish, thought only of what he wanted, not of what was good for you. He didn't even leave you a will; he had you sign on his loans and stuck you with paying them off. Think about it, Janice. What kind of a man would do that?"

"He had no way of knowing what was going to happen, Carlos. I'm not going to go on like this. I don't have to defend him. I loved him and he loved me; we knew what we shared. You don't have to understand it," I said.

"Yes, I do. If you want to stay married to me, I deserve more from you than what I'm getting and I'm tired of it. You built a shrine to this guy and you're not going to let anyone tear it down. But you're going to lose a lot in the trade-off, I can tell you that much. You'll pay a high price for the two and a half years you spent with him." He stopped to catch his breath and continued. "Was he so good in bed? What was he like with you?" Carlos was screaming, his face reddened in his attack of rage.

"Stop it, Carlos."

"Well, was he? Why can't you answer me? What's the big deal anyway?" Carlos insisted sarcastically.

I didn't have an answer or even the necessary energy to fight this battle. Carlos was cornering me into giving him an answer I didn't want to give, I couldn't give.

"Carlos, I can't. You're making an issue of something that you shouldn't."

"Fine, live in your fantasy world but don't ask me to be part of it. I don't want to live with anybody's ghost. Do you hear me?"

"Nobody's ghost. Enough is enough. I'm getting out of here!" He grabbed his leather jacket and headed for the door without looking back.

* * *

Two days later Carlos decided to come home. He didn't want to accept my explanations whatever they were. He thought that they were no more than poor excuses. I wanted to communicate with him, but he wouldn't listen.

"It's just that if I forget about him, no one else will remember him. And there's a part of me that thinks I should have called one more person, or written one more letter. Maybe I forgot something, overlooked something." My voice started to crack. "I should have gone there." That was why I couldn't forgive myself.

"You want to go to Pakistan? We'll go to Pakistan!"

"No, that's not what I want; you know that."

"If that's what it takes to get this out of your system and behind us, then we'll do it. Just tell me what you need to do. There's no way we're going to be able to go on with our lives until this is over."

I didn't know what to say to him, what to tell him.

He began again more gently, "Look, what do you think will help you get over this? You're my wife. I want you to be happy. You deserve to be happy."

"I don't know, I just don't know . . . I am happy, most of the time . . . It's just that I haven't been able to forget."

He held me. "Well, what if we do this . . . one last search, wrap up the loose ends. Maybe if you get it out of you, somehow you won't feel like you have to carry it with you."

"Maybe," I said.

He looked at me, I looked at him. We embraced. We made a covenant: a last search for Fritz, a last chance for us.

36.

The Search

T he way things were going I feared our marriage wouldn't be able to stand the pressure. So far our search went nowhere. We needed to intensify our efforts. We went through what remained of Fritz's life systematically for months.

The leather binding of one of his diaries cracked as I touched it. I smoothed the handwritten pages lightly and scanned the lines.

I remembered that during one of my sessions with Barry Taft at the UCLA parapsychology department, the name Carl had come up—that was the English equivalent for Carlos. Clues were starting to make sense. By reading Fritz's diaries, we hoped for a better feel for exactly what might have engulfed him. We followed the trail of his life. I dropped the diary on the worktable. A stack of books and correspondence cluttered the space left beside the electric typewriter. Carlos and I sent out an average of three or four letters a day, appeals and new inquiries. Every lead was worth following. One solid direction could take us to the answer, the solution to this mystery.

Carlos researched what he could find on the political situation at the time of Fritz's disappearance. Not much information had been released about the U.S. government's involvement in Afghanistan or Pakistan. It was all too recent. The war in Afghanistan was still continuing. But every once in a while we found something. "Major Zia" I wrote under the list of names. "Peshawar" under places. I put down the pen. My patience for minutiae was not great. Details did not interest me out of context. I would need some coffee before I could devote myself to the task at hand. I went to the kitchen.

I heard a door shut.

"Babe?" the familiar voice called out, half in question, half in expectation. Carlos was back from work.

"In the kitchen," I answered.

Carlos loosened his tie with one hand as he set down his briefcase. I felt spoiled on days like this when I didn't have to work and Carlos got up at six in the morning. But I stayed at the studio until seven at night on other days, I reminded myself as I stood to hug him. "Would you like some coffee?" I asked as he went into the bedroom to change.

"Sure. That sounds good," he called out behind him as he disappeared.

The next thing I knew, Carlos was in sweats and sitting at the table. He moved quickly. This was something I knew for years, but saw more so now that we were working together. Carlos got things done.

I set out two mugs and put the pot down, then sat opposite him. "So, how was your day?" I asked as he opened the mail.

"Long, but pretty good, pretty good," he mumbled under his breath as he read. Carlos was not one to complain. He skimmed the letter, then read it again more carefully, before setting it down and slitting open another envelope. When he focused his attention on something, he did not let it go.

Carlos lifted his eyes from the letter and poured coffee while glancing back at the pages he'd discarded on the table. "Well," he said, terse and exasperated, "we've started, we got something. No one said this was going to be easy. Go ahead and look them over."

I picked up the sheets. Carlos was rapidly stirring sugar into his coffee. He was already off on another thought. I looked at the letters.

One was from the CIA. "We received your request . . . We regret to inform you . . . For reasons of national security and in accordance with Executive Order 12356 . . . We can neither confirm nor deny. . . . " *Neither confirm nor deny*. If Fritz was not involved with espionage then revealing information would endanger no one. It made no sense. I put the pages aside. Carlos and I would appeal. We had thirty days to do it.

I began the next letter. It was from Interpol. Lots of thick blocks of black ink. A "released" document. They let me have the paper but took back the words. But even this was something. Initially, they'd sent back the same "we can neither confirm nor deny" form letter like the one we just received from the CIA. Carlos had insisted that we keep trying. As long as they were responding, he surmised, we had a chance. I began to read. "According to _____, _____ Stammberger was involved in covert operations along the Pakistan/Afghanistan border. According to _____ on _____, Stammberger believed to be imprisoned in Pakistan." No dates, no locations. I slapped the papers down, then picked them up and counted them again. There were four more pages that had not been sent.

Carlos took my hand. "We'll just have to write them and ask for the rest," he said calmly.

"What if I ask them for records on myself? They can't refuse to give me those. If there was anything on Fritz at that time, it would be included in my file."

"I don't want you to get involved in that. We don't want to wave a red flag in front of their faces." He stacked the letters in a neat pile.

"Do you have a better idea?" I was pushing his buttons.

He stared at me silently for a moment. "Well, it's more than you had before. You had Intertel, you had MacGeyver . . . did you ever have any documents released before this?"

"A lot of good it's doing."

"What do you mean? What do you expect? These things take time. You think they're going to give us an answer on a silver platter? You're dreaming! If they had a reason not to give you information years ago, they have a reason now.

"That's your problem," he went on. "The minute it gets difficult, you want to run away. You don't like to face things. You think things are going to fix themselves? That's not the way it happens, that's not the way life is. There's one way to do things and that's to do them yourself. The sooner you learn that the easier it's going to be."

"What are you going to do, lecture me now? That'll do a lot of good," I answered.

"Look, all I'm saying is that if you'd done this in the first place, you probably would have found him. You should have gone to Pakistan the first week!"

He said the wrong thing. "You weren't there. What do you know about it? You have no idea what I went through, what I did. How dare you judge me?"

"I know what I see. Conway took your business. You let MacGeyver screw you around. You didn't even know what your own husband was involved in because you were afraid to ask, to make things a little uncomfortable. What did it get you?"

"Let's not fight about this."

"No, we better straighten this out now. I have to be the one to sort out this mess. It's not going to happen through voices, dreams, psychics!" he spit out.

"I think you're being unfair."

"This isn't about fair. Life isn't fair."

"You're just pissed off because you haven't been able to find out any more than I have."

"Look, if you want to do this yourself, just say so, be my guest. But I know one thing and that is if you love somebody, you don't stop at anything. You don't take the easy way out!"

"Shut up, Carlos, just shut up!" I screamed as I left the room.

If this was any indication of what this was going to do to us, I didn't like it. I hated living in an angry house. I hated being wound up all the time, tense, stressed out, frustrated. This wasn't my idea of a good life, a new life. This wasn't what I wanted for myself. This isn't what we'd wanted.

I walked around the patio. It made me so mad when he got angry, when he got near the truth. I should have gone to Pakistan, Afghanistan, anywhere to find Fritz. I knew that. If only I'd done that, maybe I'd be done with this, this guilt.

Through the window I watched my husband settle down to read the notes I took during the day. He could make me so mad one minute and then, just as quickly, those feelings would disappear. He set his own notes from the library beside him. There was almost something animalistic about what he was doing for me, something guttural, honest, and direct, like sounds in the forest, the snap of a twig, the bellow of a stag.

When I thought of the situation objectively, I often wondered how he could do it, how he could keep it up: his energy, devotion, and love. To be entirely honest, I could not envision being as understanding, or as patient, had we been consumed with a former wife of his. And ninety-nine percent of the time he was tolerant. That's not to say we didn't fight. Fighting was one of the things I learned to do in our relationship. It was how we worked things out, made things better. Usually we could talk to each other about anything. I didn't want that to change. I opened the door and walked back in.

"Hey, Janice, do you know who this is?" His anger had vanished as quickly as mine.

"What?"

"Look, look at this name," he said excitedly pointing to the page. "This guy is the president of Pakistan."

The president of Pakistan? I looked over his shoulder at the page. Major Zia. Zia.

"This is it!" he exclaimed triumphantly. "This Fritz Stammberger of yours was into something big. While he was teaching English in Pakistan, he lived in Zia's house in the mid-Sixties. Zia's the president! How'd you miss this?" He went on to tell me how Zia overthrew the previous government, Bhutto's government.

"We should talk to him," he said. "I think we should go there."

He was right. "But what if President Zia won't talk with us? What if he's just like the CIA, Interpol, all of them?" I asked. "Besides, how are we going to get in to see him?"

"I don't know yet, but I think it's worth a try." Carlos had a determined look on his face. He meant business. "Truth and hard work never fail," he reassured me. "It's only a matter of time."

37.

The Law

Los Angeles
1988

I stared at the list. Nine hundred sixty dollars, first-class, Lufthansa.
Carlos and I decided to go to Pakistan. The plans were set: just the
details needed to be worked out. There was a rental car to consider
and accommodations. The night before, we sat together working out the
most economical way to do it. Now I was trying to sort out the last few
arrangements. I tapped my pencil on the table. When *Bunte* magazine
had called the day before to defer doing their story on Fritz, I fell into
a minor panic. Originally, they were going to underwrite our trip in
exchange for exclusive rights to the story, and I had counted on that
outside support more than I realized. The final payments on the remodeling were just about to come due.

Carlos and I were to meet with a lawyer, Tony Sutton, early this
morning before I went to work. Our appointment was for eight forty-
five. I contacted some of the best attorneys in the fields of human rights
and civil liberties to learn what my rights were. Mort Helperin, Paul
Young, Merrill Veneer, and today Tony Sutton. The last lawyer I
contacted didn't have much to tell me. He coughed and grunted when
I mentioned the government agencies involved, the CIA and such. I told
him that the letters said, "Unable to confirm or deny," but when I
mentioned Executive Order 12356, his interest perked. "Could you
repeat that number again?" he requested.

He told me that section 2(b) of that order authorized the withholding
of information in order to protect CIA agents. This meant that they

probably had some information on Fritz or they would not have been troubling themselves with the wording, the cryptic responses. Having others confirm my suspicions helped. Perhaps Tony Sutton would be more specific. At the very least, Carlos and I were going to see him together, in person. A different environment might elicit a different response.

The morning traffic coming over Benedict Canyon was bumper to bumper. Carlos was already upset. He hated to be late.

"Two weeks after we appealed to the CIA for the second time, we received an express letter. It asked me to call them because they had been unable to get my phone number. That seemed strange, the CIA not being able to have access to a phone number? I called them. The man with whom I spoke, Lee Strickland, Information and Privacy Coordinator, asked me why I hadn't dropped the case. He said something about my inquiries posing a threat to national security, and that my request was quite out of the ordinary. He went on to say that it was very important for the CIA, for national security reasons, to have strict control of the information flow from them to the public. That it was for the public's benefit—in the end, for my benefit—and that the agency had to insist on certain standards of classification, due to the sensitivity of the area where Fritz disappeared," I told Tony Sutton.

"What did you say after his explanation?" Sutton asked.

"I persisted that my appeal was based on humanitarian grounds and that I didn't want to drop it. Lee Strickland impressed upon me that I should withdraw my request if I didn't want to put the safety of the U.S. in jeopardy. I told him that I was a loyal American and that all I wanted was to know if Fritz was dead, alive or in jail. What did that have to do with jeopardizing our national security? He replied by saying that he would get back to me." Tony Sutton nodded as I finished.

"We did send them one more letter reiterating that Janice would not drop her appeal," Carlos broke in, "and in a few days they called to arrange for an agent to meet with us at our home."

"Well," Sutton began, "I can assure you that Fritz Stammberger had some dealings with the intelligence community; otherwise the CIA wouldn't waste so much time and energy on you. They certainly wouldn't arrange to meet with you. You struck a nerve. You might also want to consider a few other things, especially since you are going to Pakistan. The army, navy, air force, and other branches of the U.S. Armed Forces have their own intelligence operations which function separately from the CIA. Mr. Stammberger may have been involved with one of these organizations."

I had considered all along that Fritz might have been involved with an army intelligence unit. He'd been registered for the draft. He had stayed at President Zia's house when the man was a major. "What would be the best way to approach the military in Pakistan?" I asked. "Do you know anyone in that area who might be able to help us, perhaps arrange a meeting with the president or one of his aides?"

"No, unfortunately, I have no dealings in that part of the world, and I'm sorry that I don't have any other suggestions. You're probably not going to get much out of a CIA agent. He may be meeting with you to find out why you're pushing so hard. Please let me know what happens." Carlos leaned forward to shake Sutton's hand. We were on our own. We would do what I hadn't done. Go to Pakistan. We would pursue all the avenues available to have the government papers released. I wasn't going to take anyone else's word, anyone else's version of what had or hadn't happened. If nothing else, I would finish what I started. The more they told me no, the more determined I was to pursue it.

* * *

The newscaster hummed on in the background, "More drug-related violence erupted earlier in the day." Nothing that would interest me. Even though I worked on a television show, I rarely watched TV at night. Especially the news. I watched the news in the morning, when I had the rest of the day ahead of me. I didn't like seeing the news at night. It was depressing. I didn't want to go to sleep with those things on my mind. Shootings. Stabbings. Hunger.

Carlos and I were scheduled to leave for Pakistan in two weeks. I glanced at the clock. He would be home in another forty minutes or so.

The TV screen played before me. End of commercial, back to the news.

"General Mohammad Zia of Pakistan died today when his C-130 exploded after takeoff at Bahawalpur. All twenty-nine people aboard the plane, including U.S. ambassador Arnold Raphel and Brigadier General Herbert Wassom, the chief U.S. military attaché, were killed." The newscaster went on: "'The dog,' as he was known to his enemies, is dead." My eyes were riveted to the TV set. I stared at the screen in disbelief. With the general's death our trip would have to be canceled. From reading Fritz's diaries, I knew that Zia held the "key" that would solve the mystery of Fritz's disappearance.

I often asked myself who had plotted President Zia's assassination. Weeks passed, and it seemed that the investigations were being brushed under the rug. The conspirators who engineered the crash were not apprehended.

I wondered why our Justice Department wasn't pursuing the case more aggressively. Why didn't it invoke the "Long Arm" law—the law that gave the U.S. government the "legal" right to capture a fugitive hiding anywhere in the world, regardless of international laws? According to the press, the KGB and the Indian and Afghanistani governments were the main suspects. But certain intelligence sources had hinted that these were not the real culprits. It was known that the West wanted to conceal its tracks in the secret Afghanistan war. The word "cover-up" seemed to be written all over it.

38.

The Visit

Los Angeles
1988

T ry to outwait him," the lawyer said. "The CIA doesn't just send people out to meet with people at their homes. Their man is coming over for one of two reasons. He either wants to get information, or he is going to give you some." I doubted that there was anything I knew that the CIA didn't, but Tony Sutton advised me to say as little as possible.

There was no way that I could anticipate what John Wright, another information and privacy coordinator for the CIA, was going to tell me. I'd have to deal with the situation as it unfolded. Since Mr. Wright might be more likely to divulge something if there were fewer people around, I turned down Sutton's offer to be present at the meeting. His last words of advice were, "Don't sign anything saying you won't pursue your appeal asking for information regarding Fritz. Let me or someone else look over the papers first."

"No, don't worry. I won't sign," I reassured him.

I turned to face Carlos. We were both tense. He paced the room, walking quickly as if his steps would bring him closer to John Wright. The rhythm of footsteps was marked by pauses. Carlos and I experienced life so differently, yet we managed to find a middle ground. I could not imagine pacing as a way of collecting myself for this meeting. But it worked for him. I stopped analyzing these habits and just accepted them as he accepted mine. There was a balance to it. Our styles complemented each other. A perfect adjustment to an imperfect world.

We heard the car pull up. Carlos stopped pacing and we moved to open the door. John Wright came in. He was wearing a medium gray suit. His hair was sheared precisely at the edges and he wasn't carrying a briefcase. His eyes were flat and unresponsive. Even on a personal level, this man had given himself over to the CIA.

"Can I get you anything? Something to drink?" I asked. The strained words seemed mundane. This was not your average afternoon visit.

"No. No thank you," Mr. Wright responded.

"Carlos?" I asked, keeping up the facade of manners for some inexplicable reason.

"Sure. Sure, babe." He would help me out through this one. I went off to bring out the coffee I had already made for the meeting, and to regroup. The silver tray was waiting on the kitchen counter. Silver teaspoons, a bowl of sugar, and a porcelain milk pitcher sat on the gleaming surface. I removed the urn from the coffeemaker and poured the steaming dark liquid into the china pot, tall, regal, and graceful. I closed my eyes and tried to compose myself before reentering the living room. This was a confrontation, civil though it might seem. I knew what I wanted to find out from this man. Information about Fritz. I wanted to find out what Mr. Wright knew.

The living room was easily visible from the kitchen. Sounds of Mr. Wright's conversation with Carlos filtered in. Mumbles in hushed tones. Pleasantries, no doubt. I knew that Carlos would not begin without me. I picked up the tray with three cups. Perhaps John Wright would change his mind about coffee.

I set the service down on the coffee table and began to pour. As brown liquid splashed into the cups, Mr. Wright began.

"I have a letter here from the CIA. It contains our official response to your request." He reached into a breast pocket. A suit full of surprises. I set down my cup and reached out to take the letter. The thick parchment ripped as I tore open the envelope; the letter itself was rather thin. I perused the contents in disbelief, picking up the same key lines. "We regret to inform you that we cannot confirm or deny. . . ."

Before I reached the end of the document, Mr. Wright interrupted. "The agency sent me to see if I might answer any additional questions you had. Within reason, that is," he hastened to add.

"What would the CIA consider a reasonable question?" I asked. They knew exactly what I wanted to know. I looked straight at him. "What happened to Fritz Stammberger?"

"Ms. Pennington, you know that there are guidelines I must adhere to," he responded.

I sat back, waiting for him to say something more, waiting for Carlos to jump into the pause, but the two men remained silent. A quiet settled in the room.

"Are you sure you wouldn't like a cup of coffee?" I asked, filling the space.

"Actually, I would," Mr. Wright replied. "Ms. Pennington, I realize how frustrating this situation must be for you and I am sorry, but the security of our government is at stake here," he said, spooning sugar into his cup.

"Cream?" I offered.

"No thank you." He continued on, completing the formal response. I watched him sip the coffee, pinky up. His fingers were well manicured. Polished. A bureaucrat. That was what I had been sent. Not a man of action. I stared out the glass doors at the patio outside. Leaves dusted the ground. I waited for his cup to return to the saucer. Then I began.

"Mr. Wright, as I'm sure you know, Carlos and I have written many letters to the CIA, among other intelligence agencies. My contact with the CIA culminated in a phone call to Lee Strickland. Perhaps you know him?" I raised an eyebrow and watched for a response. None came. For all I knew, Lee Strickland was sitting before me. "Anyway, during our conversation, Mr. Strickland referred me to a Katherine Dyer, who, he stated, was responsible for the release of classified information."

Mr. Wright's expression remained the same.

"After further correspondence, during which I referred only to Fritz Stammberger's disappearance"—I stressed the last word—"we received a letter as follows," and I pulled a sheet out from the pile of information Carlos and I had prepared on a side table.

"'Specifically you are requesting documents pertaining to Friedrich Ludwig Stammberger and any known circumstances surrounding his death while traveling in Pakistan,'" I read. "I did not mention Fritz's death in a single letter," I finished.

Mr. Wright simply looked at me for a moment.

"Mr. Wright," I said, "please tell me: do you have a file on Friedrich Stammberger?"

"I'm sorry," he said. "I cannot confirm or deny the existence of such a file on the record."

"Why not?" My voice rose. He smoothed the sleeves on his coat.

"Ms. Pennington, you understand that it is very important to us to have strict control of the information flow from the agency to the public. This is for the public's benefit—in the end, for your benefit." I'd been told this before by Lee Strickland. Their "stories" were the same.

"My benefit? What would you know about my benefit? How can the CIA know what is for my benefit? Not telling me where Fritz was all these years was not to my benefit. Not even letting me know if he was alive was most certainly not in my benefit. I don't just process information you give me like data in a computer. This has affected my life."

The man stared at me blankfaced. "Ms. Pennington, the agency has to insist on certain standards of classification in order to safeguard its ability to work effectively. We respect the intention of the Freedom of Information Act and we have gone out of our way to offer you as much information as we possibly can, but please understand that there are some documents which are not available under the law."

The law. Here I was again, up against the brick wall of the law. Rules and regulation. Ink on paper. Not flesh and blood. Not tears. "So," I asked, "what do you expect me to do? Ignore the obvious?"

"I realize that you're still puzzled, upset perhaps. But when a request concerns foreign nationals, not U.S. citizens, we have to keep different considerations in mind. If we have any records on someone, say, from an Eastern bloc country, the mere fact that we have them is potentially ticklish for us; it might mean that we have an intelligence interest in that country. Withholding a file due to classification definitely shows an interest. So it's simply our policy to neither confirm nor deny the existence or nonexistence of information on foreign nationals."

Mr. Wright was obviously ill at ease. "I realize that your situation is different. It involves someone close to you," he said.

"Why was it," asked Carlos, who had not spoken until then, "that another intelligence agency released eight pages of information on Fritz?" He was spreading the Interpol documents, like a deck of cards, on the table.

"Which agency was that?" Mr. Wright asked, slightly taken aback.

Carlos ignored his question. "Among these eight pages there are copies of cables to Senator Ted Kennedy and Senator Gary Hart and embassies around the world regarding the matter of Fritz's disappearance. These papers say, among other things, that Fritz may have been working in covert operations along the Afghanistan/Pakistan border. Why, if this agency can release such sensitive material, can't the CIA simply tell us whether they have any files on Fritz?" Carlos was losing his patience. "Look, we have been searching for the truth for years . . ."

"I've tried so many times to put this whole matter aside," I jumped in, "but each time, something forces me to go on." I tried to appeal to Mr. Wright's humanitarian side. "If I stop now, if I just go along and pretend he never existed, he really will have disappeared from the world. Right now, the only place he exists is in my mind. Can you understand that? Can you understand what that means to me?"

Mr. Wright appeared to be considering what I'd said.

"I want you to know," he said, lowering his voice, "that this is not part of the official records or an official response from the CIA, but. . . ." He paused and sipped his coffee. "But, off the record, we were not able to find anything on your husband."

I scrutinized his face, looking for any signs that might allow me to determine whether he was telling me the truth.

"I have personally gone through the records," Mr. Wright continued. "There are no documents on Friedrich Ludwig Stammberger . . . unless he had a code name."

"Code name, what do you mean, a code name? . . . I don't know of any . . . ," I answered. "Are you saying that you may have records on him after all?"

Mr. Wright sat back in his chair. He crossed his legs. "Ms. Pennington, if there was anything else we could tell you, you would have heard it from us by now. We would never let an American citizen suffer this way. We would have sent someone not traceable to the Agency to give you the information if he was alive."

Why didn't I believe him? I waited for him to continue.

"Now, ma'am," John Wright said, "we are respectfully requesting that you withdraw your petition for information."

This was why he was here.

"I can't do that, at least not right now." I stood. It was time for him to leave. "Thank you for taking the time to come out here. Your answers have told me more than I need to know."

John Wright straightened out his coat and shook Carlos's hand. We escorted him to the door. "Thank you," I said, though I did not quite know what I was thanking him for. I stared, wordless, as he drove away. Carlos turned from the door. "I'm sorry, babe," he whispered as he gathered me in his arms. I looked over Carlos's shoulder at the vacant street outside. It was almost as if he had never been here.

"We are never going to get anything from them. All they want is to collect information, and find out what we know. It's a dead end," Carlos said.

"I know," I replied.

"One day we must go to Russia and Afghanistan. We must find out what their intelligence services know about Fritz. They may be able to provide us with the information we need to put this to rest. We cannot let our lives be destroyed by your past," Carlos said drily.

I was mad. Once again they were jerking me around. If they didn't have anything on Fritz, why didn't they tell me, or simply send me a one-paragraph letter saying that they had no files? Other U.S. intelligence services did that.

Secrecy for the sake of secrecy. I wanted to pursue it through the legal channels, but my lawyer, together with the American Civil Liberties Union, advised me not to do so. I was told that it would be a waste of my time and money. No court would require that the CIA release documents that were withheld due to "national security."

39.

It's Over

Los Angeles
1988

It had been four years since Carlos and I married. We knew that somehow our relationship was depleted. The candle was no longer lit. Since our search for Fritz came to a halt with the CIA agent's visit, Carlos no longer knew which direction to take. He hadn't delivered; he couldn't find out what happened to Fritz. For Carlos, it was a defeat. We weren't moving forward. It seemed as if our lifeline was being cut off.

In addition, we were having problems with my family, and that situation was escalating along with everything else. When Fritz disappeared, I turned to them for moral support. Now that I was remarried, a resentment was building within my family. They didn't want to relinquish the established status quo that had been built over those years.

My priorities were my marriage and my husband. Carlos tried to tolerate my past with Fritz and had encouraged my closeness with my family, but now it backlashed. It was too much.

"Sell the house, sell everything. No more second place. It's me and you and then the others," he finally said.

The painful warning signs of loss were creeping dangerously near. The infrastructure of my life was collapsing around me. I knew this feeling; I had lived this way before, and knew I had to do something drastic to get off this collision course.

The nights were long and painful. Carlos would toss and turn. He was smoking four packs of cigarettes a day. I was drinking more. What started out as a couple of glasses of wine with dinner had increased to a bottle, and sometimes two bottles a day. I was disappointed in myself, my marriage, my family, and my seeming inability to change any of it.

Tragedy reentered my life. On June 21, 1988, while taping *The Price Is Right* at the CBS studios, a new cameraman knocked me off the four-foot-high stage and onto a concrete floor below. For seventeen years, in every show we had taped, I made that same move while giving the microphone to Bob Barker at the top of the show.

My injury from the accident debilitated me physically and mentally. I had two major five-hour operations; one inch of my collarbone was cut out to repair the damage I had suffered to my right shoulder. I was lucky to be alive, even luckier that I didn't become paralyzed, but the constant pain was at times unbearable. People would often ask me: "Are you sure it was an 'accident'?"

Deepening our sadness was the news that Carlos's father had been given two months to live. His parents had returned to Lisbon, Portugal, after spending five years in South Africa. At sixty-one, he was diagnosed with generalized cancer. Two months . . . and his life would end. A race for life. Carlos embarked once again on a rescue mission, trying to save his father from death. He contacted doctors and clinics in Mexico, the United States, and Germany. He met with famous rabbis, clergymen, and healers, trying every avenue available to cancer patients. In the end he knew that he had to face his father at the doorstep of death. He traveled to Lisbon. Despite his efforts, his father passed away within the two months that the doctor had given him. Carlos's inability to save his father was a major blow. He knew now more than ever the value of time, too precious to waste. He refused to look back.

When Carlos returned from Portugal, he made a decision. We had to change our relationship. He felt that space would help clear the debris, to see if there was anything left. We were tired and beaten. Carlos left for New York.

The adversaries were many, and as if by irony or destiny, they all launched their attack at the same time: Fritz's ghost, two surgeries, one death, the CIA, and my family.

177

Carlos was lost in New York. He rented an apartment on the Upper East Side. Wanting to start anew, he sold his interest in the company to his partner, and tried to simplify his life. He was adrift. He felt the same as he did when he left Mozambique for the last time, without a purpose or destination.

I was observing life from the dark side. I had aged.

40.

U.S. Intelligence

U.S.A.
1992

After six months in New York City, Carlos decided to come back to Los Angeles. We missed each other. When he returned, we put the Encino house on the market; it reminded us of bad times. We'd bought it to start our life together, and its purchase was meant to be a symbol of change, of renewed luck. But that luck went bad. In August of 1989, the house was sold, and we moved into an apartment. Back to the simplicity of the two of us, surviving on just the basics— food, comfort, and each other. It felt good, nourishing. Our energy was no longer consumed by small, daily troubles. We were starting over.

We started a company together, a production company. Los Angeles was the city of entertainment and we would make a place for ourselves in it.

While our life was changing in small ways, on the other side of the globe a whole nation was starting over. The Soviet Union was coming apart. First Gorbachev, then Yeltsin began to reform what was once communism. The Soviet Union and the KGB were no more; the Cold War was over. The reign of secrecy and terror ended, and human rights were being restored. Even political prisoners were being freed. Carlos's battle against communism had payed off. History allowed him the pleasure of victory, to see his enemy destroyed.

In June of 1992, President Yeltsin revealed that there were Americans alive in Russia, Americans who were being kept there against their will. When we heard the news, Carlos and I both knew what it meant.

The Pandora's box was reopened. We needed to go to Russia. Fritz's statement to me that "one day you may hear that I am a Russian spy," along with the CIA's relentless refusal to release their information on Fritz, left us no option but to once again pursue the hidden truth. This time we would deal with the adversary. Before we left, we arranged several meetings with U.S. intelligence sources.

John M. G. Brown is a decorated Vietnam infantry veteran. Since his return to the United States, he had spent his time researching our national archives and interviewing intelligence and armed forces personnel who could help him in his odyssey: finding out the destiny of soldiers missing in action, not only in Vietnam, but also in other wars. He seemed to be a man of integrity. General William Westmoreland and other high-ranking American officers supported and respected his work as a historian and researcher. His wife's uncle was a U.S. ambassador, and John Brown's list of contacts included U.S. ambassador Robert Strauss in Moscow. I felt that his profound commitment and knowledge regarding prisoners of war, in particular the dynamics between the Soviet Union and our government, were of the utmost importance in our search. He was the author of the book *Moscow Bound*, a one-thousand-page manuscript documenting the destiny of thousands of American servicemen captured by the enemy and left to die in the Russian Gulag.

A meeting was arranged. We would meet Brown at a safe place where his privacy and ours wouldn't be disturbed. Brown had testified in 1992 in Washington, D.C., to the Select Committee on POW/MIA Affairs. His visibility in POW/MIA issues had raised some eyebrows. He had positioned himself into a difficult situation. Those who opposed him were powerful and relentless. They believed that no one had the right to challenge them. So far they were invincible.

The day arrived. John Brown stood out as the perfect cowboy with his weather-beaten hat and suede boots. His face showed the scars from Vietnam. He was over six feet tall, and he spoke softly. A quick smile would sometimes pass over his face as he spoke. We had two days to talk with him and learn all we could about the transport of American POWs to Russia. Even though Fritz was German, if he was captured in Afghanistan, he probably would have been transported to the U.S.S.R.

180

As we settled in around the table, John started telling us what he knew:

"It has long remained U.S. official policy to refuse to ransom American prisoners of war or civilians being held in communist nations. This policy resulted from a 1921 U.S. aid-for-hostages exchange negotiated by future president Herbert Hoover, during which the Bolsheviks secretly withheld sixty to one hundred U.S. military prisoners of war captured during the 1918-1919 American intervention in Russia. The United States government declared these POWs and MIAs to be dead, and publicly denied that any of them remained prisoners of Lenin's Bolshevik regime, even after forty to fifty of them had been reported by an eyewitness as still alive and imprisoned in 1929. In 1933 the U.S. granted diplomatic recognition of Stalin's Soviet government; the POWs disappeared. Consequently, the U.S.S.R. has little reason to return U.S. POWs or MIAs. Over the years, the Soviets have retained thousands more—U.S. POWs from World War II, the Korean War, and from Vietnam. The men are used for intelligence purposes or as forced labor in the struggle between communism and capitalism." He paused and looked at us.

"What about Pakistan and Afghanistan?" I asked. I didn't want to get into the POW issue without finding out more about the region where Fritz disappeared, the region around Afghanistan, Pakistan, and Russia.

"Well, Janice, as far as I know, it doesn't matter where the struggle takes place. If men are captured, they will be used by the Russians, be it for intelligence, technology or mere labor. Your former husband, Fritz, seemed to be a perfect target for both superpowers," he replied.

"Tell me something . . . how can we find out more about the transport of prisoners to the Soviet Union?" Carlos asked.

"Jerry Mooney, a retired National Security cryptanalyst, told me about the existence of a secret military intelligence unit comprised of fifty to sixty of the best; it's part of the National Security Agency. This highly secret unit has assembled in-depth studies of special and operational intelligence in Soviet-U.S. relations. This information was revealed to Congress," he said.

Carlos continued to probe. "Did any special operations involve the transportation of prisoners from Afghanistan or Pakistan to Russia?"

"Well, I would have to go over my papers and get back to you on that. However, I must tell you that according to Mr. Barry Toll, a former U.S. intelligence officer who has access to highly classified material, there were shipments of U.S. POWs from Vietnam and Laos to the U.S.S.R. and other Eastern bloc nations from 1973 to 1975. At the time, this intelligence was included in President Nixon's daily briefings. It was during this critical time that your former husband disappeared, right?" he asked. I nodded.

"According to a report published by researcher David Hendrix, there was a classified witness-protection type program to secretly return U.S. POWs from Indochina in the 1980s. It may have involved one hundred to three hundred Americans who were brought home clandestinely. They were not permitted to notify their families of their survival," John said.

Could Fritz have returned to the United States without letting me know?

After talking with John Brown over the course of two days, Carlos and I had a lot to think about. He had answered and confirmed many of our questions relating to Fritz's case.

When we returned to Los Angeles, Carlos and I decided to track down the man whom John Brown mentioned—Jerry Mooney. After locating him, we arranged to meet in Billings, Montana.

The Sheraton Hotel van picked us up at the airport. It took about ten minutes to reach downtown Billings. As we entered the hotel lobby, we saw, at the far left, a slight man with thick glasses. Indisputably, it was Jerry Mooney. It seemed odd, somehow, to be meeting this man under these circumstances. He was once highly respected by our government, entrusted with sensitive and secret information regarding national security. Now, he was being shunned and discredited by the government because he no longer could keep the silence; he was no longer willing to perpetuate the lie. The Defense Department, the Defense Intelligence Agency, the National Security Agency, the Central Intelligence Agency, among others, all turned their backs on him.

"Thank you for coming to meet with us," I said.

"It's a pleasure," he replied.

There was a moment of awkward silence. I wasn't sure of how to proceed.

"Should we go to our room, or do you want to stay here in the lobby?" I asked.

"No, let me check in first," Carlos said. "I think we should all go to our room. We'll have more privacy that way."

Jerry Mooney nodded in agreement. While Carlos checked us in, I talked with Jerry. He told me that he was a grandfather and that he had worked for the National Security Agency for twenty years. He was presently working in a hardware store as a clerk. He let me know that he could speak with us only once because the situation at work was becoming increasingly difficult. His employers had learned of the government's discontent with him, and he had been threatened physically and verbally. His former employer had not appreciated the fact that he had revealed what he knew from working at the National Security Agency. He had testified to the Select Committee on POW/MIA Affairs, and had indirectly pointed fingers at certain individuals in government.

He firmly believed that some of our men had been left behind, and that there was a "Moscow Bound" program for U.S. prisoners. One of his major antagonists during the hearings was Senator John McCain from Arizona, who had been a prisoner of war himself. Senator McCain was not in accord with the families of the POWs and MIAs. He was quick to back any information implying that none of our men were left behind. He defended this position in an arrogant, pompous way. I didn't like his attitude or his beliefs.

I believed Jerry Mooney. He'd never made a dime from his information, nor was he paid for any of the TV appearances in which he discussed the POW/MIA issue. Also, he was well aware of his responsibilities with respect to his code of silence in certain national matters. He always let us know when he couldn't reveal certain information. He worried about his grandchildren. Personally he felt that as a patriot he couldn't have done it otherwise. He couldn't keep secret what he saw and knew regarding our POWs and MIAs; withholding that information had made him physically ill. He had to open up, no matter what the consequences.

I was very grateful to him, but I didn't know what to think. Here I was in Billings, Montana, seventeen years after the disappearance, trying to find out whatever I could about Fritz Stammberger. Carlos seemed nervous. So was I. I didn't know if Jerry was being tailed overtly or secretly. He had certainly upset some very powerful people in the intelligence world.

As we settled in our room, we offered Jerry a drink, and then began to discuss the case. Jerry explained how he had seen documents—intercepts that mentioned certain U.S. prisoners being transferred to the Soviet Union. I wasn't sure what I should ask or say. I sat on the corner of the bed, and listened.

Jerry believed that there was a good chance Fritz was captured. If so, he felt that he was kept inside Afghanistan or Pakistan. He couldn't help us with our specific case, but he could help us analyze all the documents that we already had. He gave us advice. He told us what we should and should not do with government officials in Russia and in the United States. He explained how to ask questions, how to analyze. He tried his best to share with us in six hours what he had learned and experienced over twenty years. He smoked nonstop as Carlos asked him questions regarding our case and the Soviet transport of prisoners.

He told us about the "wink and nod" policy—you take our man and we wink, and we take your man and you nod—the two superpowers and their satellites being co-conspirators. Then he explained the "Pardon and Parole Theory"—that our prisoners of war in North Vietnam were being kept as criminals and not as POWs. As a result, the Vietnamese would not acknowledge the existence of POWs; instead they would have to pardon and parole any American "criminal" that they might still have in jail.

We had kept our radio on in the room. Jerry laughed about it and told us that the radio being on would not deter anybody from listening to our conversation. If we were being tailed, there were sophisticated ways of eavesdropping. We could be in the middle of a rock concert and they could hear every word. He seemed relaxed about it, however. After another hour of explanations and interpretations, Carlos asked a straightforward question of Jerry, one that took him and me by surprise.

"Jerry, I'm sorry, but I have to ask you this. Are you wired?" Jerry looked shocked and didn't understand what he was being asked.

Carlos repeated it again. "I mean, are you wired, do you have any microphones on you?"

"Of course not. What are you talking about?" he answered.

"Well, I'm looking at your left leg and there is something bulky in your sock," Carlos said.

Jerry laughed and pulled a spare packet of cigarettes out of his sock.

The brief tension in the room subsided. We decided at that point to take a break and have dinner in the hotel dining room. Jerry excused himself so that he could check his car. I worried for Jerry's safety. We were getting involved in a world that we didn't understand. It looked real, but it felt surreal.

After about ten minutes, Jerry came back and we all went to the top floor restaurant to eat. After another two hours, we thanked Jerry and the meeting ended. We saw him disappear into the hotel hallway; he left as he had come, quietly, as if he had never existed. One of our "invisible men."

The following morning we went back to Los Angeles. I no longer thought that we, or anybody, could keep their privacy. I knew now that if the government wanted, they could know anything and everything about me. I felt ambivalent. On one hand, I felt vulnerable and violated; on the other hand, I felt protected and proud of my country's intelligence capabilities.

41.

The Source

Moscow
October 23, 1992

B arely an hour had passed when there was a loud knock at the door. I awoke startled. Carlos stirred beside me. "Babe," I whispered. Another knock. "What . . . what is it?" Carlos asked groggily. "Someone's at the door," I answered. He woke up.

"Who is it? Who's there?" he called out. He pulled on a robe and went to look through the peephole.

"Who is it?" Carlos asked again, fully awake.

"My name is Viktor. We have to talk. Meet me downstairs in the lobby." The voice belonged to a man with a strong Russian accent.

"Who sent you?" Carlos asked.

"Emma," he said with a muffled voice. Carlos opened the door and greeted him.

"Welcome to my country," Viktor said. He was a tall man with a hefty build. There was something about the impeccable suit, the red tie that sat tightly about his thick neck, that foreshadowed a warning. He seemed friendly, but in a way I couldn't seem to trust. This was a man who could help us, or just as easily prove dangerous. Viktor had been a professional fighter, as well as an intelligence officer in the Soviet military.

"We have to move fast. I'll meet you outside. I'll be in a white BMW," he said and left, receding into the darkness of the hallway.

On October 23, 1992, we arrived at Moscow's Sheremetyevo Airport. As we waited for our turn in customs, I dropped our hand luggage, a heap of coats, and the magazines that had kept me occupied beside me. I was tired. The fourteen-hour flight from Los Angeles and the eleven-hour time difference had done a job on both of us. After we were cleared through immigration and customs, we went straight to our hotel, the Radisson-Slavjanskaya. The hotel's opulent marble floors and crystal chandeliers contrasted with the bare white walls of the lobby and hallways. There were no paintings or sculptures. No art, no color. Also, our room was small, spare. Two narrow beds. At that point, I hardly cared. We were exhausted. I finished hanging up our few belongings as Carlos fell asleep. I had just gotten into bed. Now Viktor's urgency left us no time to rest. We hurried to dress and went down to the lobby.

As we stepped outside into the street, Viktor ushered us into his car. "It is safer this way," he said. We pulled away from the hotel and onto a main street. He reached forward to increase the volume on the radio.

"So, how's Emma?" he asked, appraising us. He had waited until we were safely in traffic to start speaking.

"When we spoke with her regarding this trip, she seemed to be doing fine," Carlos responded. Emma was an underground activist whom we'd met through our network of contacts.

"Yes, yes," Viktor acknowledged, nodding his head as we stopped at a light; the pause signaled a break in the conversation. A moment later, Viktor turned toward me. "What music would you like to hear?" he asked casually.

"Anything, really . . . this is fine," I answered. I was tense. Ever since we left Los Angeles, I had a strong sense of urgency. I didn't feel safe here.

"What can I do for you?" Viktor asked.

"We are here to find out what happened to Janice's ex-husband, Fritz Stammberger," Carlos replied. "He disappeared September 27, 1975, in a restricted area near the Afghanistan, Pakistan, and Russian borders—on Tirich Mir Mountain."

"What do you mean, he disappeared?" Viktor asked.

"Exactly that. He disappeared like smoke into thin air, my friend," Carlos answered.

Viktor looked intrigued. "Why was he in that area, if I might ask?

What did he do for a living?" he inquired.

"He was a printer," I filled in. "He had a print shop in Aspen, Colorado, but he loved to climb. He was considered a top mountain climber, and he traveled all over the world to find mountains to climb— new peaks, new challenges." This information didn't seem to affect Viktor as much as the word "disappeared" that Carlos had mentioned a few seconds earlier.

"He vanished while he was climbing?" Viktor asked.

"Yes," I confirmed. "When Fritz's partner went to Pakistan to search for Fritz, he found some clues on the trail near where Fritz had planned to climb."

"So Fritz had been there?"

"Yes," I said.

Viktor pulled off to the side of the road and switched off the engine. I could see the snow dusting down, falling lightly over the Moscow River, its water flowing sluggishly, not quite frozen. On the banks, a few browned leaves still clung to the trees overhanging the current.

Viktor touched my right hand. "I'm sorry."

I nodded.

"Please tell me, when was the last time you saw Fritz?"

"The night before he left for Pakistan," I answered.

"Do you remember anything different about that night?" Viktor continued asking.

"Well . . ." I thought for a moment, reluctant to answer. I could feel Carlos tensing up in the front seat.

"Look, why do we need to get into this?" Carlos asked tersely, quietly.

"Because the details are important. I need to know as much as I can," Viktor insisted. "Go ahead," he prompted me.

"Well, I was supposed to go to Los Angeles the next day . . . I was catching a flight from Denver." I paused as I tried to recollect. "We had driven from our home, in Aspen, to Denver—to the Brown's Hotel—so we could spend a quiet night there together. . . ."

I could still see the place in my memory, the velvet couches, the mahogany front desk. "Fritz checked us in . . . we went up to the room.

For some reason, we walked up the stairs instead of taking the elevator."

Carlos stopped me. "Come on, babe, he doesn't need to know these types of details."

"No, no, it's okay," Viktor interjected.

"When we finally reached our suite, we ordered dinner in the room. We ate without saying much, then went to bed, but I couldn't sleep. . . . I knew this was the last time we would be together for weeks. . . ."

"Yes . . . ?" Viktor asked.

I couldn't tell him what I remembered; it was too intimate. We had lain there together, naked. His head on my stomach. We hadn't even made love. Fritz had said, "There's nothing like the warmth of a good woman."

"All night long I couldn't sleep. I just lay awake and thought about him and about how he would be leaving for Pakistan so soon. I wanted to stay with him, but it didn't seem possible." I stopped. Carlos had opened the car door.

"Look, I need some air," he said. I watched him as he got out of the car and started walking away.

"Carlos . . . ," I called out softly after him.

Viktor waited for me to collect myself.

I hesitated, then continued. "The next morning when we went to the airport, I had a vague sensation of wanting to reverse things," I explained.

"We stood there for so long with our arms around each other." I remembered those last few minutes at the airport . . . neither one of us wanted to move. His beard had scraped against my cheek as he kissed me one last time. "'Something doesn't feel right,' I whispered to him. 'Don't worry, everything will be okay,' he answered. 'You're going alone; if anything happens to you . . . ?' I questioned him. 'If anything ever does happen to me, don't believe what anyone tells you. Follow your own instincts. Listen to your inner voice. Besides, I'll be back soon.'" I knew what Fritz meant. "That day I knew something was different. The last thing I said to him was that I couldn't wait until Christmas. I never understood why I said Christmas—he was supposed to be back in October. I didn't want to say good-bye, but it was too late. My plane was about to leave. I walked away."

Viktor was silent.

I watched the branches dip toward the icy river. The wind had picked up, blowing slivers of frost and dead leaves along the water.

Carlos had just returned to the car; he could tell that I was upset.

"What's wrong?" Carlos asked.

"Nothing. It's okay," Viktor answered. He started the car and we drove off.

Carlos held my hand. Viktor started talking. There was a visible, twisted grin on his face.

"Well, if there is something to be found in Russia, I'll try my best to find it. There are three major information centers in our country: the presidential files, the KGB files, and the GRU or Defense Ministry files. That's where the kind of information you're looking for may be," he said, glancing back at me. Then he picked up his mobile phone and placed a call. After a few seconds, he started speaking in Russian.

Carlos and I looked at each other. It had begun. The game of finding out, of retrieving information, of trying to penetrate the inner sanctums of the intelligence world. Whether we were in Russia or in the United States, it seemed the players were the same.

"It's done," Viktor reported, hanging up the phone. I looked at his profile, the graying hair, the gold-rimmed glasses. Almost too well-groomed. Only time would tell if he could be trusted. "We will find out if the information about Fritz Stammberger is in the KGB or GRU files," he continued. "The presidential files, I cannot help you with." Carlos and I were silent for a moment.

"Thank you. We really appreciate it," I said.

Viktor changed the music to a ballad of Edith Piaf's. The car sped up as he wove through traffic, trying to make sure that we were not being followed.

I stared out the window and watched the streets of Moscow roll by. Everything in it appeared slightly aged. The modern apartments and office buildings were dirty, barren. The older churches, the onion domes of St. Basil's Cathedral, seemed ancient, as if they had begun to crumble, to fall apart in small, hidden ways, in spite of the strength that had preserved them through the centuries. A city fighting with itself, its history; a city struggling to make its way into the modern world. Carlos had told me that parts of Moscow dated back to 1147, but most of it was destroyed in 1812 after a huge fire ravaged the town. So much change in so little time. Fires, revolutions.

The car stopped at our hotel's entrance.

Viktor got out and opened my door. "I'll be in touch, then," he said.

We entered the lobby as he drove off.

42.

Susan and the Colonel

Moscow
October 24, 1992

As we cut through the crowded hotel lobby toward the Amadeus Cafe, we could see a tall woman with a Sixties Afro, clearly of the "make love, not war" school. A look of welcome spread across Susan Mesinai's face. Next to her was a distinguished, silver-haired man, Boris Yuzhin, who resembled a shorter version of George Peppard, also waiting for us. "Welcome to Russia," she said with a slight New York accent. Boris extended his hand out to Carlos, giving him a firm handshake. I embraced Susan, and we all walked into the cafe.

I felt a sense of comfort having Susan Mesinai on our side. She was a founder of the ARK Project, a human rights organization dedicated to finding lost political prisoners in the Gulag system. Former KGB colonel Boris Yuzhin worked with the ARK Project as well. Boris knew firsthand about imprisonment, about the loss of human rights. He had spent the last five years in the Siberian Gulag. While working for the KGB, he was also working with the FBI in San Francisco. A double agent. To the KGB, he was a traitor; deserving maximum punishment, the firing squad. Boris was lucky: he had been sentenced to fifteen years in the Gulag.

While in jail, his life and his family had been destroyed. They were shunned by the circles that previously welcomed them. Their privileges were revoked. No cars, no access to hard currency stores. But incarceration wasn't able to break Boris. Deep inside, he believed that one day his family and friends, the Russian people, would understand why he had done it.

The reprieve arrived in February 1992. The Iron Curtain had fallen. The Berlin Wall had come down. President Yeltsin granted amnesty to some of the political prisoners in the Gulag. Boris was freed at last.

With rebuilt hope he had decided to help others trapped in the Gulag, the invisible men in the prison system. He joined the ARK Project. Working with Susan Mesinai, he began an exhausting, endless search for the men who were alive but forgotten.

"My God, you are exactly what I expected you to be—I mean you look exactly like what I pictured," Susan said as we sat down in the cafe.

"How freely can we talk?" Carlos asked, looking around. Susan looked at Boris and smiled.

"Since the moment that you landed, you've probably been watched. This hotel is well known for being bugged . . . a lot of Americans stay here, you know. Besides, with Boris here . . . his former KGB comrades like to keep an eye on him," she replied. "But you get used to it."

Susan continued. "I'm very interested in your case. As you know, there was a lot going on in that region where Fritz disappeared, before, during, and after the Afghanistan war with the Soviets."

Her interest gave me hope. Susan and Boris had already succeeded in searches for missing Americans. They had just found a man named Victor Hamilton, who had defected to the Soviet Union thirty years before. He had been a decoder for the National Security Agency. In the U.S.S.R., he was tortured and confined. Susan and Boris had discovered him in a psychiatric hospital located thirty miles outside of Moscow.

The case made me think of the readings Barry Taft had given at UCLA's parapsychology lab. Strange, the way things people had said years before kept coming back and making sense over a decade later. When the parapsychology students had described Fritz lying on a cot with multiple injuries, when they mentioned a Russian woman standing next to him. I did not know the significance of those details. Perhaps the parapsychologists knew that one day my search would take me to Russia, that perhaps here I would discover what had happened to Fritz.

Susan's description of the man in the psychiatric hospital reminded me of how people could reappear. Hamilton was seventy-five years old when Susan found him. His only identification was a card with a "K" on it, a single letter. That was the code the KGB used to ensure that a prisoner wouldn't be discovered. A single letter, not even a name.

"I brought some of the documents and notes I accumulated during our search," I said. I offered a big manila envelope to Susan and Boris. They pulled out a few papers and looked them over. Susan adjusted her wire-rimmed glasses and Boris pulled his chair closer. We drank some coffee as they browsed through the documents.

"What do you think?" I asked Susan.

"Well, we need more information from you. The more you tell us the better we can evaluate how we can or cannot help you."

Susan gave me back the package and looked at her watch.

"We should leave. We have to meet Judi Buehrer from the *Moscow Times*. It will only take five minutes to get there. It's in this building, on the third floor," Susan said.

I felt an affinity with Susan. Boris was handsome and very polite, but I couldn't read him. Was he with us? Was he trying to help or trying to collect information? From the beginning, Carlos had agreed with Jerry Mooney, who had said: "Once intelligence, always intelligence." According to Carlos, no one ever really left Russian intelligence. We took care of the bill and went to meet the journalist at the paper.

Two days later Fritz's picture and mine appeared on half a page of the *Moscow Times*. The game would change. Russian and U.S. intelligence would make their moves.

43.

The Diplomats

Moscow
October 26, 1992

It was our fourth day in Moscow. I knew that time was of the essence. The clock was ticking. There were forces in Russia working to retain control of all information relating to foreign prisoners who had been part of the Gulag prison system. Sometimes the release of documents was inexplicably delayed; sometimes they just disappeared.

I wanted to reach President Yeltsin. I believed that he would help. He seemed to be sincere about his desire to move toward a democratic government. He was the one who had triggered this search for Fritz. His words echoed through my mind when he announced that there were Americans alive and being kept against their will in the former Soviet Union's territories. Those against him believed that he was using that revelation to pay back Mikhail Gorbachev, to show the West that as the country's new leader, he would help, where Gorbachev who knew about Americans imprisoned in the Soviet Union but never revealed such secrets to the U.S. government had not.

In spite of other people's cynicism about Yeltsin's motives, I believed him. He had everything to lose and nothing to gain if Americans were not found. I wrote a letter requesting his assistance, but Carlos and I weren't sure where to deliver it. We decided to start by inquiring at the Russian White House, only a short distance from our hotel.

As we pulled up, we saw that it was a magnificent white edifice facing the Moscow River. Flags from various Russian republics circled the building. We drove to the front door. Carlos and I got out and walked into the main lobby, where a uniformed guard approached us. Our translator told him about our desire to meet with the president. The guard looked both startled and amused; he told us that we were in the wrong place—the president was at the Kremlin.

We got back in the car, and shortly after, we arrived at the Kremlin. "The heart of the beast," Carlos said. This was the seat of power, an enormous compound, a fortress. It was surrounded by walls that stretched at least a quarter mile on each side. Brick after brick. Centuries ago, all of Moscow was contained within those walls.

I was fascinated by it. I could imagine the place as a medieval city under siege. Holes in the Kremlin walls looked as if they had been designed to shoot arrows through as knights fended off invaders. The place seemed built to withstand attacks. The old buildings in Red Square had a sturdy beauty that endured, a functional dreaminess in its architecture. The beautiful church off to the side was one example, looking like something out of Hansel and Gretel. Turrets in the shape of Hershey's Kisses. Layer upon layer of decoration resembling frosting on a huge cake. The modern monuments seemed spare by comparison. Slabs of marble. Lenin's mausoleum. The flame at the tomb of the unknown soldier. There was both grandeur and tragedy here.

We found what looked like the main entrance, and, through our translator, tried to communicate what we were looking for. The guide told us that the appropriate place to deliver my request was at another entrance, and gave us directions.

Following the outer wall, we walked for twenty minutes before we found what looked like the right place. It was near a gate that was not used much. A ramp for tourists went up and over what looked like a dried-out moat. At the top was a large door. The door we were looking for was down below, a basement door that looked fairly old, made of heavy wood with pieces nailed together and an old iron handle. Hesitantly, I rang the bell beside it. The heavy door opened and I went in.

Inside, things looked slightly modernized. There was an old man with bad teeth behind a glass counter. Our translator followed me. He told the man my story, and after much discussion the man agreed to take the envelope containing my written request for an audience with President

Yeltsin. That was it.

As I walked out, I looked up and saw one of the Kremlin clock towers. The guardian of time. For each of the years since Fritz had left, it had been there, ticking away, oblivious. Every minute of every hour that clock had faithfully documented seventeen long years, an eternity. It oversaw the recent bloodless revolution, the conversion to democracy. It had seen the demise of the last czar and the violent change to communism years before. It had watched over the square through the ages, witnessing the human events that played out within the walls below.

Like the hands of the clock, I kept coming back to the same place, turning full circle, each time regaining the illusion that I could start again. In the scale of things, mere instants had passed since Fritz had disappeared. Seventeen years, a blip in history. To me it still seemed as if it had happened yesterday. Minutes ago, hours ago. That is the illusion of time, when aging, really, is the only reality.

We climbed into the vehicle and continued on. We had several other requests and letters of inquiry to deliver. Our next stops would be the embassies of countries bordering Tirich Mir. We started with Afghanistan.

As the translator and I tried to enter the embassy compound, we were stopped by a Russian guard and two Afghanistan secret service men. They wouldn't let us in and refused to convey my request for an audience with the ambassador from Afghanistan. I tried every approach I knew. I explained the case, how long I had been searching. I said that I only had a few questions to ask. Finally, getting frustrated, the translator told the men what I did in the United States, that I was on television. I heard him say *Price Is Right*, as if it would matter. After much explaining, he was able to convince them to allow us in.

As we walked past the iron gate, we noticed how quiet the place was. In the central hall there was only a receptionist, some empty desks, and more silence. The place seemed deserted. I left the letter for the ambassador, but I was disappointed. After all that trouble trying to get in, I was told not to expect much. The situation in Afghanistan was still bad. The civil war continued. Even the mujahadin were fighting among themselves. Still, our strategy was to use the shotgun approach. Try everywhere, anywhere. Maybe then we would eventually discover some information. All it took was one source, one person willing to talk.

As we drove away, the cold breeze forced itself through the cracked glass of the car window. It was chilly, but the wind felt good, refreshing. On our way to the embassy for the People's Republic of China, we passed through the grayness of Moscow. The real Moscow was everything outside of Red Square, dilapidated buildings and streets filled with potholes. The people on the streets looked lost. They dressed in clothes and colors that reminded me of the Forties. It didn't seem like a society that could sustain a military arsenal and hide it all over the countryside. According to some political analysts, the arsenal could destroy the world or more. Yet all I saw was poverty and neglect. I felt like I was in a time warp, stuck half a century behind.

The driver slowed as we approached the Chinese embassy. I saw a single Russian guard standing out front. This time we were turned away completely. The guard took the envelope and said he would give it to the embassy staff. It might reach the ambassador, he said, but he didn't know.

Perhaps I was naive thinking I could reach these people, thinking they would help me. I went back to the car. I was getting tired and upset. After I sat beside him in the backseat once again, Carlos took my hand. "It's okay, babe. We'll do it. We'll find out," he said.

It was so frustrating to be rebuffed, ignored. Embassies, diplomats— they were supposed to help their countries, to help people from different countries communicate with each other. That's what I thought, anyhow. But that wasn't how it worked. In all these years, the embassies and the diplomats, had only gotten in my way. Our own embassy didn't even accommodate us. I was only able to contact the ambassador by phone. He'd offered to help, but words didn't mean much. They just helped to increase the inertia, prolong inaction.

"Let's go back to the hotel," I proposed. We did enough for one day.

"No, babe, we can't stop," Carlos said. "If we keep going, the door will open."

I frowned. I just didn't want to do it anymore. It felt like we were getting nowhere. Why waste our time? But I kept my thoughts to myself.

After a few more turns, the car arrived at Pakistan's embassy. Same routine. I left the car and went up to the Russian guard. The place was not as heavily protected as the others. The building was unassuming but hospitable, almost like a church with its gray stone walls. To my surprise, the guard let us in almost immediately. With some trepidation, I continued back to an entrance that appeared to come off of an alley and entered the reception area. A very friendly English-speaking woman welcomed me and asked how she might help. After we showed her the poster of Fritz and handed her our letter, she asked us to have a seat and left the room. A few minutes later, she returned and informed us that Ambassador Ashraf Qazi would see us within half an hour. We were to meet at his residence, which was connected to the embassy offices. I looked at Carlos. He smiled.

We hardly waited twenty minutes when a dark-haired, dark-eyed man in an elegant suit came through the door. He escorted us to his private house in the back of the embassy, and as we entered, I felt as though I had been transported to Pakistan. The floor was covered with thick rugs, and silk tapestries hung on the walls. With the hospitality that was so customary in that part of the world, he offered us freshly steeped tea in glass teacups. I presented him with the story, briefly, and asked him for any help he could offer me in finding Fritz.

"My dear," he began, "there have been so many changes in Pakistan during the past years; the political landscape has shifted entirely. . . . Finding any information is not going to be an easy task."

"But," I told him, "several extensive searches have already been done—within the country. There must be some records, something." I told him about the first search, the one done by Harry Conway. Harry had the cooperation of the Pakistani military. It had taken quite a bit of negotiating and paperwork for Harry to secure the Alouette helicopter he used to follow Fritz's tracks on Tirich Mir Mountain. The preparations for that trip had to be documented.

"Tirich Mir?" he reiterated. "He must have been quite a mountaineer."

"Yes, he was," I assented.

"Well, my dear, between you and me, that area has been a little out of control lately. There has been a continuous influx of mujahadin refugees from Afghanistan. It is an area of major concern, there is little the government can do . . . really. Most records have been moved around or destroyed. So much has been lost in the upheavals. . . ."

"But one of our search parties, the second one, said they saw some records. A man named Jim MacGeyver was searching for Fritz, and in the process ended up detained in Chitral. He said that he saw police files on Fritz in the Chitral police station."

"My dear, as I said, there may, at one time, have been documents pertaining to Mr. Stammberger, but it is rather unlikely that those documents still exist. Even if they did exist, it would be impossible to find them, impossible." He grumbled the last sentence almost to himself. "You have to understand," he repeated, "the region is extremely unstable. They have curfews all the time . . . people are afraid to go out on the streets," he said, his voice softening as he thought of his country.

"It wouldn't have helped that Fritz knew President Zia or Prince Burchanadin?" I approached him tentatively with that question. These had been two of the most important people in Pakistan.

The ambassador smiled wistfully. "Ms. Pennington, there is no more Zia . . . your husband's disappearance took place seventeen years ago. If what he was doing there was not to be revealed, that information has certainly been destroyed by now. Seventeen years is quite a long time in my country . . . things change so often."

"Is there anything we can do?" I asked.

"I'll tell you what," he offered. "I'm going to Pakistan in a week. I'll look into it. I'll be back at the end of the month and I'll contact you as soon as I return."

As we trudged through the snow back to the car, Carlos unleashed his frustration. "Diplomats are very polite, but they don't do shit! Pakistan, supposedly, is our ally, and look how far we got."

"Carlos, could you please keep your voice down," I whispered. He certainly turned around; he was the one who told me to be hopeful. We were barely out of the embassy—what if someone heard him?

"No," he said flatly, "I can't. I'm getting tired of this, always the same thing. 'I'll get back to you later.' I tell you right now, I don't think we're going to get anything from this guy. He already gave you an answer."

I couldn't believe this. Carlos was the last person I expected to give up that easily, to drop out when things got rough. "I don't understand you," I exclaimed. "Before you were telling me to keep on going, to just wait and someone, somewhere, would give us an answer. 'All it takes is one open door.' Now . . . now, look at you. . . . At least we got into this place."

We didn't even look at each other as we walked to the car.

As he opened the door across from the driver, I heard Carlos grunt to himself, shaking his head, "I'm so sick of this, I can't even tell you."

Silence was my companion on the ride back to the hotel. Time had become our adversary. What would happen to our relationship, to our marriage, if we didn't find the answer? I could no longer predict Carlos's reactions. He was becoming a time bomb, ready to explode at any moment.

44.

The Deceivers

Moscow
October 27, 1992

K onstantin N. Borovoi, an entrepreneur who was the chairman
of the new pro-business Economic Freedom Party, was our
next contact. One of the richest men in the Soviet Union, he
was offering financial rewards to anyone who would report the
whereabouts of Americans who were being held in the Soviet Union
against their will. He chose to involve himself with the joint task force,
created by both the Russian and the American governments to deal with
the touchy issue of American POWs and MIAs transported to Russia.
The task force dealt with all possible cases from all wars: World Wars
I and II, Korea, the Cold War, and Vietnam.

Borovoi made his money, or so we were told, by selling computer
technology, among other things, before the breakup of the Soviet Union.
He amassed a huge fortune. After the disintegration of the U.S.S.R.,
Borovoi took his place in the new order, an order in which economic
power and military force often worked in tandem. As a new capitalist,
he loved the press, and that was how we had reached out to him.

When Viktor, our military intelligence source, heard that we were to
meet with Borovoi, he warned us that some of the new entrepreneurs in the
former Soviet Union's territories were connected to the "Russian mafia."
Viktor had explained to Carlos how, after the collapse of the U.S.S.R. in
1991, segments of the underworld took advantage of the new business
opportunities in major cities. Viktor even mentioned alliances between the
Russian mobsters and collaborators in government and police agencies.

Susan and Boris had not wanted to attend the meeting with Borovoi initially. Carlos had persuaded them that they could benefit from the encounter. He didn't believe that Borovoi was part of the Russian mafia. Borovoi appeared to have a genuine interest in finding men who were persecuted. That was why we were seeing him. We were joined by Bruce Brown, a man whose father was declared missing in action during the Vietnam conflict. We sponsored his trip after watching him on an ABC-TV program, "20/20," that reported on POW/MIAs from Vietnam and other wars who may have been transported to Russia.

Bruce's father, Lieutenant Colonel Robert "Mack" Brown, was a fighter pilot who had disappeared in Vietnam on November 7, 1972, when the USAF-111 aircraft carrying him was shot down in the North Vietnamese province of Quang Binh. Brown was also an electrical engineer and scientist who had worked on our Mercury and Gemini space programs as well as the U.S. antiballistic missile system program. According to several intelligence sources, he was transported to the Soviet Union as part of the "Moscow Bound" program.

Borovoi's office was located two blocks away from what had been KGB headquarters. Our driver dropped the five of us at the door and left quickly. As we entered the aged lobby, several large men approached us. They were young, but their manner was severe. Their walk, their posture had a military aspect. Boris spoke to them in Russian.

"I let them know that we are here for the meeting," he said. One of the guards went to another room. After a few minutes, he came back, and the guards escorted us to Borovoi's office. It was not ostentatious, although it was rather comfortable by Russian standards. The desk was made of heavy oak; the chairs were upholstered in black leather. There was a mirrored wall behind the desk. I wondered whether it was a real wall or just a facade behind which someone else was watching. The guards stepped to the sides of the room but remained with us as we waited for Borovoi to arrive.

When he entered the room, Borovoi seemed like an unlikely candidate for so much power, but the guards responded to him in a way that made me nervous. It was obvious that they both respected and feared him. There was no telling what Borovoi was capable of, in spite of his benign appearance.

A short man with a raspy voice and a continuous smile, he made the pretense of deferring to us. He began to speak in a moderate tone of voice, and his translator explained to us that he would try his best to answer all of our questions. Boris said something to him in Russian to show that we understood.

Then the conversation began. First, I told him about Fritz's incident. I gave him and his assistant some of the posters and photographs I had. He listened attentively and smiled. Here and there he questioned his translator, and occasionally Boris would intercede to explain details when he felt it was important. The story had stimulated interest.

It looked as if our high hopes for this meeting with Borovoi were going to be fulfilled. He seemed like someone who would be interested in helping people like us and Bruce Brown. As the meeting progressed, first Boris, then Susan and Bruce jumped into the conversation. Everyone wanted to get their two cents in and the interactions became increasingly confusing as we all tried to speak at the same time. I was getting frustrated because the conversation was moving away from its original concerns, Fritz's case and Lieutenant Colonel Brown's disappearance. Boris kept taking over the conversation. Eventually, the translator decided no longer to continue translating.

I could see that Carlos was not happy. The meeting was getting out of control. There was no direction, and no objective was being reached. Finally, he stepped in.

"Look," he interceded, "we all want the same thing here—to find Americans who are still in Russia."

Borovoi nodded his assent.

Carlos explained his plan. It was simple: Borovoi would use his contacts in the Russian media and we would use ours in the United States. We would start a program similar to the one used to find missing children by placing their pictures on the backs of milk cartons. Every other week, we would provide the photos and the written descriptions. Then, all over the former Soviet Union, we would have one of our missing men featured. The pictures, together with some radio and television spots, Carlos explained, would give us a way of finding people who have information that could help us. There were hundreds of people like us searching for someone without a way of finding them and without the resources.

"So, why don't we start this program one case at a time," Carlos suggested. Borovoi agreed; he would begin publicizing the search for Bruce Brown's father, first with his contacts at the *Red Star*, the armed forces' newspaper. Carlos and Borovoi established a date for a press conference. Borovoi was running for a political position and would be out of town rallying votes, but his vice-chairman would represent him at the press conference to announce our new joint venture. Rumor had it that Borovoi decided that one day he would be the mayor of Moscow. Carlos told me that Borovoi reminded him of Perot. Konstantin Borovoi, the Ross Perot of Russia. He was helping us because, later, it might help him.

As Boris wrapped up the conversation, Borovoi got up. We followed to go to a photo session. Something for the papers. When Carlos and Borovoi were being set up for a shot, Carlos joked, "I hope you don't change your mind the way Perot did." Carlos had been an adviser on the California Perot Petition Executive Board. After he'd created a strategy manual for Perot's campaign, a twenty-six-page plan that had been mentioned in *Time* magazine, Perot had quit the presidential race without forewarning any of his followers.

Borovoi simply shook his head and appeared as if he didn't understand Carlos's comment. After the picture taking was over, we left.

I felt the meeting went well, but I knew that Carlos felt otherwise. His sixth sense had signaled that something was wrong.

45.

Counterintelligence

Moscow
October 30, 1992

Finally we were able to arrange for a meeting with a counter-intelligence agent. He had been highly recommended to us by a source in the U.S. intelligence network. The meeting was to take place at an old building near downtown Moscow.

It was a rainy evening. Our driver was crisscrossing through the city, unsure of how to get to the street address that we had given him. After making two stops to ask for directions, he smiled and gestured with his hand that he now knew where to go. As a matter of security, we let the drivers know our destination only after we had left the hotel, by showing them the address written on a piece of paper. We were deeply concerned with the safety of our contacts. The Russians were very good at tailing people. Their surveillance methods were less sophisticated than ours, but when it came to visual and physical shadowing they were at their best. We had nothing to hide, but we didn't want to put our sources in jeopardy.

As we approached our destination, the driver pulled up to the curb, got out, and walked around to open our door, pointing to the entrance. Carlos and I left the car and walked to a darkened lobby inside the building. The front door was ajar. It looked deserted. No lights. Suddenly, as we passed halfway through the lobby, a body leaped out at us from behind a wooden counter. I let out a shrill scream. Carlos yelled, "Who is it? We came to see Mr. Prokudin."

As fast as the body had jumped out at us, it fell back onto the floor with a loud thump. Carlos cautiously walked over to the man, who lay motionless. An empty glass bottle clutched in his hand, he adjusted himself on the cold stone floor. He was a drunken vagrant taking refuge from the rain.

I gave a sigh of relief as Carlos took my hand and we continued walking to the elevator.

The apartment was small. It looked and felt like a New York studio with a wall dividing it in two. Mr. Prokudin hadn't arrived yet. A pretty young woman opened the door and, with broken English, offered us coffee. I looked around the makeshift room. There were no photos, or books, nothing at all. It looked like a room used for drop offs and probably even for interrogations. Only God knew who had been here and for what reasons.

After ten long minutes, we heard a key unlocking the front door and Mr. Prokudin walked in. A heavyset man in his mid-thirties. He smiled as he greeted us and took off his overcoat.

"Welcome," he said.

We returned his greeting. He lit up a cigarette and started the conversation without hesitation.

"How is your search going?"

"So far we haven't been able to connect with certain people we would like to, but we are still hopeful," Carlos answered.

"I have only half an hour to spend with you; unfortunately, I have other arrangements to take care of, but maybe I can help you with your case," he said in perfect English.

Mr. Prokudin had spent considerable time in Afghanistan and Pakistan. He had watched and participated in the process of Afghanistan's invasion by the Soviet army. He knew the area, he knew the people. Apparently, he had worked with both the KGB and the GRU. A source had told us that he also had worked with Western intelligence agencies. He was sure of himself and of what he was saying. He was precise, focused, and authoritative.

"Let me ask you: Was your man, Fritz, an American citizen?" Mr. Prokudin asked.

"No. He was a German national, but he was a permanent resident in the U.S.," I replied.

"Well, that explains a lot," he said.

He rolled his eyes, pausing momentarily, then continued.

"As far as I know, your government established very strict guidelines for the Afghanistan cause. As you know, the mujahadin are men that are fighting a holy war. They can't admit that the 'big Satan,' as some Muslim fundamentalists call your government, was helping them. CIA headquarters in Langley didn't use Americans in the field, in order to avoid potential problems. If any of them were to be captured, the world would find out that the Muslim fundamentalists, the same people who overthrew the Shah of Iran and who hate the U.S. government, were being aided by American nationals." He paused and lit another cigarette before butting out the one still smoldering in the ashtray. He exhaled a cloud of gray smoke and proceeded. He seemed far, far away. Carlos and I sat speechless and shifted uncomfortably on the couch. Mr. Prokudin blinked, pushed the hair that had fallen over one eye aside, and looked at his watch before continuing.

"Let me tell you, your government had a master plan. They knew that our government was afraid of an internal Muslim revolution, like Ayatollah Khomeini's revolution in Iran." Once again he stopped and sucked on his cigarette. "George Bush was director of the CIA up to March 1977, then he was ambassador to the People's Republic of China, then he was vice-president for eight years, and finally president for four years. If you add up all those years as the head of your intelligence services, you realize that there was a consistency in direction." He paused and took a deep breath.

Again Carlos and I didn't know what to do or say; we just listened. We were warned in the U.S. by an intelligence agent that the less we knew, the better off we would be.

Carlos interceded.

"Mr. Prokudin, all we care about is what happened to Fritz Stammberger, not the policy in that area."

Mr. Prokudin became agitated. He didn't like the fact that Carlos had interrupted his speech. He looked directly at Carlos.

"You approached me, not the reverse. I'm trying to help you. This is serious business. The plan to destroy the Soviet Union." He looked at his watch again.

I froze. Carlos gave him a faint smile.

"I'm sorry," Carlos replied. "It's just that . . ."

Mr. Prokudin ignored what Carlos was saying and went on. "I have ten more minutes. I'll tell you what I know and you go your way and do whatever you have to do. Do you understand?"

We nodded in unison.

He continued: "The plan was to destroy, to break up the Soviet Union. Therefore, a massive operation of misinformation was launched in Afghanistan to lure the Soviet army. The threat of an internal insurrection by the Soviet Muslim population was too dangerous. My country believed your country's propaganda. We invaded Afghanistan in 1979."

There was a loud knock at the front door. Mr. Prokudin stopped speaking and looked at the front door in silence. I looked at Carlos, Carlos at me. I could feel my blood pulsing through my body. Two more knocks at the door. Mr. Prokudin got up and went to the door. He looked through the peephole. He opened the door. Two men in overcoats spoke with him in Russian. Maybe we had made a mistake coming to this meeting. The door closed and Mr. Prokudin came back with no apology for the interruption.

"As I was saying, your country had been working in the area. The plan was simple. Provide financial, technological, and intelligence aid to the Muslim fighters, the mujahadin. The mujahadin received arms mainly from Red China, Saudi Arabia and Egypt. They used Pakistan to warehouse the arms, distribute them, and train the fighters. The tracks of the 'great Satan' would be covered. Invisibility was the priority. Only much later were U.S. arms provided." He sighed and continued. "West Germany helped with arms shipments. Also some arms were provided by the U.S., Britain, and even Israel—captured equipment from the Arab countries obtained during the Arab/Israeli wars. In a nutshell, that was the master plan and its players. It worked. Look what happened to us. We lost."

I was afraid. Carlos looked at him.

"Mr. Prokudin, we really appreciate your time. Is there anybody else we could see regarding Afghanistan? Someone you could recommend to us?" Carlos asked.

"Last year I was run over by a truck while on business in France. My wife was badly hurt and I nearly died. 'It was an accident,' the local authorities said. . . .

"So . . . are you sure that you want to pursue this matter?" he questioned.

"Well, all we want to know is if Janice's former husband is alive. That's all," Carlos said.

"Contact the head of the Afghanistan Veterans: he is a Soviet hero; his name is Major General Ashuyev." He opened his phone book and gave Carlos a number.

Mr. Prokudin got up and shook Carlos's hand and then mine. "I must go now. Good luck with your search," he said. We walked the short distance to the door, and he opened it to let us out.

As soon as we entered the elevator, I whispered to Carlos, "Let's get out of here."

"Babe, don't worry, we'll be okay," he said.

The elevator reached the first floor and stopped. No sounds, only an eerie silence. Carlos opened the door and slowly looked out. Nothing, no one, just darkness. We walked out and moved as quickly as we could. We opened the building's door in a hurry and proceeded to where our driver was parked.

Out of nowhere, a hand grabbed Carlos's shoulder, pulling him to an abrupt stop.

"Psht . . . psht, this way . . . the car parked here." It was our driver. All we wanted was to get back to the hotel.

46.

The Security Bubble

Moscow
November 1, 1992

Our movements had been curtailed. For a few days now, two Russian men guarded our hotel floor twenty-four hours a day. Also, an American intelligence officer moved into a room down the hall. The circle was closing in.

As our access to the Russian media grew, official and unofficial parties became more interested in our plans, our actions. They were wary when I was searching for Fritz, but now they were on alert when they realized that this search extended beyond Fritz. It could affect the fate of some of the POWs and MIAs left in Russia. If we solved our case, if we solved Bruce Brown's case, there might be hope for others. Today I was going to be interviewed by Radio Russia, a station that reached over one hundred million people all across the former Soviet Union. Susan arranged the meeting.

As expected, Andrey Allahverdov, a small Russian man, arrived on time at 9:00 p.m. He looked more like a college student than a correspondent. His friendly manner made me feel at ease. Carlos and I met him in the hotel lobby and took him to our room for the actual interview. He was going to tape my story. If everything went well, he would air it within a day or two. He seemed enthusiastic and quite optimistic about the response we might get, and for good reason. After he interviewed Bruce Brown, someone had called in and revealed that, following the disappearance of Bruce's father in Vietnam, F-111 designs had been acquired by the Soviet government. That information alone brought Bruce closer to discovering what had become of his father. Under duress it was possible that anyone could have disclosed classified information, including Lieutenant Colonel Brown. I hoped that when the story of Fritz's disappearance aired, someone who knew something would be listening, someone who would be brave enough to come forward.

The interview lasted two hours. Andrey was gentle and understood my quest. He was trying his best to help democracy continue in his country, and he was interested in human rights. He was of Armenian descent and his family had known the tragedy of being caught in social upheavals, those moments of historical change. During our conversation, he briefly alluded to the massacre of the Armenian people at the hands of the Turkish government. Between 1915 and 1918, close to one and a half million perished.

It was odd that people like Andrey had always been in the Soviet Union, people who really cared about others, about society. But before the Iron Curtain was lifted, we hadn't really known that they existed. We weren't able to talk with, let alone work with, each other, even though we shared the same thoughts, the same humanitarian goals. Politics made it hard to remember that people were people; regardless of what part of the world they lived in, they had the same needs.

Andrey told us stories about the part of Russia he'd grown up in, and I told him about Los Angeles and Hollywood. We had so much to learn from each other. He was fascinated by the city of television and movies and asked question after question. He had a distant cousin living in Los Angeles, he said. I worried about what would happen to him after we left. What would happen to all the people who were helping us here? The situation was so unstable, there was no knowing what turn the government would take tomorrow. Even though things had changed, a coup could take place very quickly, and then, once again, people like Andrey would be in danger. And now we were placed in a "security bubble." God only knew who those men worked for, watching us around the clock like that. It didn't bode well.

It was nearly midnight when Andrey got up to leave. Carlos walked him to the lobby.

I had just settled in to watch some television and unwind, when suddenly, the lights went out, the TV died, and an eerie silence settled over the room. My heart started pounding heavily. The plainclothes guards were just outside in the hall. All of the stories I've heard, of people disappearing . . . this was it, this was how it happened. Carlos was gone. What would I do if someone tried to get into the room? It was pitch black. I heard footsteps in the hallway.

I locked the door. I sat still, listening, my imagination ran wild. The footsteps passed by the room. It was too dark to see. Maybe I should call Bruce. I had to find the phone. I inched my way around the furniture, trying not to bump into anything, trying not to make any sounds. Finally, I found it.

The line was dead.

What was I going to do? I couldn't just sit there waiting. I listened to the hallway again. The commotion died down and was replaced by a deathly silence. Where did the agents go?

I slowly opened the door, the hallway was blacked out. I heard voices, then a door opening and closing at the other end of the hall. I froze, straining to hear. They were coming in my direction. I stumbled back to the room and bolted the door. I told myself I was losing control, feeding the fear in my mind. This couldn't be happening. Where was Carlos?

What if they were after him? Everything was getting out of hand. Then, just as suddenly as they had left, the lights and the television popped on. I sat up and blinked, adjusting to the brilliance, the sounds. Carlos was still gone. I had to find out if he was all right.

I got up and cautiously left the room. I didn't see agents in the hall. I hurried to the elevator.

Carlos said he was going to stop in at the business center after Andrey left to take care of some paperwork. It was located on the mezzanine floor of the hotel, and it was open twenty-four hours a day. Computers. Fax machines. Copiers.

As soon as the elevator arrived, I pressed the button for the mezzanine.

What would I do if he wasn't there? I didn't want to think it, but it was possible. Anything could have happened in those minutes of darkness, and no one would have known. Maybe we were in over our heads with this whole search.

I pressed the mezzanine button again. Why was this elevator so slow? Come on, come on.

With a sudden jolt, the elevator reached its destination. There was no one at the business center, and Carlos wasn't anywhere in sight. I checked all rooms off the main area. He had to be there somewhere. A Russian man came out from one of the offices.

"Excuse me, did you see a gentleman, he has dark hair, wears glasses?" I asked.

"No, nobody has been here for the last hour," he replied. I ran to the lobby. Nothing. I looked in front of the hotel. Nothing.

I went back to the room. As soon as the elevator reached our floor, I ran to the room and fumbled with the door. It opened. There was Carlos, smiling.

"What happened?" I asked. "Where were you?" I blurted out at him.

"What do you mean?" he asked. "Are you okay?"

He put his arms around me and tried to comfort me. "The lights went out," I stammered. "I didn't know where you were."

"Lights? What lights?"

Nothing happened to the power downstairs. He didn't even know. "I was on my way to the business center, when I met this American who's working on a food aid program," Carlos explained, trying to calm me down. " Janice, it's okay," he said.

"From now on we stay together," I said.

47.

Afghanistan's Intelligence

Moscow
November 2, 1992

We just returned from delivering my request to meet with the German ambassador in Moscow, when we received a phone call confirming our meeting with Major General Ashuyev, the head of the Soviet Union's Afghanistan Veterans Organization.

Within one hour I would meet a Soviet hero and, at the same time, the enemy. The general knew the truth of what really happened in Afghanistan. He had fought that war. He believed in a greater Soviet Union, not a broken one. For him and his followers, Gorbachev and Yeltsin were cowards and traitors who had sold out to the United States.

Carlos was edgy and still upset because the German ambassador had stalled, asking for us to come back another time. Carlos always felt that the German government should have helped us more than it had. He had no patience for their stiff formalities.

As we drove to our meeting with General Ashuyev, I remembered the meetings I had with other intelligence sources. Carlos and I went through reams and reams of information as a part of our research. Through it, I learned that the Afghanistani people stemmed from vastly different and conflicting ethnic and tribal cultures. Throughout history they had united to defend their country against foreign dominance, and Western intelligence was well aware of the fiercely independent nature of the Afghanistani people.

In the early Seventies, the Afghans had opted for a neutralist line between their two suitors, the United States and the Soviet Union. On

April 27, 1978, a coup d'état took place in Kabul, led by two men, Hafizullah Amin and Nur Mohammad Taraki, who replaced President Mohammad Daoud and his regime with a Marxist-Leninist government.

In February 1979, our ambassador to Afghanistan, Adolph Dubs, was kidnapped and held hostage by guerrillas. While storming the hotel room where the ambassador was being held, the Afghan police killed him. After this incident, our government greatly reduced our aid to Afghanistan, thus adding to the political and economic crisis.

Then again in September 1979, Hafizullah Amin, the prime minister, deposed President Nur Mohammad Taraki following a bloody shoot-out at the presidential palace. A few months later, on December 27, the world had another glimpse of the inner workings of the dreaded KGB. A KGB commando group under the leadership of Colonel Bayerenov— the head of the KGB terrorist training school—executed a bloody coup, overthrowing President Amin and replacing him with Babrak Karmal.

With the help of President Amin's cook, they tried to drug Amin and his guards. The goal was to kidnap the president and to take him to the Soviet Union. The plan failed because one of the president's guards didn't eat and started shooting when he found out what was happening. Colonel Bayerenov was mistakenly killed during the raid by his own commandos. At a later date, they succeeded.

The Soviet empire wanted to solidify its position at all costs. It had to curb the spread of Islamic fundamentalism. Since 1978, the guerrilla war had been escalating in the countryside. The mujahadin would not accept communism at any price, because their war was a religious war, a holy war. With a puppet government in power and with President Karmal appealing for Soviet military assistance, the "freedom fighters" had no option but to intensify their fight for independence. For a while the Central Intelligence Agency, the Defense Intelligence Agency, and the National Security Agency leaked reports that the Soviets were up to something. Now it was confirmed. By invading Afghanistan, the Russians were trapped. The Western intelligence plan, spreading the threat of an Islamic fundamentalist holy war to the Soviet Union, had worked.

The damage to the Soviets due to their invasion was immense, particularly in the neighboring Arab world and in the People's Republic of China.

216

They feared that they might be the next target. In January 1980, our defense secretary, Harold Brown, and National Security Adviser Zbigniew Brzezinski went to Egypt and Pakistan to garner support for our covert aid to the mujahadin guerrillas. On January 20, 1981, when President Reagan was sworn in, the mujahadin cause received the biggest break that it could ever get. Reagan called the Soviet Union "the evil empire." Saudi Arabia and the CIA intensified their logistic and financial support to the mujahadin rebels. Since the Nixon administration in the early Seventies, we had had secret contacts with the Chinese. Henry Kissinger would secretly meet with the leaders of the People's Republic of China by using Pakistan as a channel. Our policy toward China was a major help in the covert global wars against the Soviet Union. Overtly or covertly, China had become our secret ally in Cambodia, Vietnam, Afghanistan, and Angola. The Soviet Union had become the common enemy.

I was eager to meet the general. I always felt that Fritz might have been captured and imprisoned there.

The car slowed and came to a halt. The building was dilapidated. As we entered the lobby, we realized that there was no elevator, so we climbed up the wide stairway. The meeting was to take place on the third floor. When we reached the appropriate door, we encountered women and old men conversing. We asked a lady for General Ashuyev. She shook her head and turned her back to us. Then a little man with a dark moustache shuffled up to us. When we asked him for General Ashuyev, he answered in perfect English.

"So, you are the Americans who want to meet with the general?" he asked.

"Yes," Carlos replied.

"I am Mr. Ruslan Khubiev—please follow me," he said and proceeded to take us down a corridor where the walls were covered with photos of military men. He took us to a room, where there were two desks and a map of the world on the wall. A few minutes later an older man came in. He greeted us in Russian and Mr. Khubiev made the introductions.

"This is Chief Leonid Biryukov. He was the head of telecommunications intelligence in Afghanistan from 1979 to 1989. He apologizes for General Ashuyev. The general had an emergency and will not be able to meet with you. The chief should be able to answer any questions you may have," he said.

Chief Biryukov pulled out a chair, sat down, and rolled a map of Afghanistan out on the table. I pulled out the poster with Fritz's photo and also gave Chief Biryukov a computerized photo that had been aged to show how Fritz might look today. Chief Biryukov picked it up, glanced at it, set it back down, and went back to his map. He spoke in Russian to Mr. Khubiev. As I listened to Chief Biryukov go on and on without, apparently, being concerned about our presence, I recalled Viktor telling us about the hard-line communist factions that still existed in his country. He said that these factions had been putting the democratic process in the new Soviet Union in jeopardy.

After a pause, Mr. Khubiev began to talk with us. He was translating some of what Chief Biryukov had said in Russian.

"During my time in Afghanistan, we had given strict orders to all parties involved to bring us any prisoners who were foreigners. This was a very strict rule. The Afghanistani commanders were well aware of it," Mr. Khubiev translated. Chief Biryukov continued.

"You see, I am sure that this man was not in any prison inside the Afghanistani territory, at least not a prison controlled by the Afghanistani government. If he was, I would have known," he said as he rose and then sat on the corner of the table.

"What if he was killed and not in prison?" I asked.

"Well, that would depend on where things took place. If he was inside of territory occupied by the mujahadin fighters, I wouldn't be aware of such an event. You see the war is over and still we have two hundred eighty Russian soldiers listed as prisoners of war or missing in action today. Also, some of our deserters were sent to the U.S. with your government's aid. They were sent to different cities. In Los Angeles alone there are a dozen or more of those," Mr. Khubiev translated. Chief Biryukov paused, looking for our reaction.

"What happened to us was a disaster. We were sold out. The present government created a joint commission to find out about American

POWs and MIAs from Vietnam, but they have done nothing about our own POWs and MIAs from Afghanistan." Mr. Khubiev tried to express his feelings with his translation but it wasn't necessary. It was very apparent from the look etched on Chief Biryukov's face exactly how he felt.

"Who else have you been working with here in Russia?" Chief Biryukov asked.

"We asked President Yeltsin for support and there's a group of human rights activists . . ."

"What people?" interrupted the chief, cutting me off. "The traitor? Yuzhin?" Mr. Khubiev and the chief looked at me and at Carlos in an accusatory way, while at the same time the chief grabbed for a red hardcover book, lifting it in the air and shaking it at us to punctuate his anger.

"I don't know if it is the same person . . . Boris Yuzhin?" I responded.

"That's the traitor! He should have been shot, not given fifteen years." He thrust the book in front of me. "Look here in the high treason list of traitors. Boris Yuzhin. Now going around trying to say that he is working for the human rights." Mr. Khubiev was very agitated as he translated while trying to show me the red book with Boris's name in it.

This meeting was taking the wrong direction. Chief Biryukov and Mr. Khubiev were hard-liners. They risked their lives fighting for their country. They believed in a greater Soviet Union. They felt the same loss Carlos did when the Portuguese government abandoned its African colonies in 1975 and left all of their people at the mercy of the communist guerrillas who had seized power. All their lives they were told that the right way was the political system they had in place, and now they were being told the opposite. All their families had fought for was lost. The "enemy" was right. Carlos had confided to me that it would give him pleasure to see the hard-line communists scrambling, trying to resurrect their own lost past. Carlos knew that devout communists never change, not even when threatened with death. During the guerrilla war in Portuguese Africa—Angola, Mozambique, and Portuguese Guinea— the hard-line communist guerrillas who had been captured by the Portuguese armed forces preferred to be killed than to reveal any information. They would be shot while shouting: "Life or death, the struggle will go on!"

Worried with Chief Biryukov and Mr. Khubiev's aggressive manner, due to our association with Boris, Carlos tried to direct the meeting back to Fritz's case.

"Were there any American prisoners in the Afghanistan jails during your ten years of war?" Carlos asked.

"No. No Americans. But there were two Frenchmen, one Englishman, and some Germans," said the chief through Mr. Khubiev.

"Some Germans," I jumped in, pointing to Fritz's poster. "Fritz was German."

This took him by surprise; he had assumed that Fritz was American because I was. I felt a sudden coldness from the chief. He refused to look at the poster of Fritz again and looked instead to Mr. Khubiev.

"No. No. I never saw anybody like him," Chief Biryukov said through his translator.

The meeting came to an abrupt end. The chief stood up and excused himself in Russian. Mr. Khubiev escorted us to the stairs and disappeared into one of the offices.

I could not believe that we came away with nothing. Who were the imprisoned Germans? I would contact the German ambassador.

It was apparent that the people we had just met were not receptive to any overtures on our part. As members of the Soviet armed forces and their intelligence services, including the GRU, they were patriots who fought hard to keep and expand their empire. The breakdown of the Soviet Union was not on their agenda. They would fight it any way they could. The new Russia would be run by those who would have the access to the military. The armed forces still had power. If the breakdown of political power continued, we would be facing a very dangerous situation here, especially due to the fragmentation of the empire into so many separate republics. This meeting had confirmed what we had been told by other sources, that there were other powerful forces to be wary of in the new Russian game.

Viktor was the one military person we met who was willing, in spite of his hard-line beliefs, to help us. The one person willing to put people before politics. He hadn't been able to collect more information for us since our last meeting, but he told us that if it was in the military files, it would be possible to find it.

The Soviet bear was deeply wounded . . . but not mortally.

48.

Spies

The snowplows cleared the roads slowly but steadily as the snow flurried down. Since our arrival on October 23, this was the worst weather yet. The mercury stayed below freezing for several days and I couldn't seem to stay warm no matter how many layers I wore. Even my wool coat felt flimsy, pierced by the chill from the river. It didn't help that the weather paralleled my mood, dismal, dark and gloomy. We were returning home soon, and so far no good news had surfaced. Time was disappearing and I was close to desperation.

Because he knew how little time we had, Carlos was working every day around the clock. He tried to find the one door that would open, the one person who had an answer, something. Carlos spent all of his time in the hotel business center, writing letters, sending faxes. He withdrew from me and became immersed in his own thoughts. The distance between us just increased my anxiety.

The Russians had continued their vigil in the hallway outside our room, even though the American officer had left. We went to great lengths not to say anything while we were in the room. If we did, we kept the television on, tuned to the constant chatter on CNN. And when we talked, we only discussed superficial matters. I felt oppressed, paranoid.

We always wondered who was listening, or following. Anyone, from a driver to a translator, was suspect. We knew that nothing happened by coincidence. The day before, we had a startling reminder of how closely we were being tracked.

That afternoon we arranged to have lunch with a former KGB colonel, one of the top men in the Russian embassy in Vietnam. He was refined, well dressed, had a Ph.D. in history and was an expert in Marxist-Leninist theories. He also spoke fluent French. Boris Yuzhin arranged for us to meet at a famous Moscow restaurant called Prague. The name sounded proprietary, taking on the name of a major city, going back to the days when this part of the world was a unit—the Eastern bloc.

Carlos and I agreed with Boris about the choice of the restaurant; it appeared to be secure. Prague was a large establishment, difficult to keep under surveillance. It was once one of the most prestigious places in Moscow, and still retained some of its old glamour, its association with the elite.

There was a line when we arrived and a doorman who decided who was suitable to deserve entry. As we walked in, I looked around at the damask curtains and gilded fixtures, the carved wood, high ceilings and chandeliers. And yet it all seemed a little tarnished, as if these were the last days of glory. As we were led to our table, I realized that the place was enormous: three floors of huge dining rooms. Perfect. It was hard for someone to listen in, to interrupt our meeting, or so I thought.

I was wrong. We discovered that we were shadowed by two young plainclothes agents. The KGB officer sitting with us recognized them, and became anxious and nervous. He just mentioned that he had seen cables regarding transportation of U.S. airplane parts captured by the North Vietnamese, parts that probably came from planes like the one Bruce Brown's father flew. He also told us that the parts were sent from the Soviet embassy in Hanoi to Moscow in the early Seventies. He had a lot to tell us, until he saw the agents. He clammed up. Carlos tried to alleviate the tension by speaking in French and diverting the conversation to personal matters. The colonel smiled here and there, but didn't say much more. He was afraid—terrified in fact. His hand trembled so badly that he couldn't hold his cigarette. He was so distracted that we finished the meal quickly and left.

Every move we made from this point on was crucial. We had to take advantage of every minute. Carlos wanted answers. We needed to arrange the press conference we discussed with Borovoi to announce our joint program, our effort to discover Americans held in the former Soviet Union against their will.

Carlos, Bruce, and I arrived at Borovoi's office and were whisked into a conference room immediately. Borovoi's assistant followed us in and we sat down. At the last minute, Susan and Boris had decided not to come.

The assistant started the meeting. "I am sorry but the person who was going to meet with you today couldn't make it," he apologized. "But, Boris—the man from the ARK Project—he has been speaking with us. We'll be in touch with him soon," he said.

This was news. Boris hadn't even mentioned that he'd been speaking with Borovoi's people. No wonder he'd canceled out on the meeting today. I could see the expression on Carlos's face change as he heard the news. He was furious.

"Listen to me," Carlos fumed at the assistant. "We flew thousands of miles, and spent many hours of our time on this project," he sputtered. "I warned Mr. Borovoi not to drop out like Ross Perot."

"Please understand"—the assistant tried to placate him—"Mr. Borovoi is out of town and we are willing to help . . ."

Carlos interrupted him. "Listen, we are leaving in two days; we have to put together a press conference in twenty-four hours. Are you willing to help with that?"

The assistant didn't answer at first. Then he started making excuses. If only Carlos would understand, he said, they would deal with Boris and continue talking with us through him. Boris had been talking with Borovoi behind our back, ruining our opportunity for a press conference, one of our last chances to publicize Fritz's case. Carlos didn't like to be misled, lied to. He didn't want to work with Boris Yuzhin any longer. Boris had double-talked him. We had been left out of the deal with Borovoi.

Carlos got up to leave. Bruce Brown and I followed. The assistant didn't know what to say or do, but simply accompanied us while uttering apologies, still unfailingly polite. As we were walking out, Carlos threw back over his shoulder, "Tell Mr. Borovoi that I'll make sure people in America know that he promises but doesn't deliver."

We returned to our car. As we drove away from Borovoi's office, Carlos took out his five-page plan, the program to help Americans who had disappeared in Russia. He intended to give it to Borovoi, to introduce it at the press conference. He stared at it for a moment, then tore it apart.

"Fuck these bastards! They want our money, they want our help, but they play games . . ." Carlos ranted. He had been betrayed in Africa by the same types of characters. They make promises but later they drop you as if nothing ever happened. As far as Carlos was concerned, Borovoi's people were flakes, just like Perot—talk, talk, talk and very little action.

The driver looked to the backseat as Carlos continued to curse. We found out later that he was part of the foreign ministry's intelligence service. We returned to the hotel to have lunch. As we stopped at the reception desk, the clerk handed us a message. The Russian Intelligence Services, Russia's new secret service, called. They had news. They would see us at 4:00 p.m.

As we ate our appetizer, we thought through what happened at Borovoi's. We didn't want Boris to think he succeeded in upsetting our plans, so instead of changing things, we decided to go ahead with the press conference. It was scheduled for 10:00 a.m. on November 6 at the Radisson-Slavjanskaya Hotel, and would take place as planned.

Even after we made our decision, Carlos was still upset. He felt that he should have known better. As I listened to him berate himself, it seemed like the idea of having a press conference was just making the situation worse.

"You know, our meeting with the people at Russian Intelligence may change everything; we might find out something. Why don't we wait until the last day of our trip to hold a conference?" I asked.

Carlos put down his soupspoon and started speaking tersely in a low voice. "Stop that shit. It's your fault—you married Fritz Stammberger, I didn't."

I couldn't believe what he was saying. It was too late for petty accusations. I had no reply to his verbal assault. I got up and said I would be in the room.

49.

Russian Intelligence

Moscow
November 3, 1992

C arlos had not said a word to me since his outburst. I felt his eyes
on me from across the room. We were tense. The stress of
having only four days left, the fact that there were no results
from the feature article in the *Moscow Times* or from my interview on
Radio Russia, and the waiting for our meeting with the Russian
Intelligence Services all increased the strain on our relationship. The
energy that had been good had gone bad, and with equal intensity. It was
almost as if our love fed the animosity between us. Someone once told
me that the opposite of love was not hate, that they were the same
thing—strong, inescapable. No, the opposite of love was indifference.

From my hotel room, I stared out the window at the Kiev train station
across the street. People sat on the stairs—teenagers loafing, middle-
aged women returning home laden with bags, a coarsely dressed man,
and one who looked too slick to trust.

In less than half an hour we would have to leave for our meeting at
the Russian Intelligence Services. It was hard for me to anticipate what
they might say, what they might reveal about Fritz's destiny. In the past,
I tried to discuss with Carlos what might happen if we were able to
retrieve Fritz alive. He always tended to evade the question, even the
thought of it. I felt that whatever would happen was meant to be. I knew
that there were major problems behind such a "happy ending." The
drama of this possibility—having two husbands alive—would sometimes make us laugh. I don't know if it was because it made us nervous,

or because sometimes tragedy matched comedy. All those years, the thought of a phone call from Fritz, of him knocking at our door, never left my mind. According to Jim MacGeyver, Fritz was imprisoned in Chitral. He could have been shipped to Russia; he could be here. MacGeyver had heard that Fritz was alive as late as October 1982.

"What's on your mind?" Carlos broke into my thoughts abruptly. "You look like you're off in space." His voice was rough.

"I was thinking about—about, well . . . what if Fritz is alive? What if they tell us that?"

Carlos just stared at me. "We'll deal with it when we have to," he said. "Look, we've talked about it a thousand times." We had.

Carlos was a planner, always thinking ahead. The meeting with the intelligence services—he had to have thought of what that might mean.

"You don't really think we're going to find him alive, do you?" he said sarcastically.

"If you don't think he might be alive, then why the hell are we here?" I asked. "If you're so sure he's a corpse, why bother?"

"Why?" he asked. "Why? Because that's the only way to get this thing out of your head. Look at you, staring out of windows, daydreaming. You're not here with me. You never were."

I couldn't believe he said that, meant that. He felt alone . . . the one thing I never wanted Carlos to feel was that kind of abandonment. I loved him. It was a different kind of love from the love I had for Fritz. I always thought Carlos knew that, that he was secure in my love for him, in our relationship. . . .

"Carlos, please," I said.

"I don't want to hear it. No more. We'll know what's what soon enough," Carlos replied.

I kept silent.

In my fantasy, I was somehow always able to reconcile my present life with my past one, to envision living—somehow—with both men in my life. But I had never seemed to work out the details, the logistics.

Carlos and I worked so differently. I was amazed at how well he planned our strategy. Whenever he faced a problem, he broke it down into parts. When it came to Fritz, he'd said: "Let's approach the situation step by step: first, find him; second, bring him out; and third, deal with the repercussions." But we had to talk now. The repercussions were upon us.

I tried again, "Carlos, don't you think—"

"No!" he cut me off again, more vehemently this time. "I don't want to talk about it! When we get there, we'll see."

I couldn't deal with this. I hadn't thought this through, that wasn't my way. I only saw the end of things, the resolution, nothing before or after. I saw only the joy, the happiness—rescuing Fritz. I'd never thought about the hard questions. If Carlos and I found Fritz, what would happen? Could I be friends with one and lovers with the other? Would I stay married to Carlos? Would I go back to Fritz?

Fritz would have been through a lot . . . he would be changed, aged. And I declared him dead. Or he might have another life. He might not even want to see me. . . .

No, it was easier to do this Carlos's way. We would wait until the search was over, and then deal with what we found.

* * *

We pulled into a parking space across the street. Maneuvering into it was tricky; the curbs were lined with Volgas, and traffic was fairly brisk. Unlike the grandeur of Red Square and its ambiance created by people with the leisure to stroll about and take in sights, this place was defined by business, movement. We were in a hub of activity.

The building was rather unassuming. It hardly looked like an office building, it was kept up so poorly. The pale blue clapboard walls contrasted with the fat stripe of a royal blue concrete foundation that rose several feet out of the wet sidewalk. The sidewalk, the street, everything was slick with melted snow and a smattering of light rain. The weather was stuck somewhere between autumn and winter and the streets were permanently covered with a thin layer of water, just enough to freeze at night when the temperature dropped. It made getting around hazardous.

We waited for a lull in traffic so that we could cross the street. As we watched, two rough-looking men in leather jackets arrived in front of the pale blue building and disappeared inside. They were casually holding packages wrapped in newspaper. Agents or delivery boys. Maybe both, I thought. We dodged across the street.

The doorway did not seem like the entrance to a high-security establishment. It was more like the door of an apartment building, gentrified with cement moldings that mimicked Roman archways. It reminded me of buildings I saw in Portugal. Carlos's family lived there now. At first he didn't want to go there. He felt that the Portuguese government had abandoned him in Africa, left him to his fate. However, as time went by, he softened. He took me to visit his family a few times. When I heard people speaking Russian, it sounded almost like Portuguese to me. By the time this trip came to an end, Carlos and I would have traveled nearly around the globe together. A landmark of sorts. I looked at him; I was glad he was with me.

As we entered the building, we were led through a series of doorways. The security precautions seemed especially rigorous, until the initial formalities ended. Once we reached the hallways, the security measures relaxed. There weren't even any guards—uniformed or plainclothes. Most of the hallways were empty, and some of the offices looked vacant. A shell of what it must have been before. Finally, we reached the office of Agent Labusov.

We were seated in thinly padded, square red chairs that looked modern and spare. They contrasted with the room: high ceilings, a large, tall window with panes draped with white lace curtains. An antique cabinet with beveled glass panels stood behind a modern light wood desk that seemed to go with the red chairs. Carlos remained standing. He was too tense to sit. To the side of the desk, a long hallway stretched back toward what appeared to be a suite of offices. As I stared down the hall, a good-looking man with blond hair came out of a side office and walked toward us. It was Agent Labusov. He seemed almost nondescript as he approached. His hair and his features could fit into any role—a bureaucrat, a worker, a Russian, a European, an American. I could almost picture him in the Midwest as a college professor or a farmer. The only feature that disrupted this malleability were his eyes. They were like a wolf's eyes—clear, blue, elusive. They seemed to go back forever and ever, revealing nothing. Perfect for a shape-changer.

We stood and introduced ourselves. He started with a formal response, addressing us in English. I braced to hear the news.

"We have no information on your former husband," he said. The words reverberated in my head.

"No information?" I questioned. If they didn't have any information on Fritz, then he couldn't have worked with them.

"No. No information," he assured me shaking his head. "We checked all our records and there was nothing, nothing at all."

"He wasn't employed by you—I mean, by your agency?" I asked. I had to be sure.

"That's correct," he replied shortly.

So Fritz was not a KGB agent. I was stunned and I was relieved.

"Don't believe anyone if they tell you one day that I am a Russian spy," Fritz had said. He was telling me the truth. He was not a Russian spy.

Agent Labusov was still looking at me. He meant for this to be a short meeting, informal and brief. But now that he finished the official response, he appeared relieved, helpful even.

"I was told that he was traveling alone, wasn't he?" the agent inquired.

"Yes," I replied hesitantly. They had no records on him, but the agent knew the details of Fritz's case. That was unsettling.

"Well, that makes it more difficult to find out what happened to him," he said gently, shrugging.

"Is there anywhere else I can look?" I asked. "Have you checked everything?"

He shook his head. "Only our records, the former KGB records—you could still look in other places, the Ministry of Defense," he suggested.

Military intelligence, once again, I thought. And we hadn't heard from Viktor in several days. He was the direct link to the military records.

I thanked Agent Labusov for his time and for his agency's help. Carlos shook the man's hand without saying a word. The KGB had been

Carlos's main enemy throughout his African ordeal. He believed that regardless of the drastic changes taking place in Russia, the KGB was still the KGB. It just had a new face, and a different building. Decades had to pass before any real change took place, he said to me on our drive over.

As we left the building, I felt depleted, emptied. I expected that they would have been able to tell me what happened to Fritz.

If Fritz was not a KGB spy, then what was he?

50.

The General

Moscow
November 4, 1992

I t was about 10:00 a.m. on November 4, 1992. We were up all night at the hotel's U.S. presidential election party. It was filled with Americans living or vacationing in Moscow. We met the correspondent of the *Washington Times*, Gerald Nader, and his wife. Bruce Brown came as well. We stayed up listening to the votes being tallied. We rooted for Bill Clinton. A new president, a new start. So it was a tiring evening, but a rewarding one once the results were confirmed.

We just returned to our hotel room at the break of dawn, when the call came. It was from the Ministry of Security. President Yeltsin's office arranged for us to meet with General Dmitry Volkogonov, the man in charge of the presidential and the KGB files. The presidential files were the most secret documents in the country, only accessible by the president, the vice-president, and the general. He was also an adviser to President Yeltsin. Since Yeltsin was unable to meet with us personally, he provided one of his top men to assist with the case. The meeting was set for 4:00 p.m. at the Ministry of Security in downtown Moscow. Our determination and tenacity were paying off. Also we were privileged to have the opportunity to meet a Russian source with direct access to President Yeltsin's inner circle.

Carlos and I were excited, even though there was an underlying fear or dread. We tried to go back to sleep, but it was difficult. General Volkogonov held the key to the secrets of the Soviet Union. We were hours away from knowing the truth.

Just as we began to nod off, there was another phone call. The embassy of the People's Republic of China. The spokesperson had said that the ambassador would do whatever he could to initiate an investigation into Fritz's disappearance. All this goodwill so soon after the election. Clinton was good news. During the past ten days in Russia, we'd had few results. Now embassies and officials were calling us instead of our having to negotiate with their guards in hopes of getting a response.

The winds of history were changing. Bill Clinton's victory unsettled the international leadership. A democrat in the White House would focus on human rights, on people instead of business conglomerates.

And perhaps General Volkogonov would be more open to change, more open to helping us instead of playing political games. After all, he had released documents clearing the name of one of the most infamous men in recent history: State Department attorney Alger Hiss. Volkogonov had let the Western press representatives know that Hiss had not been a Russian spy, even though he had been convicted for it. Later Volkogonov also released information related to the massacre of Polish nationals during Russia's occupation of Poland. He seemed like a man who might have a soft spot for human rights, even though we knew that he was a leader of the Soviet Union's propaganda machine for years. I had mixed feelings about the man.

* * *

We arrived at the general's fourth-floor office, consisting of a suite of rooms rather than a single office, and were escorted to one of the conference rooms on the left. The walls were paneled in wood, and the table was long—solid and polished. Aside from a large flag, there wasn't much else there.

As we entered, Mr. Sergei, a man in his forties, greeted us in Russian. He introduced himself as an assistant to the general. An intelligence officer. He seated us along one side of the table and sat down opposite us.

Since General Volkogonov also headed the Russian task force on POWs and MIAs, Bruce Brown came with us to the meeting. He sat down beside me. Off to the side, a pitcher and some glasses were set on the table. After offering us some water, Mr. Sergei started talking to our translator. He said that President Yeltsin's office sent him my request for information on Fritz and Lieutenant Colonel Brown; in front of him was my letter. Across the top of it was a small red tag labeled "Urgent" in Russian. But first, Mr. Sergei discussed Bruce's father.

He explained that they hadn't found anything on Lieutenant Colonel Robert "Mack" Brown. He implied that some of the information he had seen in our documents seemed inaccurate, such as the reports that there were transfers of U.S. F-111 parts and planes from Vietnam to the Soviet Union. He denied that there had been technological espionage by the Soviet Union. It seemed unlikely that his office could help with Colonel Brown's case, but he would try.

I looked at Mr. Sergei and wondered. He was taking his time, being very polite, but I knew that I had collected fairly reliable information which didn't match what he was saying. And there was the report we received from Radio Russia, the account of F-111 designs being used by the Soviet government. We also knew that Russian intelligence officers interrogated POWs in Vietnam. General Oleg Kalugan of the KGB had testified to the U.S. Senate's committee on POWs and MIAs; he revealed that, yes, the KGB had interrogated U.S. prisoners during the Vietnam War. "A handful, maybe ten," he said, but nevertheless, it had been done. Also, that living American POWs were left, after 1973, in Southeast Asia.

Bruce Brown just sat there quietly listening to Mr. Sergei. I could feel his disappointment. He had already met with Colonel Pusey of the U.S. task force and other U.S. military intelligence officers at the American embassy, and he hadn't found out anything more. When Bruce described his encounters with various intelligence sources to me, it sounded as though Bruce had done most of the talking. Somehow, he ended up answering more questions than he asked. All they did was collect information from Bruce. That's one of the things I learned through my searches. Intelligence agents rarely disclose anything of value or anything that can help. To them, information is power, and they aren't going to give out any of it.

Millions of dollars went to fund intelligence projects—from satellites to operatives in the field. The agencies simply accumulated massive amounts of data, most of which they never managed to analyze. If they did process it, they rarely took action. The reports sat on a bureaucrat's desk until they were filed away. It was odd to speak with intelligence sources from different countries and realize how, basically, they were all the same. They thought they were more important, more worldly, just because they had access to information. In spite of its arrogance, its self-importance, the U.S. intelligence community hadn't been able to stop the fall of either South Vietnam or the Shah of Iran. And communism succeeded in the takeover of Cuba by Fidel Castro, the takeover of Nicaragua by the Sandinistas, the takeover of Angola by the MPLA, the takeover of Mozambique by the communist Frelimo, and on and on. On the other side, Soviet intelligence services, including the KGB and the GRU, were unable to prevent the fall of the Soviet empire.

Mr. Sergei finished by explaining that, with regard to Fritz's case, the information we were looking for could be in the military files. Mr. Sergei suggested that we let General Volkogonov go over our information, and indicated that we should move to the other conference room. The general was waiting.

An elderly man stood as we entered. His appearance seemed anything but threatening. He was wearing a pin-striped suit with a pin of the Russian Federation flag on his lapel. General Dmitry Volkogonov could be anybody's grandfather. Cordially, he shook my hand, then Carlos's and Bruce Brown's. The general's eyes crinkled under bushy, "mad-scientist" eyebrows. He had a small turned-up nose and a reddened complexion. He had a mischievous look about him. His eyes were alive; he took everything in. In addition to being an adviser to President Yeltsin and head of the KGB archives, General Volkogonov was also a scholar, a member of the Russian Academy of Sciences, a published writer, Stalin's biographer, and one of the main Soviet propagandists during the Cold War era. A master of misinformation.

The general beamed at Bruce and said that he looked like his father. A chill ran down my spine. I couldn't help but think that the general must have once sat across the table from Bruce Brown's father, just as he sat across from Bruce now. Bruce grinned back. The general said that he knew about Bruce's case and that he would do whatever he could to help. He understood Bruce's plight because his own father had disappeared during a war. As for my case, he said, "I will see what I can do."

"Aren't there any files on Fritz in the archives?" I asked.

General Volkogonov cleared his throat, and glanced at the translator. "I am sorry to have to disappoint you," he said through the translator, "but . . . ," here the general paused and looked at me, "so far I have been unable to find anything about Fritz Stammberger in the presidential files." He went on to explain what Viktor had told us when we first arrived. There were three major networks of information in the Soviet Union: the presidential files, the KGB files, and the military intelligence files. All told, he confided, there were close to seventeen thousand different locations with government archives located throughout the former Soviet Union's territories. When it came to military intelligence, though, it would be more difficult for him to help us.

Susan and Boris already discussed with us how unwilling the military leaders were to open their files to the West. Power in the Soviet Union was scattered. There was so much infighting—one office against another, agency against agency—the balance of control was always shifting.

The general inquired, "He was German, yes?"

"Yes," I said.

"This makes it more difficult," he said shaking his head. "All files that involved foreign people were coded by the KGB. The folders were marked by a secret code. Often, only one letter is used to identify the prisoner and there is rarely any way to trace the person." He stopped.

"General, could you tell me just one thing . . . could Fritz be in prison here in Russia?"

The general was silent for a moment.

"When we entered Afghanistan in 1979, we asked the Afghanistani government to inform us of any foreign prisoners in their prison system. So, to answer your question, if Fritz was in jail inside Afghanistan in territory controlled by the government, and was transported to the Soviet

Union, I will be able to track him down. Be patient," the general advised.

As the meeting ended, he promised to get back to me as soon as possible. He told me that he would be going to Washington, D.C., on November 10th to testify to the Select Committee on POW/MIA Affairs. Even though I knew that the general was a propagandist, I somehow liked him, his gentle manner. We left the building through a private elevator and headed back to the hotel.

51.

Human Rights

Moscow
November 6, 1992

As scheduled, we held our press conference on November 6 at 10:00 a. m. In spite of Borovoi's defection from our cause, we managed to obtain a panel of experts on the issue of human rights and Americans held against their will in the former Soviet Union territories. Susan and Boris came, and brought none other than Leonid Abramkin, the director of the Gulag prisoner network. They had also arranged for Dr. Emile Gushansky, vice-president of the Independent Psychiatric Association in the former Soviet Union, to participate. According to Susan, up to fifteen thousand "special prisoners" remained hidden away in psychiatric hospitals by the KGB, and worldwide there were at least three hundred thousand people jailed without having even been charged.

To focus attention on the personal human aspect of the issue, we placed displays around the hotel conference room with enlarged photographs and news stories of American servicemen who had disappeared, men who were believed to have been transported to the Soviet Union. Often, politics can overshadow the basic issue of human rights. We wanted the press to see these men as individuals, with families and hobbies and homes. We chose a few select cases, but it was still daunting to see how many of the grainy reproductions circled the room. I watched the reporters and photographers mill about as they entered, glancing at the displays. The room filled up quickly.

Fritz's and Colonel Brown's pictures were placed in front, next to a table decorated in swathes of blue fabric. Behind it was a makeshift backdrop, a folding wall, with panels which opened like a handmade fan. It was time to get started. We and the other guests seated ourselves and waited for the room to settle down.

All my life I had been very private about personal matters, personal concerns, but now I was going to let it all out. I wanted to share my ordeal, my experiences, and to help others who found themselves in similar situations, to help the families of all those men missing in action. The nature of our press release had appealed to the news desks. As I looked around the room, I saw that all three networks came—ABC, CBS, and NBC—as well as many journalists and news service correspondents.

I opened the press conference by thanking President Yeltsin and General Volkogonov for their assistance with respect to Fritz's case; then I pleaded with President Clinton and President Yeltsin to improve cooperation between the two countries on human rights issues, such as the treatment of prisoners. I brought up the fact that there had been minimal cooperation from Russian officials because they feared future retribution if a different administration took over in Russia. I also asked President Clinton to pass legislation that would create less stringent rules for the declassification of government documents in the United States.

After addressing these concerns, I introduced our panel of guests. Susan started by explaining difficulties that she had encountered while trying to verify sightings of Americans in remote parts of the former U.S.S.R. She mentioned that sections of the archives that she needed to check would suddenly catch fire a day or two before she arrived. She also described how recently, an informant was beaten and threatened with severe punishment if he assisted her or Boris any further in the search for American POWs in the Soviet prison system.

As Dr. Emile Gushansky, a middle-aged man, listened to Susan speak, he rubbed his forehead. The circles around his eyes showed how much misery he had seen, how many injustices had been committed. Only now was he able to let the world know; all those years of silence. With the help of a translator, after Susan had finished speaking, the

240

Bel Air Hotel. April 20, 1984. Carlos and I at our wedding.

Encino, California. New Year's Eve, 1987.

Los Angeles. April 20, 1992.

Carlos and I celebrating our eighth wedding anniversary.

Written response from Senators John Kerry and Bob Smith, chairman and vice-chairman, respectively, of the Select Committee on POW/MIA Affairs.

Once again, a typical format letter saying no. Even if Fritz had been considered a POW/MIA, the response would probably have been similar. Our guest, Bruce Brown, whose father was Lieutenant Colonel Robert "Mack" Brown, a USAF-111 fighter pilot who disappeared in Vietnam on November 7, 1972, had been stonewalled over the years regarding his father's case, even though Colonel Brown was a highly decorated officer and had been a scientist in the Mercury and Gemini space programs.

JOHN F. KERRY, MASSACHUSETTS,
Chairman
THOMAS A. DASCHLE, SOUTH DAKOTA
HARRY REID, NEVADA
CHARLES S. ROBB, VIRGINIA
J. ROBERT KERREY, NEBRASKA
HERBERT H. KOHL, WISCONSIN

BOB SMITH, NEW HAMPSHIRE,
Vice Chairman
JOHN McCAIN, ARIZONA
HANK BROWN, COLORADO
CHUCK GRASSLEY, IOWA
NANCY LANDON KASSEBAUM, KANSAS
JESSE HELMS, NORTH CAROLINA

FRANCES A. ZWENIG, STAFF DIRECTOR
DINO CARLUCCIO, DEPUTY STAFF DIRECTOR
J. WILLIAM CODINHA, GENERAL COUNSEL

United States Senate

SELECT COMMITTEE ON POW/MIA AFFAIRS
WASHINGTON, DC 20510-6500

March 5, 1992

Carlos de Abreu

Dear Mr. de Abreu:

Thank you for your letter and packet of information on Fritz Ludwig Stammberger's disappearance in Pakistan in 1975.

Regrettably, the Select Committee's authority only extends to missing American servicemen, and we are unable to look into the disappearance of Ms. Pennington's husband.

Last November, Congress passed, and the President signed, a law giving families more access to information about their POW/MIAs. The Committee is pressing for further declassification of documents and we hope that this work will usher in more openess on the part of the Defense Department, CIA and other agencies.

Please convey our best wishes to Ms. Pennington in her search and our high regard for her continuing efforts to learn the fate of her husband.

Sincerely,

Bob Smith
Vice Chairman

John F. Kerry
Chairman

/dd

PRINTED ON RECYCLED PAPER

Above: At Salt Lake City Airport on my way to Billings, Montana, to meet Jerry Mooney.

Above: Jerry Mooney, former cryptanalyst for the National Security Agency. *Right:* John M. G. Brown, author of *Moscow Bound*, historian, and researcher.

Red Square

The Kremlin

Moscow. October 1992. In front of the tomb of the unknown soldier and the Kremlin wall during our trip to Russia to search for Fritz.

Moscow. October 1992.
Entering the residence of
Pakistani ambassador
Ashraf Qazi.

Delivering a package to the German embassy in Moscow.

Moscow. October 1992. At the back door of the Kremlin delivering a letter to President Yeltsin.

Right: Delivering another letter to former prime minister Gaidar.

October 1992. Feature article about my quest in the *Moscow Times*.

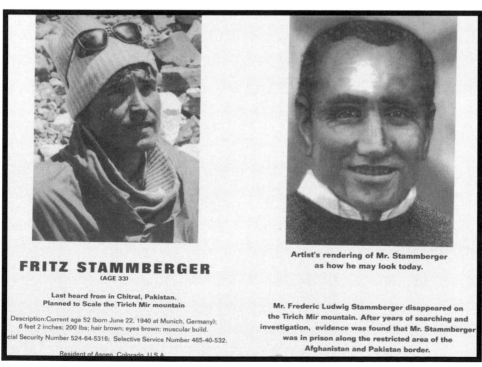

Poster distributed in Russia showing how Fritz looked in 1975 and how he might look today.

Moscow. October 1992. At Konstantin Borovoi's office. One of the richest men in Russia and chairman of the Moscow Stock Exchange, he offers financial rewards to anyone who reports the whereabouts of Americans held in the territories of the former Soviet Union against their will.

Above: Carlos telling Borovoi not to back out on him as Ross Perot did during the 1992 U.S. presidential elections. *Left:* Borovoi and I. *Below:* Shaking hands on a joint program to help find POWs and MIAs.

Moscow. November 1992. Left to right: Former KGB colonel Boris Yuzhin, our guest Bruce Brown, me, and former KGB officer Alexander Chermensky.

At the offices of the Committee on Afghanistan Combatants. Left to right: Ruslan Khubiev, me, and Chief Leonid Biryukov. Biryukov was in charge of telecommunications and intelligence on foreign prisoners in Afghanistan until 1989.

Moscow. October 1992. *Left:*
Inside the American embassy
with a U.S. intelligence officer.

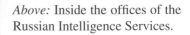

Above: Inside the offices of the
Russian Intelligence Services.

Left: Waiting at the front door
of KGB headquarters.

Moscow. November 1992. At the Ministry of Security with General Dmitry Volkogonov, adviser to President Yeltsin and head of the presidential and KGB files.

Moscow. November 1992. Inside the offices of the Russian Intelligence
Services, discussing Fritz's case. The RIS is the new Russian intelligence
agency that took over the KGB's functions.

Russian intelligence agent Labusov
informing me of his findings with respect
to the whereabouts of Fritz.

Moscow. November 6, 1992. At our press conference discussing the joint efforts between the U.S. and Russia to find American POWs and MIAs in the Soviet territories.

Left to right: Bruce Brown, me, Susan Mesinai, former KGB colonel Boris Yuzhin, doctor Emile Gushansky, vice-president of the Independent Psychiatric Association in the former Soviet Union, and Valery Abramkin, director of the Gulag prisoner network.

Right: Susan Mesinai, director of the ARK Project. In 1992, her human rights organization was able to discover a U.S. National Security Agency defector, Victor Hamilton, who had been imprisoned for 30 years in a psychiatric institution located 20 miles from Moscow.

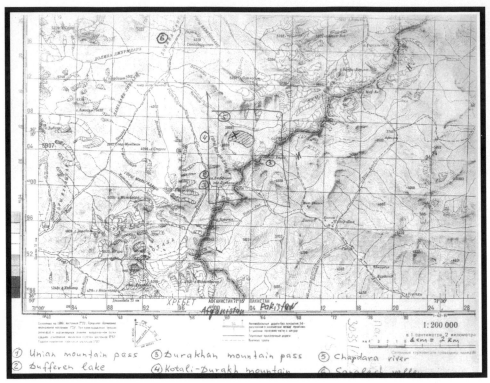

Soviet military intelligence map of the restricted area at the borders of Afghanistan and Pakistan, provided by Viktor.

Blow-up of area inside Afghanistan territory two miles from the Pakistan border.

Los Angeles. June 1993. Celebrating our 4,265th show. Bob Barker and I taped the pilot of *The Price Is Right* in September 1971.

Left: Celebrating the beginning of our 22nd consecutive year together on the show. From left to right: Kathleen Bradley, Holly Hallstrom, Bob Barker, me, and Rod Roddy.

doctor began to explain how the psychiatric institutions functioned in Russia and how, up until a month before, the intelligence services had used them to punish political prisoners. He said that it was close to impossible to trace those same prisoners because of the special coding systems used. He concluded by expressing great concern regarding the continuous lack of human rights that still persisted in the psychiatric institutions.

When he finished, Leonid Abramkin, who had been a Gulag prisoner for fifteen years himself, confirmed Susan's and Dr. Gushansky's revelations that there were foreigners still in the Soviet prison system; then he let Boris speak. Boris started by condemning the government's intimidation of potential witnesses and informers who provided leads concerning missing Americans in the Soviet Union territories. In fact, he said, as recently as three years before there were up to ten Americans from Vietnam still alive in the Soviet prison system.

The journalists started scribbling notes furiously. This was a news bomb waiting to explode. Vietnam vets marooned in Russia. Boris came through. Whatever deals he was negotiating with Borovoi, it looked like they were to aid in the search for live Americans. Boris was on our side.

The Associated Press correspondent interrupted Boris and asked him to confirm the information.

"You're saying that there are American POWs from the Vietnam War held in Russian jails?"

"That's right," Boris replied. The reporters became agitated; they all wanted to ask questions. The ABC reporter jumped in.

"Could you tell us where they are?"

"For obvious reasons, it wouldn't be advisable to release such information. I'm sorry," Boris answered apologetically. The press corps' curiosity refused to abate. They wanted to know where these Americans were imprisoned. Another reporter pounded Boris with questions, asking for locations, addresses. Boris didn't break. He knew how to handle pressure. As a former KGB colonel and a prisoner in the Gulag for five years, he had developed mental devices that wouldn't allow anyone or anything to penetrate his defensive wall. Susan had told us how dangerous it was to release information. It could jeopardize the

241

safety of those prisoners. At the very least, they could be transported to another location, but more likely, they would be eliminated. There was a "policy of denial" being pursued by some of those in power in Moscow. Despite their pledge to cooperate in the search for Americans being kept against their will, they refused to release meaningful information on the fate of those missing.

Boris told the press that he would gladly speak with them after the press conference, and he introduced Bruce Brown. Bruce presented a five-point program to help the joint task force to find POWs and MIAs. Then he opened the conference to questions.

The ABC correspondent asked me, "Janice, did the CIA ever ask you or force you to stop searching for Fritz?"

"Yes, they asked me to drop my request for information because of national security reasons," I replied to the reporter.

He asked once again, "Did they threaten you?"

"I think I answered your question . . . any other questions?"

Another reporter asked Boris for more details regarding the physical threats to informers. As Boris started to answer, I spotted Carlos by the door; he was signaling for me to get up and go to him. I tried to communicate with a gesture that this was not the best time to leave, but he kept motioning insistently, to no avail. There was no way for me to leave graciously without creating a stir. I waited for the question period to end and then I hurriedly got up. Carlos was distraught. As he spoke, he took my arm and led me through the crowd of journalists.

"Why—?" I started to ask.

"Shh," he whispered in my ear, "we have to go. I just spoke with Viktor. He's at the Peking restaurant and he has major news, something really important."

I wasn't feeling well. The stress of the press conference, together with the expectancy of finding out what Viktor had to reveal, was too much for me to handle. The pressure was unbearable.

What news did Viktor have? What did he discover? Perhaps what MacGeyver told me was true, that Fritz was in a high-security prison in the Chitral area. If he was alive, what would he have thought all these years? Would he think that he was forgotten? That he was betrayed?

What would he think about me remarrying? I always knew that I should have gone to Pakistan, regardless of the circumstances, regardless of what anybody told me. By not doing so, I suffered from guilt all these years. I had already paid a price, but soon I would know how much higher that price would be. Only with the final piece of the puzzle would the love triangle be broken, and I would be set free.

Choices. Everything in life came down to choices.

52.

The File

G olden monkeys and dragons were carved on the door of Peking restaurant. As we passed between the large columns framing the entrance, a doorman ushered us in. "Welcome," he said. "Would you like to enjoy the ruble or the hard currency dining room?" He explained: "You may pay with dollars on the hard currency side."

"The ruble room is fine," I answered. Those were Viktor's instructions.

Unlike Prague restaurant, this place was close to empty. The tables were placed in rows like a dining car on a train. The spare arrangement served to emphasize how large the room was; its immense ceilings made the place look palatial. As we were led to a table, we looked around for Viktor; he wasn't anywhere to be seen. The hostess seated us and handed us the menus. "We need a few minutes," Carlos said to her. She understood and left.

I scanned the choices without much appetite. I wasn't hungry. My stomach was all nerves. I felt like a ball of string being batted about by a kitten. Skittish. Carlos glanced around restlessly to see if Viktor had arrived.

"I'm going to go to the hard currency side of the restaurant to see if he's there," Carlos said.

A few minutes later he returned.

"I didn't see him." He stood still for a few seconds, not quite ready to sit down.

"It's possible that he's waiting for us somewhere else," he said.

"Wait here and don't go anywhere." He walked off again. I saw him disappear in the direction of the restroom.

I toyed nervously with the edge of my menu, then opened it and studied it some more.

Carlos walked into the restroom and looked around. He noticed someone in the next stall. Carlos washed his hands. The restroom door opened. An older man entered, relieved himself, and left. The door to the stall gradually opened; Viktor appeared. He pulled a manila envelope from his overcoat and handed it to Carlos. "According to our military files, Fritz is dead. He died fighting for the mujahadin," Viktor quietly related. He cautiously explained what had happened to Fritz. Then they left the restroom and came to the table. Carlos looked ashen.

"I have something for you, Janice," Viktor said as he sat down. Seeming ill at ease, he handed me a white brocade box covered with silver embroidery. It had a small gold clasp. I opened it carefully. It was a religious icon. Inside were pictures of Mary and Jesus.

"To help you in difficult times," he said with his thick Russian accent. He became a Christian after the breakup of his country. I thanked him.

"I'm sorry, but I can't stay for lunch," he said, excusing himself as he stood, but I wish you luck."

As we watched him walk away, I asked Carlos, "What happened? Where did you find him?"

"He found out," Carlos replied. "I'd rather tell you on the way to the hotel. Let's go."

We got up to leave, and Carlos pulled out a wad of rubles, leaving them on the table to cover the bill. He held my coat for me while I put it on. As we made our way toward the door, he reached for my hand.

We stepped outside. It was windy. The gray sky had covered over the sun and a light drizzle was falling. I watched the trails of exhaust streaming out behind the cars as they disappeared down the street. Carlos hailed a taxi.

I stared at it while it made a U-turn and pulled around in front of us. I was worried.

The cab was at the curb. We got in and Carlos gave the driver directions to our hotel. He made a left turn onto the main road. As we drove away, I looked out the window and watched the Peking restaurant vanish, replaced by washed-out buildings.

"Carlos," I asked again, "what happened?" I could not read his eyes.

He looked at me, touched his hand to my face.

"Janice," he said in a strained voice, "Fritz is dead."

"Dead . . . ," I uttered, ". . . how?"

"He was recruited by the CIA in 1974. He collected information . . . he helped organize bases in Afghanistan and Pakistan."

"But, how . . . how did he die?" I asked hoarsely.

Carlos took both my hands in his, pressed them tightly.

"He was involved in the mujahadin struggle against the Soviet Union, Janice. . . . He died in the early Eighties, inside Afghanistan," Carlos whispered.

"My God, he was alive all those years!" I said. Nellie Hendricks's psychic readings. Mike Hillman's phone call. Bob Peloquin's decision to end his search. Jim MacGeyver's call from Pakistan in 1982 saying that Fritz was alive. The CIA's refusal to release documents on Fritz and their request for me to drop my appeal. Now it all made sense. I felt hot and cold at the same time. I wanted to cry, but I couldn't.

"Viktor gave us a military map showing where Fritz's remains are buried. It's about two miles from the Pakistani border, inside Afghanistan," Carlos finished.

As the car continued on, I vaguely sensed that I was being held, comforted. Carlos was cradling my head, stroking my hair. "I love you," I heard him whisper through the voiceless wail inside my body. Fritz was a spy after all.

53.

Phantom Love

Moscow
November 6, 1992

I felt confined in the hotel room. The bed was lumpy. I turned on my side toward the wall, pulling my knees up, trying to get comfortable. I stared at the plain beige striped wallpaper that was peeling and curling at the edges. Like me. Frayed. Carlos sat in the chair near the window. Viktor's revelation about Fritz was not what I had expected. I wanted to find him alive, find him in a prison somewhere, free him, and bring him back. Viktor brought us very different news. I felt strangely changed. I never thought of Fritz as dead before, but he was gone. My "phantom love" was over.

I had been able to put off accepting this for seventeen years, years of living with my thoughts and dreams, no matter how farfetched they seemed. When I married Fritz, I thought he was the man of my dreams. Instead my life had turned into a nightmare. There was no one to blame but myself for the decisions made during those years. Before we left for Russia, I told myself that no matter what the results, this would be my last effort to find out what happened to Fritz. Now it was over. The news that Fritz had been alive for years after his disappearance was disconcerting and painful. It felt like a betrayal. I couldn't understand why he had never contacted me, why he had never let me know that he was alive. Even if he was incarcerated, he didn't share his real reason for going to Tirich Mir. Was it to protect me from unseen potential danger? When we were together, he once asked me if there was anything in my past that I hadn't told him, anything that he should know. I told him no, I didn't have any skeletons. Why was he so concerned about my past?

Now I wondered if he considered how his actions would affect my life. His own interests were more important than our love. He didn't think of me, of us. It hurt. His secret life was his priority.

Expecting Carlos to fight my battle had been selfish, but he did it. He was the one who deserved my devotion. He was the real hero.

He was so giving of himself, of his ideas—always ready to discuss or to listen, to be supportive. He wanted me to be happy. He told me he would change his life for me when we met, and he had kept his promise. I was thankful that I hadn't lost him. Carlos never wavered in his love for me. I had been blind at times, not realizing what it must have been like for him to shoulder all of my personal demons. He took my pain and made it his so that I could be free of my past, and we could have our life together.

Secretly I reminded myself that Carlos was the only man on the planet who would do what he did—search for Fritz. I finally realized the gift that I had been given in Carlos.

This trip to Russia sealed off the door to my past. "Look forward, not backward; try harder, there is no time to waste"—that's what Carlos believed in. That's what I wanted to do. I got up from the bed and walked to him.

"Forgive me. I'm sorry for everything that you've had to go through. I want you to know that I love you and I need you." I put my arms around his neck and kissed him.

"It's over, babe. No more ghosts. No more lies. We have the future," he said.

I couldn't wait to get home. I wanted to share my love and life with Carlos, play with Menina, our dog, to cut roses from our garden, to make pasta. The simple things.

We left Russia on November 7, 1992.

54.

Rebirth

Malibu
April 1993

I pulled out my makeup bag for work and twisted my hair into a braid. Two decades working on *The Price Is Right*. I stayed with it because it kept me going—it was something I depended on when everything else was being turned upside down. Bob Barker knew of my plight and always respected my privacy. The zipper on the makeup bag jammed as I tried to open it. I yanked it. My hand shook as I dabbed concealer on my face.

I wanted others to know that what had happened to me could happen to them. I was led through a maze of changes, a long and drawn out chase. As in the Nancy Drew mysteries, resolution to my own life mystery materialized. Carlos rescued me. The happy endings of the movies from my childhood were a writer's fantasy; in real life it is up to us to write our own happy endings by the choices we make.

The vicissitudes of foreign policy and international intrigue, and its changing tides, had buffeted my life for nearly twenty years. I was affected by forces I could hardly see, let alone measure. Now, suddenly, it was over. That was the way politics and the realms of intelligence affected most people: their lives were altered and they didn't even know how or why.

After our return, General Volkogonov's offices in Moscow informed us that there were no records relating to Fritz in either the presidential or KGB files. Also, Pakistan's ambassador Ashraf Qazi advised against going to Afghanistan to unearth the body because of our vulnerability to politically and criminally motivated attacks on foreigners.

On April 15, 1993, the U.S. State Department refused to assist us in retrieving Fritz's remains. Upon my return from Russia, I had requested assistance from Secretary of State Warren Christopher and President Clinton. The president never replied.

Fritz never had a proper burial. Carlos and I had a ceremony in his memory. We went to the foot of the Santa Monica Mountains, by the ocean.

After the last hedge of storefronts, the turns widened, deepened. There were few traffic lights past this point. A series of graceful arabesque arcs led to the ocean. The wheels rolled beneath the vehicle, logging the bumps. An arrhythmic unevenness, a pattern for survival. Each pothole offered a note, each lengthened crack a repetition. Arpeggio, trill. An ascension in the symphony, a burst of speed, a variation on the theme. Do one thing over and over again in different keys, different places on the scale, and a core of harmony will be revealed. I had learned that. I had searched. I had driven this road so many times.

The last climb fell away, and the ocean spread out before us and on into the horizon. I savored the view, wanting it to last past the descent. There was a grandeur in everything. It was a meeting, moving toward the ocean as its waves tumbled toward me. There was something right about this, something that could not be captured, but only experienced. A truth. Real truths were undeniable.

We parked the car along the side of the road and got out into the wind. The brisk air whipped hair into my face, blinding me for an instant. I brushed it back, then turned to take Carlos's hand. The current blew my hair back behind me as we walked toward the water. Use the opposition, don't resist it, I thought. A rule for life. As far back as I could remember, I had something to work against. There were always conflicts. Personal conflicts. Political conflicts.

The waves drew closer as we approached the edge of the water. Carlos and I were both attracted to the ocean. He grew up with it; I always came here to find peace. Peace of mind. When I was at the water,

250

everything else, the whole continent, stretched out behind me and I could release it all. I was calm.

Sea gulls arrayed themselves along the surf. Sentinels. Guarding. Waiting. What kept them there, staring out, lined up? It was almost as if they did not notice one another in expectation of what might arrive. The one farthest back spread its wings as I neared, but it did not take flight. It tottered a short distance, then settled again, never turning its neck.

The waves rolled in as the sun declined. Patterns of seven. A cycle pulled by the moon. The inclined light shimmered on the surface, creating dark ripples, shadows of the deep rising up. The sea gulls took to flight, one by one skimming above the water, wings crooked, heads craned to see below their reflections. They stayed out beyond the fringe.

I dropped my bag down on the sand. We could see the mountains and the water. With our hands, Carlos and I dug a pit just deep enough to shield the flame from the wind.

The world had to be let go before it could be found, before it would return of its own accord. Life could not be forced. That was what I learned. Sand sifted through my fingers while the moon rose. It emerged from the mountains, a pale bald round, full and skeletal. The birth squeezed from the earth; this was a crowning. The sky lavendered as the mountains turned agate.

"Ashes to ashes, dust to dust . . . ," I whispered, adding kindling to the fire. It blazed and snapped in the wind. I placed the shirt with red and yellow Volkswagens in the flame. The shirt Fritz wore when we met. Beside it went newspaper clippings. Articles about him, his climbs and mishaps, his prowess. Column after column puzzling over his disappearance.

Then I dropped in the talisman I had kept all these years. The silver rolled around, charred. The last thing I had of his was the cap to his antique pen. He wore it on a thin chain around his neck. After his disappearance, I found the cap, the chain, but not the pen. Fritz had left so many things behind. I wanted to lay them to rest, to release him—and myself.

I lit a candle from the fire burning in the pit. As long as the candle burned I would mourn him. That was the pact I made with myself. I gave him the funeral he never had.

On the other side, over the waves, the sun died, extinguished in the darkening abyss.

Simultaneously, moon and sun hung suspended: birth and death in one instant. Earth, fire, air, water. Carlos and I watched, and listened.

Time had played into our hands . . .

EPILOGUE

The New World Order

Los Angeles
October 1993

T he men I loved, the men who were my life, had both been scarred, injured in the mortal struggle against communism. They fought against it in Africa and in Afghanistan. Their sacrifices, together with millions of others caught in the same "games of destruction," seemed to have been in vain. From Angola to Mozambique, Yugoslavia to Afghanistan, hate, destruction, and death are even more rampant now than they were before the fall of communism. With the breakup of the Soviet Union there is a renewed threat to the world, a nuclear, biological, and chemical threat, the proliferation of arms. The U.S.S.R.'s arsenal of warheads is spread throughout its former territories. Those weapons of mass destruction may fall into the wrong hands.

Billions of taxpayer dollars have been spent yearly by our intelligence agencies. These dollars were channeled into financial, strategic, and military assistance that, in previous years, was meant to fight communism around the globe. Still, the world is in chaos. Regional and factional wars are exploding all over, the most formidable being the Muslim fundamentalist jihad, the "holy war."

Ironically, it was the CIA that trained and supplied the Muslim fundamentalists in Afghanistan, the mujahadin fighters. Yet after a decade of support, we abandoned them. When the Soviet Union fell, the bulk of U.S. aid to Afghanistan ceased. Feeling bitter and betrayed, some of them went into exile. Today the mujahadin fighters have shifted their focus to fighting the "international Satan," the West. Even some

253

of the diehard supporters of U.S. involvement in Afghanistan, people like Congressman Charles Wilson, are now afraid of the consequences of the CIA having trained and armed religious zealots.

We are paying the price for our pattern, training and financing fighters in other countries and then dropping them as soon as they are no longer useful for our strategies. On January 25, 1993, two CIA agents were killed in Langley by a Pakistani national. This incident was soon followed by the World Trade Center bombing on February 26, 1993, and the subsequent botched attempts to blow up the FBI building in downtown New York, the United Nations building, and two Manhattan tunnels in June of 1993. Whether at home or abroad, Americans are no longer as safe as they once were. We are walking targets.

Some of our leaders never bothered to ask what would happen after the superpowers left Afghanistan, what would happen when civil wars were begun and abandoned in Africa, what would happen when the different territories of the Soviet Union were left to battle for power among themselves. They didn't ask what would happen to the huge arsenal of nuclear, biological, and chemical arms.

Now the United States is scrambling, competing with Iran, Syria, and Iraq, among others, to buy up weapons that have found their way into the international market since the withdrawal of the former Soviet Union from Afghanistan. U.S. weapons. The same weapons we provided to the mujahadin just a few years ago.

As the most powerful country in the world, we should not allow men without vision to create and implement strategies that, if gone awry, may cost millions of lives. Cash and guns can influence people, but only through well-planned programs that strengthen the infrastructures of countries and their people can we create lasting change. It's time to make sure that those who concoct idiotic short-term policies in the protected marble hallways of government buildings no longer wield power.

No more human rights violations in the name of religion and ideology. No more madness in the interest of selfish, corrupt leaders and greedy financial conglomerates. As a global community, we must change. Our society is spiritually bankrupt. It's time to believe in a higher law, God's law.

Documents

October 15, 1987

Director
Freedom Of Information Act Unit
Central Intelligence Agency
Washington D.C. 20505

Dear Sir:

Pursuant to 5 USC 552, the Freedom of Information Act, would you please supply me with any documents or information you have on the following individual:

Friedrich Ludwig Stammberger

Social Security # 524-64-5316
Selective Service # 465-40532
Date of Birth: June 22, 1940
West German Citizen
Resident of Aspen, CO

Stammberger disappeared under unknown circumstances in September, 1975 while travelling in Pakistan. Missing person reports were filed here in the U.S. the following year.

I would appreciate any information you have in your files on this case. I shall of course immediately remit any costs involved.

Yours sincerely,

J. Pennington

Letter sent to the CIA requesting information on Fritz.

EXPLANATION OF EXEMPTIONS

FREEDOM OF INFORMATION ACT:

(b)(1)   applies to material which is properly classified pursuant to an Executive order in the interest of national defense or foreign policy;

(b)(2)   applies to information which pertains solely to the internal rules and practices of the Agency;

(b)(3)   applies to the Director's statutory obligations to protect from disclosure intelligence sources and methods, as well as the organization, functions, names, official titles, salaries or numbers of personnel employed by the Agency, in accord with the National Security Act of 1947 and the CIA Act of 1949, respectively;

(b)(4)   applies to information such as trade secrets and commercial or financial information obtained from a person on a privileged or confidential basis;

(b)(5)   applies to inter- and intra-agency memoranda which are advisory in nature;

(b)(6)   applies to information release of which would constitute an unwarranted invasion of the personal privacy of other individuals; and

(b)(7)   applies to investigatory records, release of which could (C) constitute an unwarranted invasion of the personal privacy of others, (D) disclose the identity of a confidential source, (E) disclose investigative techniques and procedures, or (F) endanger the life or physical safety of law enforcement personnel.

PRIVACY ACT:

(b)   applies to information concerning other individuals which may not be released without their written consent;

(j)(1)   applies to polygraph records; documents or segregable portions of documents, release of which would disclose intelligence sources and methods, including names of certain Agency employees and organizational components; and, documents or information provided by foreign governments;

(k)(1)   applies to information and material properly classified pursuant to an Executive order in the interest of national defense or foreign policy;

(k)(5)   applies to investigatory material compiled solely for the purpose of determining suitability, eligibility, or qualifications for Federal civilian employment, or access to classified information, release of which would disclose a confidential source; and

(k)(6)   testing or examination material used to determine individual qualifications for appointment or promotion in Federal Government service the release of which would compromise the testing or examination process.

Central Intelligence Agency

Washington D.C. 20505

2 8 OCT 1987

Janice Pennington

Reference: F87-1287

Dear Ms. Pennington:

Your letter dated 15 October 1987 requesting documents under the provisions of the Freedom of Information Act has been received in the office of the Information and Privacy Coordinator. Reference Number F87-1287, cited above, has been assigned for identification purposes.

Specifically, you are requesting documents pertaining to Friedrich Ludwig Stammberger and any known circumstances surrounding his death while traveling in Pakistan.

I must advise you that, in all requests such as yours, the CIA can neither confirm nor deny the existence or non-existence of any CIA records responsive to your request. Such information—unless, of course, it has been officially acknowledged—would be classified for reasons of national security under Section 1.3(a)(5) (foreign relations) of Executive Order 12356.

Accordingly, you request is denied on the basis of FOIA exemption (b)(1). By this action, we are neither confirming nor denying the existence or non-existence of such records. An explanation of the FOIA exemption cited above is enclosed.

The CIA official responsible for this denial is Kathryn I. Dyer, Information Review Officer for the Directorate of Intelligence. You may appeal this decision by addressing your appeal to the CIA Information Review Committee, in my care. Should you choose to do this, Please explain the basis of your appeal.

We regret that we could not be of greater assistance in this matter.

Sincerely,

Lee S. Strickland
Information and Privacy Coordinator

Enclosure

Denial from the Central Intelligence Agency to my request regarding information on Fritz.

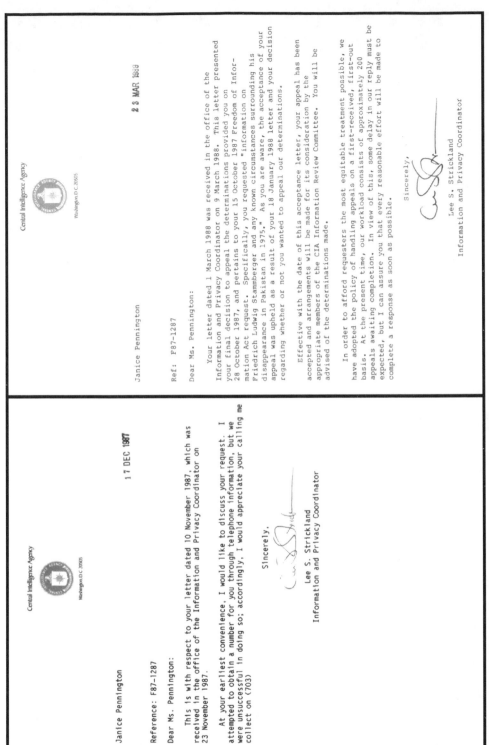

Central Intelligence Agency

Washington, D.C. 20505

17 DEC 1987

Janice Pennington

Reference: F87-1287

Dear Ms. Pennington:

This is with respect to your letter dated 10 November 1987, which was received in the office of the Information and Privacy Coordinator on 23 November 1987.

At your earliest convenience, I would like to discuss your request. I attempted to obtain a number for you through telephone information, but we were unsuccessful in doing so; accordingly, I would appreciate your calling me collect on (703)

Sincerely,

Lee S. Strickland
Information and Privacy Coordinator

Central Intelligence Agency

Washington, D.C. 20505

23 MAR 1988

Janice Pennington

Ref: F87-1287

Dear Ms. Pennington:

Your letter dated 1 March 1988 was received in the office of the Information and Privacy Coordinator on 9 March 1988. This letter presented your final decision to appeal the determinations provided you on 28 October 1987, and pertains to your 15 October 1987 Freedom of Information Act request. Specifically, you requested "information on Friedrich Ludwig Stammberger and any known circumstances surrounding his disappearance in Pakistan in 1975." As you are aware, the acceptance of your appeal was upheld as a result of your 18 January 1988 letter and your decision regarding whether or not you wanted to appeal our determinations.

Effective with the date of this acceptance letter, your appeal has been accepted and arrangements will be made for its consideration by the appropriate members of the CIA Information Review Committee. You will be advised of the determinations made.

In order to afford requesters the most equitable treatment possible, we have adopted the policy of handling appeals on a first-received, first-out basis. At the present time, our workload consists of approximately 200 appeals awaiting completion. In view of this, some delay in our reply must be expected, but I can assure you that every reasonable effort will be made to complete a response as soon as possible.

Sincerely,

Lee S. Strickland
Information and Privacy Coordinator

My appeal was accepted by the CIA Information Review Committee. After their review, they requested that I telephone them.

259

Central Intelligence Agency

Washington. D.C. 20505

15 SEP 1988

Janice Pennington

Reference: F87-1287

Dear Ms. Pennington:

This is concerning your 15 October 1987 Freedom of Information Act (FOIA) request and subsequent appeal for information on your husband, "Friedrich Ludwig Stammberger and any known circumstances surrounding his disappearance in Pakistan in 1975."

The processing of your request has now been completed, and the CIA Information Review Committee has provided my office with their final determinations regarding your request. Although my office has attempted to obtain a telephone number for you from the information operator, we have been unable to do so. At your earliest convenience, I would appreciate it if you would call me collect at (703) ___ to discuss your case. If I should be unavailable when you call, please leave a phone number where you can be reached and I will return your call.

Sincerely,

John H. Wright
Information and Privacy Coordinator

Central Intelligence Agency

Washington. D.C. 20505

29 September 1988

Ms. Janice Pennington

Dear Ms. Pennington:

This is in response to your letter of 1 March 1988 in which you state your final decision to appeal the determination of this Agency, dated 28 October 1987, neither to confirm nor deny the existence or nonexistence of records responsive to your Freedom of Information Act (FOIA) request of 15 October 1987. In that request you asked for records pertaining to Friedrich Ludwig Stammberger and any known circumstances concerning his disappearance while travelling in Pakistan in 1975.

Your appeal has been presented to the Central Intelligence Agency Information Review Committee. Pursuant to the authority delegated under paragraph 1900.51(a) of Chapter XIX, Title 32 of the Code of Federal Regulations, Mr. Richard J. Kerr, Deputy Director for Intelligence, has determined that we must neither confirm nor deny the existence or nonexistence of any documents responsive to your request. He has further determined that such information would be classified for reasons of national security under Section 1.3(a)(5) [foreign relations] of Executive Order 12356. Accordingly, pursuant to FOIA exemption (b)(1), your appeal is denied. By this statement, we are neither confirming nor denying that any such documents or records exist.

In accordance with the provisions of the FOIA, you have the right to seek judicial review of the above determinations in a United States district court.

We appreciate your patience while your appeal was being considered.

Sincerely,

R. M. Huffstutler
Chairman
Information Review Committee

After my appeal, the CIA contacted me by telephone and, once again, asked me to put a halt to my probing into the reasons for Fritz's disappearance. Because of my determination to find the truth, they offered to send an agent to my home to meet with me.

AMERICAN CIVIL LIBERTIES UNION

WASHINGTON OFFICE

122 Maryland Avenue, NE
Washington, DC 20002
(202) 544-1681

National Headquarters
132 West 43rd Street
New York, NY 10036
(212) 944-9800

Norman Dorsen
PRESIDENT

Ira Glasser
EXECUTIVE DIRECTOR

Eleanor Holmes Norton
CHAIR
NATIONAL ADVISORY COUNCIL

December 7, 1988

Janice M. Pennington

Dear Ms. Pennington:

After reviewing them at his request, I am returning the documents which you sent to Dr. Morton Halperin concerning your Freedom of Information Act (FOIA) requests for information on Friedrich Stammberger.

It is our opinion that a lawsuit against the CIA pursuant to the Freedom of Information Act will prove unavailing. Based upon prior court decisions in these matters, it is likely that a court will uphold the CIA's right to refuse to confirm or deny the existence of records concerning Mr. Stammberger in the context of allegations, however ill-founded, that Mr. Stammberger was supposedly involved in a covert operation along the Pakistan-Afghanistan border. Even if a court were to require the CIA to confirm or deny the existence of records, it is likely that there will be no records other than what you have obtained from other agencies, or the CIA will be upheld in its assertion that any records it has are properly classified and withheld.

The materials you received from the State Department appear to be genuine and there is no basis at present to suspect that any of these agencies have acted in bad faith.

Beyond this, we have no additional advice or opinion to offer.

Sincerely,

Al

Legislative Counsel

a:Penningt.ltr
12/07/88
PC #4

The ACLU response to my request for legal assistance regarding the possibility of filing a lawsuit against the CIA. Based on existing laws, they recommended against my doing so.

U.S. Department of Justice

National Central Bureau - INTERPOL

Washington, D.C. 20530

February 12, 1988

Mrs. Janice Pennington

Dear Mrs. Pennington:

This is in response to your Freedom of Information/Privacy Act request seeking information concerning Friedrich Ludwig Stammberger.

Twelve documents were discovered pertaining to Mr. Stammberger. Eight documents are being provided to you under the provisions of the Freedom of Information/Privacy Acts. However, portions of these documents have been deleted pursuant to Title 5 U.S.C., §552 (b)(2), which exempts the release of information related solely to the internal practices of a Federal agency; Title 5 U.S.C., §552 (b)(7)(C), which exempts the release of information which constitutes an unwarranted invasion of personal privacy, and Title 5 U.S.C., §552 (b)(7)(D), which exempts disclosing the identity of a foreign source.

Four documents are being withheld in their entirety pursuant to Title 5 U.S.C., §552 (b)(2), (b)(7)(C) and (b)(7)(D) as listed above.

Should you desire to appeal this action, you may do so by contacting the office of Privacy and Information Appeals, U.S. Department of Justice, Washington, D.C. 20530, within 30 days of receipt of this correspondence.

Sincerely,

Richard C. Stiener
Chief

Enclosures (8)

U.S. Department of Justice

National Central Bureau - INTERPOL

Washington, D.C. 20530

May 11, 1988

FOI/PA# 87-0109

Mrs. Janice Pennington

Dear Mrs. Pennington:

This is in response to your administrative appeal to the Office of Privacy and Information Appeals, U.S. Department of Justice, concerning your Freedom of Information/Privacy Acts (FOIA) request sent to this office dated November 17, 1987.

An attorney from the Office of Privacy and Information Appeals reviewed the FOIA documents and determined that one additional document was releasable, and that additional information contained in three documents could be released.

The newly released document has deletions pursuant to Title 5 U.S.C., §552 (b)(2) which exempts the release of information related solely to the internal practices of a Federal agency and Title 5 U.S.C., §552 (b)(7)(C) which exempts the release of information which constitutes an unwarranted invasion of personal privacy.

Should you desire to appeal this action, you may do so by contacting the office of Privacy and Information Appeals, U.S. Department of Justice, Washington, D.C. 20530, within 30 days of receipt of this correspondence.

Sincerely,

Richard C. Stiener
Chief

Enclosures (4)

Denial from the Justice Department to release some documents with information related to Fritz.

U.S. Department of Justice

Office of Legal Policy

Office of Information and Privacy

Washington, D.C. 20530   MAY 2 7 1988

Mrs. Janice Pennington

Re: Appeal No. 88-0433
     RLH:WLW:CAK

Dear Mrs. Pennington:

    You appealed from the action of Interpol on your request for access to records pertaining to Friedrich Ludwig Stammberger.

    As a result of discussions between Interpol personnel and members of my staff, a supplemental release of records either has been or will soon be made to you directly by Interpol. In light of this fact and after careful consideration of your appeal, I have otherwise decided to affirm the action in this case. Certain information was properly withheld from you pursuant to 5 U.S.C. §552(b)(2), (7)(C) and (7)(D). These provisions pertain to purely internal agency practices and to records or information compiled for law enforcement purposes, the release of which could reasonably be expected to constitute an unwarranted invasion of the personal privacy of third parties and to disclose the identities of confidential sources. Names of Interpol employees were among the items excised on the basis of 5 U.S.C. §552(b)(7)(C). None of the information being withheld is appropriate for discretionary release.

    Judicial review of my action on this appeal is available to you in the United States District Court for the judicial district in which you reside or have your principal place of business, or in the District of Columbia, which is also where the records you seek are located.

                    Sincerely,

                    [signature]

                    Richard L. Huff, Co-Director
                    Office of Information and Privacy

Due to my appeal, the Justice Department finally decided to release the documents they had on Fritz.

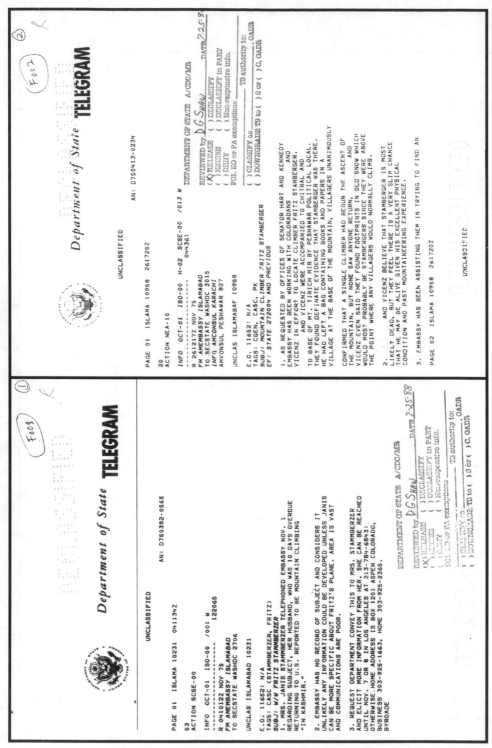

UNCLASSIFIED

Telegram ①

Department of State TELEGRAM

UNCLASSIFIED

AN: D750382-0565

PAGE 01 ISLAMA 10231 041134Z

53
ACTION SCSE-00

INFO OCT-01 ISO-00 /001 W
------------------ 122065
R 041012Z NOV 75
FM AMEMBASSY ISLAMABAD
TO SECSTATE WASHDC 2706

UNCLAS ISLAMABAD 10231

E.O. 11652: N/A
TAGS: CASC (STAMMBERZER, FRITZ)
SUBJ: M/W FRITZ STAMMBERZER

1. MRS. JANIS STAMMBERZER TELEPHONED EMBASSY NOV. 1 REGARDING SUBJECT, HER HUSBAND, WHO WAS 10 DAYS OVERDUE RETURNING TO U.S. REPORTED TO BE MOUNTAIN CLIMBING "IN KASHMIR."

2. EMBASSY HAS NO RECORD OF SUBJECT AND CONSIDERS IT UNLIKELY ANY INFORMATION COULD BE DEVELOPED UNLESS JANIS CAN BE MORE SPECIFIC ABOUT FRITZ'S PLANE. AREA IS VAST AND COMMUNICATIONS ARE POOR.

3. REQUEST DEPARTMENT CONVEY THIS TO MRS. STAMMBERZER AND ELICIT MORE INFORMATION FROM HER. SHE CAN BE REACHED UNTIL NOV. 7 OR 8 IN LOS ANGELES AT 213-784-6843. OTHERWISE HOME ADDRESS IS BOX 1201 ASPEN COLORADO, BUSINESS 303-925-1663, HOME 303-925-2365.
BYROADE

DEPARTMENT OF STATE A/CDC/MR DATE 2-25-88
REVIEWED by D G Shaw
(X) RELEASE ( ) DECLASSIFY
( ) EXCISE ( ) DECLASSIFY in PART
( ) DENY ( ) Non-responsive info.
FOI, EO or PA exemptions ___ TS authority to:
( ) CLASSIFY as
( ) DOWNGRADE TS to ( ) S or ( ) C, OADR

Telegram ②

Department of State TELEGRAM

UNCLASSIFIED

AN: D750413-0234

PAGE 01 ISLAMA 10958 261720Z

20
ACTION NEA-10

INFO OCT-01 ISO-00 H-02 SCSE-00 /013 W
------------------ 044361
R 261217Z NOV 75
FM AMEMBASSY ISLAMABAD
TO SECSTATE WASHDC 3015
INFO AMCONSUL KARACHI
AMVONSUL PESHAWAR 827

UNCLAS ISLAMABAF 10958

E.O. 11652: N/A
TAGS: CGEN, CASC, PK
SUBJ: MOUNTAIN CLIMBER FRITZ STAMBERGER
EF: STATE 272004 AND PREVIOUS

1. AS REQUESTED BY OFFICES OF SENATOR HART AND KENNEDY EMBASSY HAS BEEN WORKING WITH COLORADANS AND VICENZ IN EFFORT TO LOCATE CLIMBER FRITZ STAMBERGER. AND VICENZ WERE ACCOMPANIED TO CHITRAL AND TO BASE OF MT. TIRICH MIR BY PESHAWAR POLITICAL LOCAL. THEY FOUND DEFINATE EVIDENCE THAT STAMBERGER WAS THERE. HE HAD LEFT A BAG CONTAINING BOOKS AND PAPERS IN A VILLAGE AT THE BASE OF THE MOUNTAIN, VILLAGERS UNANIMOUSLY CONFIRMED THAT A SINGLE CLIMBER HAD BEGUN THE ASCENT OF THE MOUNTAIN, BUT NONE SAW ANYONE RETURN, AND VICENZ EVEN SAID THEY FOUND FOOTPRINTS IN OLD SNOW WHICH WOULD MOST PROBABLY BE STAMBERGERS SINCE THEY WERE ABOVE THE POINT WHERE ANY VILLAGERS WOULD NORMALLY CLIMB.

2. AND VICENZ BELIEVE THAT STAMBERGER IS MOST LIKELY DEAD, BUT THEY FEEL THERE IS A VERY SLIM CHANCE THAT HE MAY BE ALIVE GIVEN HIS EXCELLENT PHYSICAL CONDITION AND PAST MOUNTAINEERING EXPERIENCE.

3. EMBASSY HAS BEEN ASSISTING THEM IN TRYING TO FIND AN

PAGE 02 ISLAMA 10958 261720Z

UNCLASSIFIED

DEPARTMENT OF STATE A/CDC/MR DATE 2-25-88
REVIEWED by D G Shaw
(X) RELEASE ( ) DECLASSIFY
( ) EXCISE ( ) DECLASSIFY in PART
( ) DENY ( ) Non-responsive info.
FOI, EO or PA exemptions ___ TS authority to:
( ) CLASSIFY as
( ) DOWNGRADE TS to ( ) S or ( ) C, OADR

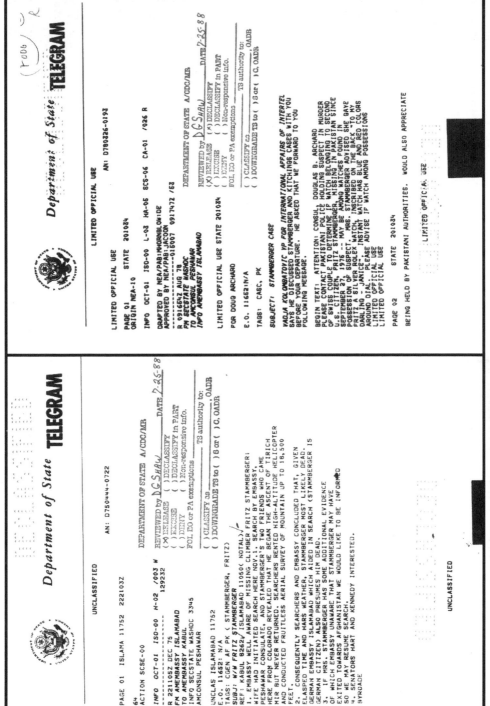

UNCLASSIFIED

Department of State TELEGRAM

AN: D750444-0722

DEPARTMENT OF STATE A/CDC/MR

REVIEWED by D G SHAW   DATE 7-25-88
(X) RELEASE   ( ) DECLASSIFY
( ) EXCISE   ( ) DECLASSIFY in PART
( ) DENY   ( ) Non-responsive info.
FOI, EO or PA exemptions _____
( ) CLASSIFY as _____ TS authority to:
( ) DOWNGRADE TS to ( ) S or ( ) C, OADR

PAGE 01 ISLAMA 11752 222103Z

64
ACTION SCSE-00

INFO OCT-01 ISO-00 H-02 /003 W
129232

R 221105Z DEC 75
FM AMEMBASSY ISLAMABAD
TO AMEMBASSY KABUL
INFO SECSTATE WASHDC 3345
AMCONSUL PESHAWAR

UNCLAS ISLAMABAD 11752
E.O. 11652: N/A
TAGS: CGEN AF PK (STAMMBERGER, FRITZ)
SUBJ: W/W FRITZ STAMMBERGER
REF: KABUL 8262/ ISLAMABAD 11050(NOTAL)
1. EMBASSY WELL AWARE OF MISSING CLIMBER FRITZ STAMMBERGER; WIFE HAD INITIATED SEARCH HERE NOV.1. SEARCH BY EMBASSY, PESHAWAR CONSULATE, AND STAMMBERGER'S TWO FRIENDS WHO CAME HERE FROM COLORADO REVEALED THAT HE BEGAN THE ASCENT OF TIRICH MIR BUT NEVER RETURNED. SEARCHERS RENTED HIGH-ALTITUDE HELICOPTER AND CONDUCTED FRUITLESS AERIAL SURVEY OF MOUNTAIN UP TO 18,500 FEET.
2. CONSEQUENTLY SEARCHERS AND EMBASSY CONCLUDED THAT, GIVEN ELASPED TIME AND HARS WEATHER, STAMMBERGER MOST LIKELY DEAD. GERMAN EMBASSY (STAMMBERGER A GERMAN CITIZEN) ALSO PRESUMES HIM DEAD.
3. IF MRS. STAMMBERGER HAS SOME ADDITIONAL EVIDENCE OF WHICH EMBASSY UNAWARE THAT STAMMBERGER MAY HAVE EXITED TOWARDS AFGHANISTAN WE WOULD LIKE TO BE INFORMED SO WE MAY RESUME SEARCH.
4. SENATORS HART AND KENNEDY INTERESTED.
BYROADE

UNCLASSIFIED

LIMITED OFFICIAL USE

Department of State TELEGRAM

AN: D790326-0193

DEPARTMENT OF STATE A/CDC/MR

REVIEWED by D G SHAW   DATE 7-25-88
(X) RELEASE   (X) DECLASSIFY
( ) EXCISE   ( ) DECLASSIFY in PART
( ) DENY   ( ) Non-responsive info.
FOI, EO or PA exemptions _____
( ) CLASSIFY as _____ TS authority to:
( ) DOWNGRADE TS to ( ) S or ( ) C, OADR

PAGE 01 STATE 201034
ORIGIN NEA-10

INFO OCT-01 ISO-00 L-03 HA-06 SCS-06 CA-01 /026 R

DRAFTED BY NEA/PAB:MHORNBLOW10DE
APPROVED BY NEA/PAB:JACON -015007 0917472 /63
FM SECSTATE WASHDC
TO AMCONSUL PESHAWAR
INFO AMEMBASSY ISLAMABAD

R 091646Z AUG 78

LIMITED OFFICIAL USE STATE 201034

FOR DOUG ARCHARD

E.O. 11652:N/A
TAGS: CASC, PK

SUBJECT: STAMMBERGER CASE

NADJA KOLOWRATOVIC VP FOR INTERNATIONAL AFFAIRS OF INTERTEL SAYS HE DISCUSSED STAMMBERGER AND KITCHING CASES WITH YOU BEFORE YOUR DEPARTURE. HE ASKED THAT WE FORWARD TO YOU FOLLOWING MESSAGE.

BEGIN TEXT: ATTENTION: CONSUL, DOUGLAS B. ARCHARD PLEASE CONTACT PAKISTANI POLICE HOLDING SUSPECT IN MURDER OF SWISS COUPLE TO DETERMINE IF WATCH BELONGING TO SECOND U.S. CITIZEN, FRITZ STAMMBERGER, MISSING IN PAKISTAN SINCE SEPTEMBER 27, 1976 -- MAY BE AMONG WATCHES FOUND IN POSSESSION OF SUSPECT. MRS. STAMMBERGER ADVISED SHE GAVE FRITZ A SILVER ROLEX WATCH, INSCRIBED ON THE BACK "TO MY DARLING - JANICE." INSTANT WATCH HAS BLUE AND RED COLORS AROUND DIAL. PLEASE ADVISE IF WATCH AMONG POSSESSIONS

PAGE 02 STATE 201034
BEING HELD BY PAKISTANI AUTHORITIES. WOULD ALSO APPRECIATE

LIMITED OFFICIAL USE

UNCLASSIFIED
Department of State
389

PAGE 01   NEW DE 00259   051033Z
ACTION NEA-07

INFO   OCT-01   ISO-00   H-02   /010 W
------------------077247   051738Z /43

R 050956Z JAN 79
FM AMEMBASSY NEW DELHI
TO SECSTATE WASHDC 6340
AMEMBASSY ISLAMABAD
AMCONSUL PESHAWAR

UNCLAS NEW DELHI 0259

E.O. 12065: N/A
TAGS: CASC (STAMMBERGER, FRITZ)
SUBJECT: MOUNTAINEERING ACCIDENT OF FRITZ STAMMBERGER

REF: (1) STATE 01441 (2) ISLAMABAD 0124

INDIAN MOUNTAINEERING FOUNDATION CONTACTED AND THEY INFORMED
EMBASSY THAT THEY HAVE NO KNOWLEDGE OF STAMMBERGER. EMBASSY
UNABLE TO CONFIRM STORY REFTEL THROUGH ANY OTHER SOURCE.
GOHEEN

Department of State   TELEGRAM
7697

PAGE 01   STATE 001441
ORIGIN NEA-07

INFO   OCT-01   ISO-00   H-02   /010 R

DRAFTED BY NEA:PWLANDE:BJS
APPROVED BY NEA:PWLANDE
PAB:MHORNBLOW
H:RFLATEN (INFO)
------------------065520   040429Z /70

R 032356Z JAN 79
FM SECSTATE WASHDC
TO AMEMBASSY ISLAMABAD
AMEMBASSY NEW DELHI
AMCONSUL PESHAWAR

UNCLAS STATE 001441

E.O. 12065: N/A

TAGS:

SUBJECT: MOUNTAINEERING ACCIDENT

1. WE UNDERSTAND THAT A PROMINENT GERMAN MOUNTAIN CLIMBER,
FRITZ STAMMBERGER, DISAPPEARED WHILE CLIMBING TIRITH MIR IN
SEPTEMBER 1975. HIS BODY WAS NOT FOUND AT THE TIME.
ACCORDING TO RECENT INFORMATION A POLISH MOUNTAINEERING
GROUP FOUND HIS BODY WHILE CLIMBING TIRITH MIR LAST YEAR.

2. COULD YOU CONFIRM THIS INFORMATION. WHILE THE ACCIDENT
TOOK PLACE IN PAKISTAN, THE INFORMATION WE ARE TRYING TO
CONFIRM WAS OBTAINED IN NEW DELHI. VANCE

Documents released by the Department of State regarding Fritz.

UNCLASSIFIED

AN: D750443-0738

Department of State **TELEGRAM**

PAGE 01 KABUL 08262 220405Z
ACTION SCSE-00

73
INFO OCT-01 NEA-10 ISO-00 /011 W
121174

R 210640Z DEC 75
FM AMEMBASSY KABUL
TO AMEMBASSY ISLAMABAD
AMCONSUL PESHAWAR
INFO SECSTATE WASHDC 5469

UNCLAS KABUL 8262

E.O. 11652: N/A
TAGS: CASC, AF (STAMMBERGER, FRITZ)
SUBJ: C/W FRITZ STAMMBERGER
1 FOLLOWING COMMERCIAL TELEGRAM RECEIVED BY CONSULAR SECTION ON DECEMBER 20 1975 FROM MRS. JANICE STAMMBERGER CONCERNING HER HUSBAND FRITZ STAMMBERGER: MY HUSBAND IS MISSING. HE WAS CLIMBING THE MOUNTAIN OF TRISCHMIR IN PAKISTAN. BELIEVED TO HAVE EXITED OFF THE MOUNTAIN TOWARDS AFGHANISTAN. WOULD LIKE TO INITIATE ENQUIRIES IN REMOTE VILLAGES AND HOSPITALS BORDER OF AFGHANISTAN. PLEASE SEND ME ANY INFO YOU MAY RECEIVE. JANICZ FHAMMBERGER. SHERMAN OAKS, CALIF..

2. AS ADDRESSEES WELL AWARE THERE ARE NO HOSPITALS ON BORDER PLUS AFGHAN COMMO LINKS TO VILLAGES NONEXISTENT; THUS OBTAINING INFO ON SUBJECT'S W/W HIGHLY UNLIKELY UNTIL HE WOULD REACH MAJOR TOWN OR CITY. WOULD APPRECIATE KNOWING IF SUBJECT HAD GOP PERMISSION TO CLIMB MOUNTAIN. IF OBTAINED PERHAPS GOP WOULD HAVE INFO RE HIS PLANS FOR MOUNTAIN. DID SUBJECT REGISTER WITH EMBASSY OR CONSULATE? WOULD APPRECIATE ANY INFO YOU MAY HAVE ON SUBJECT SO WE CAN PASS IT ON TO MRS. STAMMBERGER.
ELIOT

UNCLASSIFIED

UNCLASSIFIED

AN: D750444-0722

Department of State **TEL**

PAGE 01 ISLAMA 11752 222103Z
ACTION SCSE-00

64
INFO OCT-01 ISO-00 H-02 /003 W
129232

R 221105Z DEC 75
FM AMEMBASSY ISLAMABAD
TO AMEMBASSY KABUL
INFO SECSTATE WASHDC 3345
AMCONSUL PESHAWAR

UNCLAS ISLAMABAD 11752
E.O. 11652: N/A
TAGS: CGEN AF PK (STAMMBERGER, FRITZ)
SUBJ: W/W FRITZ STAMMBERGER
REF: KABUL 8262, ISLAMABAD 11050(NOTAL)
1. EMBASSY WELL AWARE OF MISSING CLIMBER FRITZ STAMMBERGER; WIFE HAD INITIATED SEARCH HERE NOV.1. SEARCH BY EMBASSY, PESHAWAR CONSULATE, AND STAMMBERGER'S TWO FRIENDS WHO CAME HERE FROM COLORADO REVEALED THAT HE BEGAN THE ASCENT OF TIRICH MIR BUT NEVER RETURNED. SEARCHERS RENTED HIGH-ALTITUDE HELICOPTER AND CONDUCTED FRUITLESS AERIAL SURVEY OF MOUNTAIN UP TO 18,500 FEET.
2. CONSEQUENTLY SEARCHERS AND EMBASSY CONCLUDED THAT, GIVEN ELAPSED TIME AND HARS WEATHER, STAMMBERGER MOST LIKELY DEAD. GERMAN EMBASSY ISLAMABAD WHICH AIDED IN SEARCH (STAMMBERGER IS GERMAN CITIZEN) ALSO PRESUMES HIM DEAD.
3. IF MRS. STAMMBERGER HAS SOME ADDITIONAL EVIDENCE OF WHICH EMBASSY UNAWARE THAT STAMMBERGER MAY HAVE EXITED TOWARDS AFGHANISTAN WE WOULD LIKE TO BE INFORMED SO WE MAY RESUME SEARCH.
4. SENATORS HART AND KENNEDY INTERESTED.
BYROADE

Left Telegram

Department of State TELEGRAM

LIMITED OFFICIAL USE

AN: D780326-0193

PAGE 01   STATE 201034
ORIGIN NEA-10

INFO OCT-01 ISO-00 L-03 HA-05 SCS-06 CA-01 /026 R
------------------015007 091747Z /63
DRAFTED BY NEA/PAB:MHORNBLOW:DE
APPROVED BY NEA/PAB:JACCON
R 091652Z AUG 78
FM SECSTATE WASHDC
TO AMCONSUL PESHAWAR
INFO AMEMBASSY ISLAMABAD

LIMITED OFFICIAL USE STATE 201034

FOR DOUG ARCHARD

E.O. 11652:N/A

TAGS: CASC, PK

SUBJECT: *STAMMBERGER CASE*

VADJA KOLOMBATOVIC VP FOR INTERNATIONAL AFFAIRS OF INTERTEL
SAYS HE DISCUSSED STAMMBERGER AND KITCHINGS CASES WITH YOU
BEFORE YOUR DEPARTURE. HE ASKED THAT WE FORWARD TO YOU
FOLLOWING MESSAGE.

BEGIN TEXT: ATTENTION: CONSUL, DOUGLAS B. ARCHARD
PLEASE CONTACT PAKISTANI POLICE HOLDING SUSPECT IN MURDER
OF SWISS COUPLE TO DETERMINE IF WATCH BELONGING TO SECOND
U.S. CITIZEN, FRITZ STAMMBERGER, MISSING IN PAKISTAN SINCE
SEPTEMBER 27, 1975.-- MAY BE AMONG WATCHES FOUND IN
POSSESSION OF SUSPECT. MRS. STAMMBERGER ADVISED SHE GAVE
FRITZ A SILVER ROLEX WATCH, INSCRIBED ON THE BACK "TO MY
DARLING - JANICE". INSTANT WATCH HAS BLUE AND RED COLORS
AROUND DIAL. PLEASE ADVISE IF WATCH AMONG POSSESSIONS
LIMITED OFFICIAL USE
LIMITED OFFICIAL USE

PAGE 02   STATE 201034

BEING HELD BY PAKISTANI AUTHORITIES. WOULD ALSO APPRECIATE

Right Telegram

Department of State TELEGRAM

UNCLASSIFIED

AN: D790014-0360

PAGE 01   WARSAW 00263 101033Z
ACTION NEA-07

INFO OCT-01 EUR-12 ISO-00 H-02 /022 W
------------------118410 110213Z /64
R 100956Z JAN 79
FM AMEMBASSY WARSAW
TO SECSTATE WASHDC 9952
INFO AMEMBASSY ISLAMABAD
AMEMBASSY NEW DELHI
AMCONSUL PESHAWAR

UNCLAS WARSAW 0263.

E.O. 12065: N/A
TAGS: PL, US, CASC, CGEN, PK (STAMMBERGER, FRITZ)
SUBJECT: *MOUNTAINEERING ACCIDENT*

REF: ISLAMABAD 0012<

1. AN EMBASSY OFFICER TALKED WITH A REPRESENTATIVE OF THE POLISH
ALPINE CLUB IN WARSAW ON JANUARY 5. AFTER CONSULTATIONS WITH
MEMBERS WHO PARTICIPATED IN CLIMBS IN PAKISTAN DURING 1978,
THIS REPRESENTATIVE INFORMED US THAT A CANADIAN ALPINE GROUP
DISCOVERED AN UNIDENTIFIED BODY IN SEPTEMBER, 1978, WHILE CLIMBING
IN THE TIRITH MIR REGION. SUBSEQUENTLY, MEMBERS OF THE CANADIAN
GROUP COMMUNICATED THIS INFORMATION TO THE POLISH CLUB'S CHAPTER
IN GDANSK BECAUSE IT WAS GENERALLY KNOWN WITHIN CLIMBING
CIRCLES THAT THE POLISH CLUB HAD LOST A TEAM MEMBER IN THAT SAME
AREA EARLIER IN THE 1978 CLIMBING SEASON. THE UNIDENTIFIED BODY,
HOWEVER, WAS NOT THE REMAINS OF THE LOST POLISH CLIMBER WHOSE
BODY HAS SINCE BEEN LOCATED AND BURIED.

2. IN INVESTIGATING THE INITIAL REPORT OF THE UNIDENTIFIED BODY,
THE POLISH CLUB WAS TOLD BY LOCAL VILLAGERS THAT A WESTERNER HAD
BEEN IN THE AREA ATTEMPTING TO CLIMB ALONE AND THAT HE HAD
DISAPPEARED WITHOUT TRACE. BECAUSE OF THIS INFORMATION FROM THE
LOCAL VILLAGERS AS WELL AS FOR OTHER UNCLEAR REASONS, MEMBERS OF
UNCLASSIFIED
UNCLASSIFIED

PAGE 02   WARSAW 00263 101033Z

THE POLISH CLUB IN GDANSK SUSPECTED THAT THE UNIDENTIFIED BODY

UNCLASSIFIED

Documents released by the Department of State regarding Fritz.

Department of State TELEGRAM

AN: D790013-0883

PAGE 01   PESHAW 00002   100244Z
ACTION NEA-07

INFO OCT-01 EUR-12 ISO-00 H-02 /022 W
------------------114237 102003Z /46
R 070740Z JAN 79 ZDK
FM AMCONSUL PESHAWAR
TO SECSTATE WASHDC 428
INFO RUEHLBAMEMBASSY ISLAMABAD 867
AMEMBASSY WARSAW

UNCLAS PESHAWAR 0002

E.O. 12065: N/A
TAGS: CASC, PK (STAMMBERGER, FRITZ)
SUBJ: MOUNTAINEERING ACCIDENT

REF : STATE 01441 AND ISLAMABAD 00124

A SENIOR OFFICER OF THE NORTH WEST FRONTIER PROVINCIAL POLICE
WHO HAVE JURISDICTION OVER CHITCAL WHERE TIRITH MIR IS
LOCATED, TELLS US THAT HE HAS RECEIVED NO REPORT THAT FRITZ
STAMMBERGER'S BODY HAS BEEN FOUND. HE WOULD CERTAINLY HAVE
BEEN INFORMED IF THE POLISH MOUNTAINEERING GROUP, WHICH IS
REPORTED TO HAVE FOUND STAMMBERGER'S BODY, HAD BROUGHT
IT TO THE NOTICE OF THE LOCAL POLICE. THE OFFICIAL DOUBTS
THE ACCURACY OF THE REPORT.
ARCHARD

UNCLASSIFIED

Document released by the Department of State regarding Fritz.

269

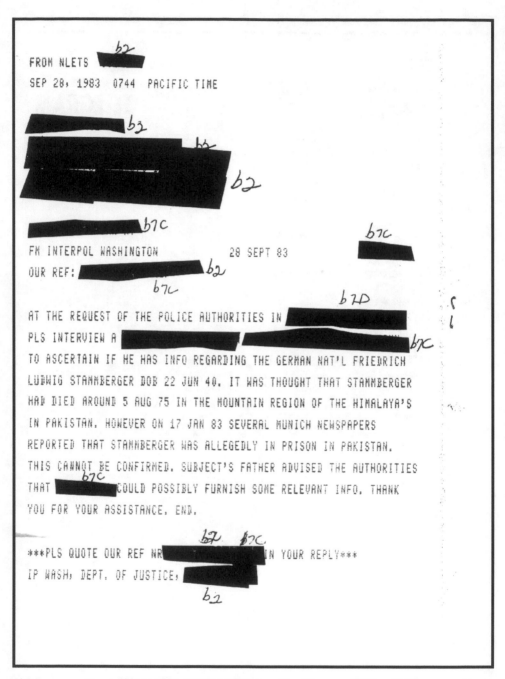

FROM NLETS [redacted] *b2*

SEP 28, 1983 0744 PACIFIC TIME

[redacted] *b3*

[redacted] *b3*

[redacted] *b2*

[redacted] *b7C*

FM INTERPOL WASHINGTON   28 SEPT 83

OUR REF: [redacted] *b2*

[redacted] *b7C*

AT THE REQUEST OF THE POLICE AUTHORITIES IN [redacted] *b7D*

PLS INTERVIEW A [redacted] [redacted] *b7C*

TO ASCERTAIN IF HE HAS INFO REGARDING THE GERMAN NAT'L FRIEDRICH
LUDWIG STAMMBERGER DOB 22 JUN 40. IT WAS THOUGHT THAT STAMMBERGER
HAD DIED AROUND 5 AUG 75 IN THE MOUNTAIN REGION OF THE HIMALAYA'S
IN PAKISTAN. HOWEVER ON 17 JAN 83 SEVERAL MUNICH NEWSPAPERS
REPORTED THAT STAMMBERGER WAS ALLEGEDLY IN PRISON IN PAKISTAN.
THIS CANNOT BE CONFIRMED. SUBJECT'S FATHER ADVISED THE AUTHORITIES
THAT [redacted] *b7C* COULD POSSIBLY FURNISH SOME RELEVANT INFO. THANK
YOU FOR YOUR ASSISTANCE. END.

PLS QUOTE OUR REF NR [redacted] *b2* *b7C* IN YOUR REPLY

IP WASH, DEPT. OF JUSTICE, [redacted]

b2

Document released by the Department of State regarding Fritz.

Travel Warning

United States Department of State
Bureau of Consular Affairs
Washington, D.C. 20520   For recorded travel information, call 202-647-5225.
To access the Consular Affairs Bulletin Board, call 202-647-9225.

Afghanistan — Warning

Afghanistan - Warning
February 12, 1993

The Department of State warns all U.S. citizens against travel to Afghanistan. Westerners remain vulnerable to politically and criminally-motivated attacks and violence, including robbery, kidnapping and hostage-taking. Land mines are still prevalent throughout the countryside. All U.S. personnel at the U.S. Embassy in Kabul were evacuated in 1989, and no other diplomatic mission represents U.S. interests or provides consular services. More information can be found in the Department of State consular information sheet on Afghanistan.

No. 93-009

This replaces the Department of State Travel Warning of January 8, 1993 to clarify the status of the U.S. Embassy in Afghanistan.

PRIORITY

March 23, 1993

President Bill Clinton
The White House
1600 Pensylvania Avenue N.W. 20500
Washington D.C.

The Honorable President Bill Clinton

Dear President Clinton:

I am a citizen of the United States, and I am the hostess of the U.S. TV show "The Price Is Right," with a daily viewership of 15 million Americans. Based on humanitarian grounds, I would like to request an audience and/or engage your help in seeking the Truth in my quest to learn the final destiny of my former husband, Fritz Ludwig Stammberger, a citizen of Germany and a permanent resident of the United States, who disappeared in the restricted area along the Afghanistan/Pakistan and Russian borders in 1975.

Through the Freedom of Information and Privacy Acts, search teams, interviews with intelligence sources, and most recently with my trip to Russia and the help of President Yeltsin, I received information that he may have been involved in covert operations for which he was captured, imprisoned and killed. I was told that his body is buried inside Afghanistan.

In 1988 the C.I.A. sent an agent to my residence in Encino, California informing me that they would neither confirm or deny the existence of records in respect to Fritz. Since my return from Russia last November I received new information that leads me to believe that he was recruited by the Agency in 1974.

For the past eighteen years this matter has troubled me greatly. Once again I ask the help of my Government. My interest is not what he was doing, but rather his fate.

I am arranging to fly to Afghanistan to retrieve his body within the next two months, therefore it is of the utmost importance to receive any and all information regarding this matter.

I know that you are coming to Los Angeles soon (NAACP Dinner), and if it is possible I would like to meet with you then.

Yours sincerely,

Janice Pennington

Janice Pennington

Letter sent to the president requesting his help. He never replied.   Document sent by the State Department advising us not to travel.